ROCKFORD PUBLIC LIBRARY

W9-BHL-240

3 1 1 1 2 0 2 1 0 5 5 4 7 6

WITHDRAWN

HISTORY 326.8 ZOELLNER
Zoellner, Tom,
Island on fire :

08/03/2021

ISLAND ON FIRE

ISLAND ON
FIRE

The Revolt That Ended Slavery
in the British Empire

TOM ZOELLNER

Harvard University Press

CAMBRIDGE, MASSACHUSETTS · LONDON, ENGLAND · 2020

ROCKFORD PUBLIC LIBRARY

Copyright © 2020 by Tom Zoellner

All rights reserved

Printed in the United States of America

First printing

Library of Congress Cataloging-in-Publication Data

Names: Zoellner, Tom, author.

Title: Island on fire : the revolt that ended slavery in the
   British Empire / Tom Zoellner.

Description: Cambridge, Massachusetts : Harvard
   University Press, 2020. | Includes bibliographical
   references and index.

Identifiers: LCCN 2019045203 | ISBN 9780674984301 (cloth)

Subjects: LCSH: Sharpe, Sam, 1801–1832. | Slavery—Jamaica—
   History—19th century. | Slavery—Great Britain—
   History—19th century. | Jamaica—History—Slave
   Insurrection, 1831.

Classification: LCC HT1096 .Z54 2020 | DDC 326/
   .8097292—dc23

LC record available at https://lccn.loc.gov/2019045203

CONTENTS

ISLAND ON FIRE

House/Estate

Fortress

Battle

N
W   *E*
S

Lucea

Montego Bay

Falmouth

Great River

Martha Brae R.

Cabarita R.

THE COCKPIT
COUNTRY

Savanna-
la-Mar

Black R.

Rio M.

Black River

Mandeville

Milk R.

C a r i b b e a n   S e a

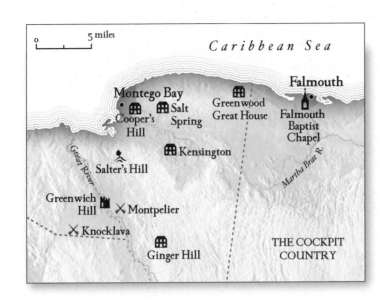

Caribbean Sea

Montego Bay

Cooper's Hill

Salt Spring

Greenwood Great House

Falmouth

Falmouth Baptist Chapel

Kensington

Salter's Hill

Greenwich Hill

Montpelier

Knocklava

Ginger Hill

THE COCKPIT COUNTRY

Great River

Martha Brae R.

5 miles

Caribbean Sea

Ocho Rios

Port Antonio

Rio Magno

SPANISH TOWN

Kingston

Port Royal

Rio Grande

Morant R.

Morant Bay

25 miles

Jamaica, 1831–1832

INTRODUCTION

ON THE NIGHT OF DECEMBER 27, 1831, a watchman standing on top of the courthouse in the Jamaican city of Montego Bay spotted a fire on a hillside south of town. Then another fire appeared close by. And then another.[1]

The meaning of this chain of fire was instantly clear to the watchman, Colonel George Lawson, who had been—like the rest of his militia unit—in a state of high alert because of credible evidence that the slave population of the northwest shore of Jamaica was about to rise up in revolt.[2]

Lawson reported the fires to John Roby, the collector of customs at the port, who had almost certainly already seen them. As the Caribbean night sky gradually turned the color of copper, Roby wrote an urgent message to the governor of Jamaica underlining two words, a gesture almost never seen in official correspondence:

> Sir, I consider it my duty to inform you that there is at this moment a serious fire raging in a southeasterly direction from this town, apparently 8 or 10 miles distant, and it is supposed at Hampton Estate but from the glare I fear it extends to other estates in its vicinity lying more to the southward. From the late insubordination of the negroes on many estates in the neighborhood, which has caused the militia to be under arms since Sunday last, it is feared that this fire is <u>not</u> from accidental causes

and I beg the favor of your giving his Excellency the governor immediate information thereof.

He then added a postscript, knowing that one company of a badly trained militia would not be sufficient to prevent the white population from being massacred:

½ past 9
I have just been informed that Kensington pen and Mr. Tullock's settlement have been burned—we have one company of the 22nd regiment in this town.[3]

Lawson and Roby had no way of knowing if the family had been left alive or not. By ten o'clock, the men had counted at least six fires that seemed to blend into a terrifying orange crown on the hills. By this point, Lawson "feared the east part of the parish would be destroyed by morning."[4] If anything, this was an underestimation. Fires were breaking out all over northwestern Jamaica.

One man on a plantation in Cornwall started a letter and kept revising it throughout the night:

The work of destruction has commenced. We now see two fires, evidently in the direction of St. James.

Ten o'clock—We have just received intelligence that the fire at Palmyra estate was extinguished, after burning down one trash house.

Eleven o'clock at night—The work of destruction is going on. The whole sky, in the southwest is illuminated—From our office we at this moment perceive five distinct fires—one apparently in this parish, the others in St. James's and at no great distance from us.

Midnight—One fire is raging with unabated fury. We apprehend it to be the whole of the works and buildings on the York estate, in this parish.[5]

Nobody who saw them ever forgot the plantation fires. They would burn and reignite across northwestern Jamaica for the better part of two weeks and rain a curtain of ash down on the trees. Various awestruck witnesses described them as "one solid mass of flame," "a vast furnace," the skies "lighted up in all directions," a chain of signaling lamps that seemed the fruits of a biblical judgment. "The whole country," concluded a minister, "seemed given up to destruction." More than two hundred blazes were reported in the opening days of the revolt, and in the daytime, they magnified the glare of the tropics and tinted the sun with menace as an organized army of enslaved people held their masters hostage and fought off attacks from the volunteer militia.[6]

The gathering inferno frightened George Lawson to the point that he ordered his post abandoned. "I am convinced the contest must be decided in the streets of Montego Bay," he hurriedly wrote the governor before he left for the countryside to link up with another regiment. Professional British soldiers sailed into the harbor three days later and quickly became ensnared in a guerilla war they were ill prepared to fight. Many of them expressed astonishment at the military talent of the enslaved people, who outnumbered whites on the island by ten to one. The rebels built a fortress atop Greenwich Hill and won at least one direct head-to-head confrontation on the battlefield. Indicating an unprecedented level of preparation, some of the dead fighters were found wearing uniforms: blue coats with red sashes.[7]

The entire plantation society of Jamaica came under attack in the largest revolt it had ever faced. One of the richest sugar growers in Jamaica, Richard Barrett, watched the fires with mounting fear from a house in Montego Bay. A fierce defender of slavery, he was the cousin of the poet Elizabeth Barrett Browning and well connected in British society. Barrett scratched out a note to the colonial governor on the fourth night of the insurrection: "The militia to a man are zealous and loyal, and no praise can be too high for their courage and conduct." A hint of his panic, however, can be seen in the drops of ink carelessly spilled onto his note.[8]

"It is supposed that a hundred plantations and settlements are already in ashes," Barrett wrote. "If the rebellion spreads, our force is quite insufficient to put it down—all depends on the moral effect of the employment of the King's troops. Five rebels have been tried by court martial and shot. A woman also condemned was spared—I think she should be hanged."[9]

Those first nights full of fire touched off five weeks of burning, looting, crop destruction, courts-martial, on-the-spot executions, severed heads mounted atop poles, and outright human hunting for sport that shook slaveholding Jamaica to its foundations and sent authorities on a manhunt for the renegade Baptist deacon Samuel Sharpe, who had told his followers the revolt would be a peaceful sit-down strike, only to watch it gyrate out of control and erupt into an inferno. The violence created alarming newspaper headlines across the ocean, forcing Richard Barrett to return to London to answer for the embarrassment in an attempt to save the three-century-old institution of British slavery.

But he could not; the costs were too high. The violence on the Christmas holiday played a central role in convincing the British public that slavery could no longer be countenanced and spurring them to demand change from a dysfunctional Parliament. The effects would also ripple in the United States, where politicians with Southern sympathies had just weathered the revolt of Nat Turner in Virginia and seen how Sharpe's rebellion in Jamaica had led directly to British abolition.

Periodic slave insurrections were taken as a fact of life in Jamaica—even as a routine cost of doing business. But Sharpe's movement was different: resistance on a dazzling scale. It was well organized, spread across a wide geographic area, and inspired by Baptist salvation thinking. More than thirty thousand enslaved people were eventually brought into a plot rooted in nonviolent idealism that anticipated twentieth-century movements such as those led by Mahatma Gandhi, Martin Luther King Jr., and the proponents of liberation theology in Latin America.[10]

Samuel Sharpe's rebellion was not the only key to ending slavery in the British Empire. The tumultuous economics of Caribbean sugar, the work of the abolitionist movement, the reform of Parliament, the rising clout of Britain's new industrialized classes—all of these forces made British slavery's long-term survival unlikely. But the five-week uprising in Jamaica, even though it was confined to the northwest shore and was put down in a decisive military victory, proved to be the spark that ignited the movement to end British slavery less than two and a half years later and an invigorating example for abolitionists who then turned their attention to the overthrow of slavery in the United States.

How this remarkable story unfolded—how such a seemingly isolated set of events involving some of the globe's most despised human beings should have resulted in such tectonic change—is the central question animating this book, which will argue, first, that Sam Sharpe's movement was not predicated on anything more than seeking liberty for himself and his fellow enslaved people and, second, that it sent an unambiguous message to London that slavery was no longer sustainable—not economically, not militarily, and not morally. Sharpe's rebellion did not spur emancipation all by itself, but it certainly hastened the forces that were already in play.

The first six chapters examine the colonial society of Jamaica—an island culture beset with alcoholism, sexual predation, petty corruption, obsession with money, routine cruelty, absentee ownership, and disease. British settlers came here to make money fast or die trying, supplying the parent country with as much sugar as they could grow. To be a successful West Indian planter was to be in possession of some of the most rapidly accruing wealth in the entire British Empire, thanks to a widespread passion for creams, whips, cakes, tarts, pancakes, puddings, and the omnipresent hot tea with sugar. Feeding this addiction on a grand scale was made possible by the labor of the approximately 860,000 kidnapped Africans transported to Jamaica as slaves between 1600 and 1807.[11]

The next three chapters provide a day-by-day account of what happened during the five active weeks of the insurrection, as houses burned and the militia conducted on-the-spot executions.

The last four chapters are largely a political story: we see how the news landed in Britain, how it broke the back of the West Indian Interest in Parliament, and how it resulted, improbably enough, in Samuel Sharpe's ultimate goal of bringing freedom to enslaved people not just in Jamaica but across the whole empire.

Sharpe's insurrection took place at the beginning of the 1830s, a decade when cracks formed in the global order of transatlantic mercantilism that would soon collapse the system entirely. Revolutionary movements threatened old institutions in both hemispheres. The first railways had begun spiderwebbing across northern England's coal country, moving cargo and people at the astonishing speed of twenty-five miles per hour between smog-choked boomtowns teeming with new factories and textile mills. A medieval-era Parliament stuffed with noblemen faced a challenge from the growing numbers of poor and middle-class people who demanded representation through riots and strikes, and the nation teetered on the brink of revolt for several weeks. The French got rid of their Bourbon king Charles X, even as the Parisian Louis-Jacques-Mandé Daguerre tinkered with the precursor to the photograph. Americans worked on their own pioneering railroads, founded a lakefront settlement named Chicago, traveled overland in wagons to the Oregon Territory, and elected as their president the hot-headed military hero Andrew Jackson in order to snub the elites and break up the national bank. Richard Wagner wrote his first opera; the inventor Samuel Morse experimented with electric pulses sent through a new device called a telegraph; powerful steamboats replaced hand-rowed barges, and a farm boy in upstate New York named Joseph Smith began telling his neighbors that he had excavated a set of golden plates bearing strange symbols that he would soon translate into *The Book of Mormon*. On December 27, 1831, the young naturalist Charles Darwin set sail on HMS *Beagle* for the Galapagos Islands. Later on that same night, the first fires of Samuel Sharpe's rebellion were lit at Kensington.

At that point in time, approximately 800,000 British slaves lived in a state of grinding captivity, forced to work fourteen hours a day in sweltering cane fields or sugar-boiling houses, dwelling in flimsy thatched huts and using primitive tools, their lifespans shortened by decades and punctuated with frequent lashings, systematic rapes, and bouts of near starvation. Jamaica was a vast agricultural prison camp with nearly twenty enslaved black people for every free white person. But less than two years after Sharpe and his allies made their stand, Parliament was convinced to end the practice of slavery for good. By the time the decade was out, every enslaved person was made a full citizen. This is the story of how that happened.[12]

ONE

A SUBURB OF HELL

JAMAICA HAD LONG THRIVED on its image of easy wealth amid tropical breezes, long manor lanes shaded by coconut trees, plenty of fresh mangoes, languid afternoons spent drinking rum-and-lime punch on the veranda while watching one's human property chopping rows of sleek sugarcane. From this vantage point, it was easy to appreciate why this bead of volcanic rock in the midst of a turquoise sea had been singled out by Christopher Columbus as the most beautiful of the islands he had seen in his four voyages to the West Indies.

Cooling trade winds buffeted the coasts, the Caribbean looked like a plate of cobalt when spread out for miles against the edges of wide beaches, and the island's soils proved ideal for growing the cash crop that planters called Creole cane, the sharp stalks of grass that concealed sweet fiber in their interiors. Assuming no disruptions from hurricanes or slave mutinies, a man who had been given eighty acres of land and enough capital to buy one hundred enslaved Africans could expect to produce eighty tons of sugar in a year, enough for a comfortable living. With more land and human property, he could become dazzlingly prosperous.[1]

The British had grabbed the island in a dishonorable manner. After Oliver Cromwell had taken control of Parliament in 1653 and overseen the beheading of King Charles I, he laid out a plan for seizing more territory from the Spanish as part of an anti-Catholic crusade. Cromwell aimed to secure a bigger share of gold by issuing merchant seamen "letters of marque and reprisal," which made it legal for them to hijack Spanish galleons and claim the stolen cargo for themselves. Not coincidentally, this scheme also created a foreign adventure through which to distract from the divisions and potential counterrevolutions at home. The aggressive "Western Design" campaign led to a 1654 British invasion of the island of Hispaniola with 8,200 amateur soldiers drawn largely from poor white laborers from the neighboring sugar island of Barbados.[2]

Nothing went right. Cannons went missing, approximately one thousand troops immediately died from malaria and yellow fever, squadrons got lost in the jungle, and the generals grew contemptuous of their own men; one called them lowlifes and braggarts "so cowardly as not to be made to fight." Another lamented having to march into the jungle with "common cheats, thieves, cutpurses, and such like lewd persons" who were fit more for prison than military service. After blundering around for three weeks, the generals William Penn and Robert Venables decided to switch islands, and they headed to the more lightly defended island of Jamaica, which took its name from a corruption of the name given by the native Taino people, Xaymaca, "the land of wood and water."[3]

The Spanish had already carved it up into plantations and made slaves of the Taino. Here the British had better luck, burning down the main settlement of Villa de la Vega and then rebuilding it under the new name Spanish Town. After the restoration of the monarchy with the crowning of Charles II, Jamaica became known as a wild frontier outpost where those who sided with Cromwell and helped murder the king could safely hide out from the authorities.[4]

An early governor named Thomas Modyford encouraged settlement by doling out land patents—many to his own family and friends—and importing boiling pots and cane presses from Britain. While a few gentlemen farmers set out patches of coffee, pimento, cocoa, indigo, ginger, or cotton, sugar was always the biggest game; it was the root of the local monoculture and the way to make truly staggering amounts of money. One of those pioneer sugar planters,

Hersey Barrett, had fought the Spanish in the first invasion force and had bragged to friends that he had been the one to personally chop off the head of King Charles I. He would go on to found one of the most prominent dynasties in Jamaica: the family that would produce the future Speaker of the Jamaica Assembly, Richard Barrett.[5]

These first Jamaican sugar boomers wiped out most of the native Taino people through disease and slavery, and built a city, Port Royal, at the tip of a slender thread of land that curved around one of the biggest natural harbors in the world—one that could easily have sheltered the entire British fleet. Port Royal's streets were tight and labyrinthine; they were especially dangerous when a ship full of thirsty sailors disgorged its crew after the six-week journey from Britain or the slaving grounds of Africa. Only slightly less populated than Boston, but far more carnal, Port Royal fed off sugar and piracy to support a knot of tailors, blacksmiths, brothels, bakers, gambling dens, alehouses, a few churches, and even a small synagogue tucked out of the way to serve a small population of Sephardic Jews who spoke Portuguese and had migrated from Brazil. The former pirate Henry Morgan soon learned he could make far more money planting sugar than he could raiding ships.[6]

Heavy drinking was acceptable at all hours, and Jamaicans enjoyed many choices: brandy, Madeira wine, ale in casks imported from the mother country, and a coarse rum called kill devil, cut with fruit juice. "The Spaniards wondered much at the sickness of our people, until they knew the strength of their drinks," wrote Modyford, "but then wondered more why they were not dead." Ships from Britain ferried in almost as much alcohol as food. A tip of land named Gallows Point was reserved for the dead bodies of the condemned, who dangled from iron cages known as gibbets, their intestines food for gulls. This display was among the first sights of the island for newcomers.[7]

A popular writer named Ned Ward visited in the late seventeenth century and collected impressions for a pamphlet titled *A Trip to*

Jamaica, which painted the island as a haven for prostitutes, drunks, cutpurses, and the general scum of the empire, while Port Royal itself was described as "a shapeless pile of rubbish." Though Ward hoped to entertain through humorous exaggeration, readers in England were scandalized and not a little bit fascinated with what he called the Sodom of the Indies. Jamaica came to stand for the entire British West Indies and the other sugar colonies: a ne plus ultra of debauchery. The mythology surrounding the island was not unlike that which the Wild West would take on for a later generation of American readers, except without the heroics. Nobody here came off looking good; Jamaica earned the nickname Dunghill of the Universe.[8]

Shortly before noon on June 7, 1692, an earthquake leveled Port Royal, sending a large portion of it into the ocean and leaving fresh corpses floating in the saltwater next to skeletons that had been liberated from their coffins. In need of a new port, Jamaica's sugar grandees moved off the coastal spit and built a town at the far end of the harbor at a place they named Kingston, this time with a geometric street pattern that left room on the outskirts for a parade ground. One observer said Kingston had "no pretensions to beauty" and compared it to "a large town entirely composed of booths at a race-course." But Kingston was not about raiding; it was about stocking up sugar for the overseas trade. The reckless criminal spirit of the island—born of regicide, piracy, and territorial theft—had survived the destruction of Port Royal and shifted over to agriculture.[9]

The newly arrived had to act fast, because they did not know when they would die. One doctor estimated that a third of young men died within three weeks of stepping off a ship in Kingston, and no insurance company in England would issue a policy for anyone traveling to Jamaica. When Robert Renny took his first look at the island in 1800, he watched from the deck of his ship as a small group of black women approached in a canoe to sell fruit to the newcomers. As they paddled away, they began to sing a song about *buckra*—a catch-all term for white people:

> New-come buckra
> He get sick
> He take fever
> He be die
> He be die[10]

The woods were alive with the hum of disease-bearing mosquitos, joined by the alien chatter of tree frogs, lizards, owls, and grasshoppers, and all the ominous noise was made even more noticeable by the motionless air. Fields that had been recently cleared of trees grew in again quickly if left untended, the jungle reasserting itself as if humans had never been there. The sun was so relentless that objects seemed to cast no shadows and the very atmosphere seemed to advertise the idea of a short life tinged with corruption. Not for nothing did the evangelist William Jones call the island "the suburbs of hell."[11]

Malaria was the most common killer; those who caught it endured fevers, chills, sweats, diarrhea, and enlarged livers before a trip to a tropical grave. Yellow fever was an even more grotesque way to die. A person appeared normal for several days after a bite from an infected mosquito before suffering a headache so fierce as to make the skull feel as though it were exploding. The skin then became jaundiced, taking on the color of a ripe banana. Victims perished after a final struggle during which they vomited dark ooze. "A man, well in the morning, is seized, perhaps at noon; and on the third day is often a corpse," wrote Theodore Foulks. "The effects of this fever are so astonishingly rapid, and a few hours of suffering so effectually change the appearance, that it is sometimes difficult to recognize even an intimate friend. The face assumes a yellow and ghastly hue." An indentured servant from Yorkshire named William Fisher survived his ordeal, but he was so sick at one point that he wrote his father, "You would scarce know me if you met me. My blood is reduced to water, almost, and I am a mere sceleton." He fully expected to be dead before he could leave Jamaica.[12]

A febrile death in the night was common enough to be considered rather unremarkable. The victim was buried immediately and rarely spoken of again; it was as if the person had never existed at all. Lady Maria Nugent, the English-born wife of a colonial governor, was shocked by how nonchalantly her new friends took the passing of a friend. "Rise at 6," she wrote in her diary on August 30, 1801, "and was told, at breakfast, that the usual occurrence of a death had taken place. Poor Mr. Sandford had died at 4 o'clock in the morning. My dear N. and I feel it very much, but all around us appear to be quite callous."[13]

An astonishing 10 percent of the whites died in an average year, creating open jobs for fresh shiploads of British strivers from lower social orders, eager for opportunities they never would have had back home. They typically started on a sugar estate as "bookkeepers," which had almost nothing to do with accounting but instead meant tending pigs, supervising the harvests, and administering whippings. If a man worked hard, he could become an overseer, and then an "attorney"—the local property manager for whatever London plutocrat held the deed to the plantation. An average attorney, wrote resident Robert Charles Dallas, was a "plain plodding man" who got by on his own dependable mediocrity and eventually became "stark mad with pride." But this was how real money could be made, because attorneys took 6 percent on every transaction. The average white male resident of Jamaica was 52.3 times wealthier than his peer back in England, and 57.6 times as wealthy as a white man living in New England.[14]

Such a harried pace of life left no time for beauty. Among the staple crop civilizations of the nineteenth century, Jamaica was noteworthy for what it *didn't* have in abundance: granite monuments, private

MARIA, LADY NUGENT.

Lady Maria Nugent. Her diary paints a picture of a hedonistic society dedicated to consumption and surrounded by death. *(British Library)*

gardens, schools, parks, beautiful churches, columned public halls. Nobody thought to bring a printing press until sixty-six years after the British takeover. Graceful mansions like those built in the American South were less common in Jamaica and generally seen only around Kingston and on the shore of St. James Parish, where the wealthier planters aimed to impress their neighbors with blood-wood floors, wine cellars, silverware, china sets, and ancestral portraits on the walls. But the master's "Great House" was more commonly made of crude materials and sometimes looked no better than a barn with windows. As a government secretary described them, many country estates were "miserable, thatched hovels, hastily put together with wattles and plaster, damp, unwholesome and infested with every species of vermin."[15]

Having children in Jamaica's pestilential climate was a chancy matter; only the most prosperous planters seemed to have more than two that survived. The wealthiest sought to send their children to England after the age of six, because schools were never built to any appreciable degree and tutors were despised—"looked upon as contemptible," wrote one resident, "and no Gentleman keeps company with one of that character." Boys typically started drinking alcohol and sleeping with enslaved girls around the age of fourteen, whereas girls were expected to occupy themselves with theater and dances, and rarely learned to read. "Here in Jamaica, the unfortunate children learn nothing at all," wrote a young German visitor in 1778. "The people here are very rich, but they don't spend any of this wealth on their children."[16]

One of those elite children sent off to England for a formal education was Edward Barrett Moulton-Barrett, the offspring of the regicidal soldier Hersey Barrett. By the end of the eighteenth century, the Barrett descendants would control three thousand enslaved people and a good portion of the countryside in St. James Parish. Moulton-Barrett never really returned to the island; he became one of the legions of absentee sugar lords and married an even wealthier woman in Britain, with whom he had twelve children.

For reasons that remain hazy, Edward refused to let any of his children marry. He may have been unhealthily fixated on preserving their virginity or—as others speculated—he wanted the Barrett line to die out. Though she was sickly, reclusive, and addicted to opiates, his oldest daughter, the poet Elizabeth Barrett Browning, defied his wishes. She and Robert Browning eloped, then moved to Italy when she was forty years old, and she lived with him there for the rest of her life. Embarrassed by her family's slave-owning history, she never visited Jamaica and confessed to being "haunted" by the possibility of being taken there.[17]

The Barretts were among the cream of the fifty or so elite families who had control over Jamaica. Like the rest of their dazzlingly wealthy peers, most of the tropical aristocracy made a full-time home in England or spent lavishly to take their families on vacations away from the island, especially in the broiling summers. American residents of port cities like Charleston, New Orleans, and New York looked on visiting West Indian sugar barons with a mixture of envy and disgust. One letter writer said they could always be identified by their "carbuncled faces, slender legs and thighs and large prominent bellies." Another suggested that hotels should design advertisements in the shape of "the worn-out West Indian, dying of a dropsy from intemperate living." The visible decrepitude of the sugar grandees was even more remarkable because the decay happened so early. Old men in Jamaica were a rarity, and even the middle-aged were in short supply. Most planters were single men in their twenties and thirties.[18]

Few unmarried white women were ever induced to emigrate, and those who were suffered the scorn of those back home, for "'tis impossible for a Woman to live at *Jamaica* and preserve her Virtue," wrote William Pittis, who satirized the island's loose morals in his novel *The Jamaica Lady.* Upper-class British women who visited the island remarked critically on the high-pitched and whiny patterns of speech of the housewives there, as well as their ostentatious dress and love of dancing. British soldiers stationed in Kingston found them easy to seduce.[19]

Even Jamaican families who had been living there for generations displayed what one historian called a "remarkable rootlessness." Nothing seemed permanent; almost everything was built for cheapness, utility, and disposal. Those who were best equipped and educated to build a lasting society—those of the moneyed overclass— were away in England. Roads were muddy and narrow; bridges were rickety and prone to collapse. Kingston went for years without a custom house because not even the city dwellers who would have most benefited from the revenue would agree to pay for it. "The want of public spirit for noble and liberal undertakings, has long been a striking feature of this island," lamented John Stewart, "while the inhabitants will heedlessly throw away thousands upon some trifling amusement." Vulgar wealth, he said, was "the great desideratum" of life in Jamaica.[20]

This was how it went, for Jamaica was the "Kingdom of I," in the words of the disgusted observer James Ramsay: the place where the glorification of the individual took precedence over public spirit, over building anything to last, and over the suffering of others—indeed, over everything. For the materially fortunate, the vast prison camp of Jamaica was the zenith of freedom. Democratic informality and arriviste style prevailed among the white colonists, along with a coarseness of speech, manners, and behavior. The stultifying class system that reigned back home in England was completely reframed in the West Indies. Social distinction among whites was founded instead on how much money, and how many slaves, a man had accumulated. People were used to casually wandering into each other's houses and helping themselves to a glass of rum punch. One landowner commented that "visitors, negroes, dogs, cats, poultry, all walk in and out, and up and down your living-rooms, without the slightest ceremony." Some of the most notable political figures in the colony had hot tempers and would shoot at one another if they felt insulted. There was no real police force outside the capital; law enforcement in the countryside was in the hands of the plantation bosses and their muskets and whips. In this sense, white Jamaican society resembled contemporary settlements on the Australian and US frontiers and developed for itself a global reputation for hedonism, sensuality, bluff manners, easy money, and unpredictable violence.[21]

What made Jamaica's know-nothingness so noteworthy was that it had previously displayed some affection for the ideas of the

Enlightenment. A handful of debating and scientific societies formed, then withered as Jamaica seemed to retreat into a defensive crouch. Planters with cosmopolitan sensibilities displayed books and the latest newspapers from London in their parlors, but many of their white neighbors could not even read and had to have legal documents reviewed by others. The Anglican Church was an official partner of the Crown as a registrar of births, deaths, and marriages—as well as a taker of confessions from convicted criminals—but Jamaicans were largely an irreligious lot, and Sunday masses were attended only by a smattering of older women. Churches filled up only for the funerals of the rich. The Bishop of London, Beilby Porteous, lamented that he had tried his best to recruit good priests, but they could "scarce be tempted by any advantage to go to the West Indies where they are in dread of the climate." A local judge was more blunt when he characterized local Anglican pastors as on an antinomian spree, addicted to "lewdness, drinking, gambling and iniquity," more fit to be pirates or fishmongers than clergymen.[22]

The English settlers had still tried their best to re-create the basic political geometries of their homeland in the tropics. They had divided the island into nineteen parishes—official divisions of the Anglican Church, but really local governing units—and given them names of Old Albion, like Hanover, St. James, Trelawny, and Westmoreland. They sent two representatives apiece to the legislature, the Jamaica Assembly, which met in the sleepy capital of Spanish Town from October to December, watched over by a governor—typically a minor aristocrat in the civil service—appointed by the Colonial Office in London. The home government gave the island special diplomatic attention. Not only was it a check against French and Spanish ambitions in the New World, it was a massive money generator at the heart of the British Empire. "Jamaica is a Constant Mine, whence Britain draws prodigious riches," wrote Charles Leslie in 1739. Though it was a rough place across the ocean, it was never treated like a backwater.[23]

All free men between the ages of sixteen and sixty, whites and colored alike, were required to join the Jamaican militia, the amateur paramilitary force that was supposed to put down rebellions if they should start, but many did so without any feelings of patriotism or esprit de corps. One eighteenth-century governor had characterized it as full of disgruntled Irish immigrants known for their "backwardnesse, mutinys and desertion." Everyone had to supply their own weapons and uniforms and show up once a month for drilling. Officers tended to get their commissions based on wealth and social rank rather than any measure of ability.[24]

The militia displayed a noteworthy ineptitude, and its chief benefit may have been to provide a psychological comfort to whites who knew they were surrounded at all times by an abused majority that could crush them if they ever successfully unified. In times of war with other European powers in the Caribbean, the colony had to depend on the Royal Navy to ward off invasions. When slave rebellions erupted, the crimson-clad King's Grenadiers were the last, best hope. In slave nations like Jamaica, remarked planter Bryan Edwards, "the leading principle on which the government is supported is fear."[25]

Perhaps because of the looming specter of rebellion and death, Jamaicans spared themselves no luxury at the dining table. At their feasts, the gentry served up to each other an array of papayas, pineapples, meat pies, anchovies, bacon, potato puddings, snapper, lobster, candied fruits, oysters, and custards—the more color and variety, the better. Evening dinners could last for as long as five hours.[26]

The gluttony at the table was complemented by heavy drinking; chronic alcoholism was another of the diseases endemic to colonial Jamaica. Planters customarily set out a bowl of rum laced with lime, sugar, and nutmeg in their halls, and many would take cups of this punch throughout the day. As an appalled visitor observed, the white inhabitants "live like the people of Sodom and Gomorrah of biblical times; they drink, eat, play and dance, become pale as death and die like flies." Maria Nugent, the wife of a colonial governor, also marveled at the drunken lunches. The Jamaican men were sending themselves to early graves, she concluded, because they "drink like porpoises." She noted in a diary entry for February 4, 1802:

> I don't wonder now at the fever the people suffer from here—such eating and drinking I never saw! Such loads of all sorts of high, rich, and seasoned things, and really gallons of wine and mixed liquors as they drink! I observed some of the party, to-day, eat of late breakfasts, as if they had never eaten before—a dish of tea, another of coffee, a bumper of claret, another one of hock-negus; then Madeira, sangaree, hot and cold meat, stews and fries, hot and cold fish pickled and plain, peppers, gingers sweetmeats, acid fruit, sweet jellies—in short, it was all as astonishing as it was disgusting.[27]

Thomas Thistlewood was a man of these voracious appetites who represented his time and place. He came to Jamaica in 1750 at the age of twenty-nine, having failed to make a living as a farmer in his native Lincolnshire. He brought with him a case of razors, a rack of liquor, surveying tools, nine waistcoats, a partially filled diary of his travels, and an inheritance of sixty pounds from his parents. Almost immediately after he landed in the town of Savanna-la-Mar, he was offered a job as an overseer at Egypt Estate and watched with apparent disgust as his new boss, the planter William Dorrill, punished runaway slaves by having them whipped until they bled in multiple places and then rubbing lime, pepper, and salt into the wounds.[28]

But before long Thistlewood was ordering the whipping himself, having come to believe that his charges were "a Nest of Thieves and Villains." He whipped them for making noise at night, for speaking impudently, for letting cattle into the wrong pasture, or for eating sugarcane. It was Thistlewood who invented a punishment called Derby's dose, named for a recalcitrant slave, which involved forcing another slave to defecate directly into Derby's open mouth, which he then wrapped shut with wire for several hours. His diary is filled with fragmental notations of when he beat his enslaved people, how many lashes he administered, the state of the weather that day, whom he saw on business, and—eventually—the details of his sexual encounters with female slaves, which he rendered in a primitive Latin code. "Sup Terr," for example, was his way of saying "on the ground." In the thirty-seven years he spent in Jamaica until his death in 1786, he recorded 3,852 couplings with 138 different women. He ordered some of them whipped later in the same day. His enslaved people nicknamed him "No for Play" on account of his menacing temperament.[29]

One is tempted to think Thistlewood a monster after reading his nonchalant account of his lusts and cruelties. But a broader look at the Jamaica of the day brings to light the even more awful realization of just how unremarkable he was, for he epitomized the eerie change in personality that came to Jamaican newcomers after even a few weeks' exposure to the routine degradations of slavery. People who would have been horrified at the idea of whipping another human were soon doing it themselves; men who had sworn chastity and fidelity were soon bedding slave women. The seventeen-year-old bookkeeper Zachary Macaulay wrote home to a friend in 1785, "The air of this island must have some peculiar quality in it, for no sooner does a person set foot on it than his former ways of thinking are entirely changed. The contagion of an universal example must indeed have its effect." Or as J. B. Moreton had observed near the same time, moral character tended to melt like wax in the heat of the Caribbean.[30]

Thousands of white newcomers to Jamaica would see the inexplicable personality distortions in themselves after a few weeks and become living examples of the great moral truth later articulated by the escaped slave Frederick Douglass: that slavery corrupts the master even more than it ruins the enslaved, and that "the fatal poison of irresponsible power" is a powerful intoxicant. William

Fisher of Yorkshire wrote with disgust at the vicious punishments he saw: "I was sick when I first came here and saw the negroes flogged every day" until their backs were "all chattered." Yet Fisher did not utter any protests on their behalf, and the daily cries of anguish soon became routine to him. A Jamaican newspaper, the *Falmouth Post,* would later describe the corrupting power of money and violence on any number of young men who were suddenly made "a little king" over hundreds of people who had to be forced to work. Could a man with such power retain "the last shreds of his moral being? He could not—he must have seen that to bend or break was inevitable."[31]

As it had been for Thistlewood, the whip handle was typically the point where the personality change started. Estate manager William Taylor recalled that an overseer on a neighboring property had been "most humane and benevolent" but found that having his workers lashed and even tortured was the only way to "establish his authority."[32]

Sex was the other primary arena of corruption in Jamaica. An average sugar estate was an erotic free-for-all for white overseers, who enjoyed a sort of droit du seigneur over their charges. As one observer put it, an estate proprietor was automatically granted "unlimited power over the body of his female slaves." The topsy-turvy morality of Jamaica was such that a man who didn't regularly have sex with as many enslaved women as he could was subject to public scorn. Few lower-class married men lived in Jamaica, and they were usually denied employment on sugar estates because they were perceived as killjoys. Casual rape was a customary part of the famous Jamaican hospitality. In addition to the copious liquor and food, it was common to offer a male visitor a young girl for a night's pleasure. A parliamentary committee heard testimony in 1833 that white neighbors would customarily gather at different estates on Sunday evenings for parties where it was "not unusual for the female slaves to be collected and shown, that each [white male guest] may choose a companion for the night."[33]

Sex with white men was compulsory for enslaved women, for, as one British witness testified, "if an overseer sends for a girl for such purposes she is obliged to come, or else flogged." These beckonings usually started when the girl turned fourteen, and sometimes when she was as young as nine. Those who became the mistresses of a white man often did so out of self-preservation. Submitting to the rape of a white man of even low standing could mean easier work, better food, occasional liquor, kinder treatment, the authority to help manage the great house, and the possibility one day of being set free. If the woman had a black male partner, he was obliged to endure the cuckolding without protest lest he be submitted to a fierce lashing as the woman stood by. Conversations between enslaved partners after these encounters must have been excruciating.[34]

TWO

DEACON SHARPE

WILLIAM KNIBB FELT a sense of doom as he approached the island of Jamaica. This was the same garden of lost souls that had killed his brother Thomas, who had succumbed to yellow fever at the age of twenty-five, and now here he was, to carry on the same work, without knowing if it would also send him to his grave. After landing in January 1825, he sent a letter to his friend Samuel Nichols. "I have now reached the land of sin, disease, and death," he wrote, "where Satan reigns with awful power, and carried multitudes captive at his will. Here religion is scoffed at, and those who profess it ridiculed and insulted."[1]

Knibb had a hot temper from the start and may have suffered from what is today called attention deficit disorder. His first schoolteacher described him as "a good boy, but somewhat volatile," and a later classmate said he was "chiefly distinguished for the exuberance of his animal spirits" and that he was "marked rather by incessant activity than by any deep or earnest thoughtfulness." As he grew into manhood, he cut an unimpressive figure. One man who met him briefly described him as "a common vulgar shop man" with a "great, fat over-grown body, very restless, and a short, quick manner, which has a degree of coarseness added to it."[2]

The members of the Baptist Missionary Society had clearly thought more highly of his late brother, Thomas, yet the dull-looking William Knibb had also volunteered to risk his life in Jamaica for the sake of preaching. They got more than they expected or wanted. The torture Knibb soon witnessed on the plantations shocked his conscience to the point of his having what amounted to a second conversion.

"The cursed blast of slavery has, like a pestilence, withered almost every moral bloom," Knibb confided in a letter to his mother. But missionaries had to keep quiet about what they saw in Jamaica if they wanted to avoid being kicked off the island. As a Baptist directive put it, "Maintain toward all in authority a respectful demeanor. Treat them with the honor to which their office entitles them. Political and party discussion avoid as beneath your office." They were not to meddle in political life and were under strict instructions to keep silent about its signature feature.[3]

More than a few enslaved people told newly arrived missionaries like Knibb that they were troubled by the concept of sin and punishment, for it seemed to them that they were already living in a version of hell. Sin involved an awareness of individual agency and dignity, a concept that had been under assault for most enslaved people from the moment they touched Jamaican soil, either by birth or by abduction. But those who accepted the message—especially in the Baptist Church—received an astonishingly vivid welcome: hymns, white robes, reading lessons, and an immersion in water, either in a river or in the sea.

The Christianity preached by the white missionaries quickly fused with African influences, giving rise to a style of worship that came to be called Native Baptist or Black Baptist. These congregations operated to the side of the traditional churches, and, instead of the staid and patterned form of worship advocated by the British, they put a premium on ecstatic spiritual experiences and emotive expressions of faith. Operating in a kind of gray zone between Protestantism and traditional African beliefs, this style of worship spread more effectively than the more formal message preached by the white missionaries, who were suspicious of these unorthodoxies and their joyous noises. Yet these small groups sprouted like flowers wherever the

Gospel was preached in Jamaica, and they enjoyed a measure of self-governance. Free from oversight by the whites, members of an enslaved congregation could choose leaders among themselves as "teachers" or "daddies" to lead worship, and some of them were given the privilege to travel between plantations to spread the message. These types of loose churches were known colloquially as the Black Family.[4]

An important locus for these semisecret groups was a modest building in the town of Montego Bay: a new Baptist church founded by Thomas Burchell, a quiet and cultured man from Gloucestershire who was thought to be more politically astute than his more excitable colleague William Knibb. He grew the church to a size of 4,600 worshippers in seven years and took on a number of enslaved people as junior partners in the Gospel, naming them deacons, even though some of them had double roles in the Black Family. They had the authority to hand out the bread and wine of Communion, distribute money for the needy, pay visits to the sick, and give religious instruction.

One of the new deacons was especially educated and charismatic, a fine public speaker and a dedicated reader of the Bible. His name was Samuel Sharpe.

Frustratingly little is known of Samuel Sharpe's early life, and this makes him entirely characteristic of the enslaved people of Jamaica whose names might be written down once—if at all—in a bookkeeper's ledger before their bodies were discarded in an unmarked grave when their working life was over.

What is known for certain from documentary evidence is that a white lawyer named Samuel Sharpe, the owner of an estate named Cooper's Hill, filed a legal document called a slave owner's return to British authorities that listed his human property on June 28, 1817. He claimed a total of twelve enslaved people, including adult males named Hamlet, Ned, and Paisley. Among them was a twelve-year-old boy named Archer, the son of a forty-year-old woman, Eve, who was listed as "African" and not "Creole," meaning she had been brought to Jamaica from an unspecified region of Africa.[5]

A later document filed by the same lawyer-slaveholder in 1832 lists a twenty-seven-year-old man, "Archer alias Sam Sharpe," indicating that the boy Archer had taken on the name of his owner, a common custom of the time. The lawyer Sharpe owned only a moderate number of enslaved people; the *Jamaica Almanack* for 1828 shows him with thirty-two. The master Sharpe is also listed as a captain in the St. James Regiment of the militia.[6]

The younger Samuel Sharpe was said to have been a favorite of his owner, "brought up as a playmate for the juvenile members of the family," said an acquaintance, and even "a pet." The white members of the family had always been kind to him, Sharpe told people near the end of his life. He had never been flogged, or even punished, except for "the occasional and slight correction which he had received when a boy."[7]

Significantly, he learned to read and write—likely under the tutelage of a Baptist missionary, possibly a free colored American migrant named Moses Baker—and he showed an early gift for speaking and persuasion. The religious influence in Sharpe's life is represented in an anecdote: at some point, it was said, he was rented or sold to a Miss Williams who owned a hotel in Montego Bay, but was sent back to the lawyer Sharpe after he destroyed one of her musical instruments in a fit of religious piety. In his early adulthood, he had been named as a Baptist deacon, and he was permitted to travel around the countryside of northwestern Jamaica to give instruction in the Bible. In this way he was able to meet more fellow enslaved people than almost anybody, and he developed an encyclopedic knowledge of plantations and the roads that connected them. Sharpe was also a devoted husband: he married an enslaved woman who lived at Content Estate, where he seems to have been a regular presence.

His followers later said he took pains to visit her, even after religious meetings ran late into the night. Her name remains unknown.[8]

No portrait of Sharpe was painted in his lifetime, but a vivid description of him survives from Rev. Henry Bleby, who visited him shortly before his death. Bleby's account of Sharpe's ebony skin seems to discount the possibility that he was an offspring of a tryst involving a white overseer and to confirm that his father was likely one of the three adult enslaved men listed in the 1817 return document from Cooper's Hill. According to Bleby,

> He was of the middle size; his fine sinewy frame was handsomely molded, and his skin as perfect a jet as can well be imagined. His forehead was high and broad, while his nose and lips exhibited the usual characteristics of the Negro race. He has teeth whose regularity and pearly whiteness a court-beauty might have envied, and with an eye whose brilliance was almost dazzling.[9]

Bleby also took note of the young preacher's considerable rhetorical gifts, recalling the effect they had on one of his followers, a man named Gardner, who had not been committed to the idea of rebellion but then "entered into it with all his soul" once he heard Sharpe expound on man's inherent right to be free. While visiting Sharpe in prison, Bleby witnessed these charismatic powers firsthand, writing afterward,

> I heard him two or three times deliver a brief extemporaneous address to his fellow-prisoners on religious topics, many of them being confined together in the same cell; and I was amazed both at the power and freedom with which he spoke, and at the effect which was produced upon his auditory. He appeared to have the feelings and passions of his hearers completely at his command; and when I listened to him once, I

ceased to be surprised at what Gardner had told me, "that when Sharpe spoke to him and others on the subject of slavery," he, Gardner, was "wrought up almost to a state of madness."[10]

Because Sharpe also had the gift of literacy, he had access to a powerful source of knowledge denied to most enslaved people: the newspapers from Britain thrown off the ships in bundles onto the docks at Montego Bay. He picked discarded copies from the trash, received them from his nephew who worked in a newspaper office, and had them put into his hands by friendly passersby, and he made a habit of telling his students what he had learned of the outside world.[11]

In those gray columns printed an ocean away, Sharpe would certainly have read of the parliamentary elections of 1830 that replaced the slave-friendly Tory government with the moderate Whig government led by Prime Minister Charles Grey and composed of more representation from the cities. This had reenergized the popular activism against slavery, and drawn the aging humanitarian lions Thomas Clarkson and William Wilberforce back into the long argument about Britain's national crime.

Wilberforce was an evangelical Christian and an ally of the missionaries who had befriended Prime Minister William Pitt. He was barely five feet tall, and dumpy, but possessed of abundant charm. He made a key acquaintance in Clarkson, a onetime Cambridge University student for whom an essay assignment in college had morphed into an obsession with the evils of slavery. Clarkson rode on horseback all over England, displaying thumbscrews, shackles, whips, and other tools of brutality he had collected from former slave owners.

These two men—different in personality but united by a goal—had helped form a group named the Committee for the Abolition of the Slave Trade. In a masterstroke of propaganda, they enlisted the potter Josiah Wedgwood to design a widely distributed clay medallion featuring an African kneeling in chains with the accompanying legend, "Am I Not a Man and a Brother?" In March 1807, after Parliament heard testimony of gross abuses, it passed the Slave Trade Act. This act banned the kidnapping and importation of Africans into British colonies while still permitting an internal trade. But then Wilberforce retreated, saying he did not want to further antagonize the West Indian planters. He also believed slavery would die of natural causes without new African bodies to sustain it.[12]

A quarter century later, it was increasingly clear that no such thing would happen. Clarkson was ailing, and Wilberforce had retired from Parliament, but both found renewed determination to continue the fight. Their committee had since transformed into the Anti-Slavery Society, publisher of the *Anti-Slavery Reporter*, and by 1830, Wilberforce had dropped his long-held view that abolition should be a gradual affair. Now he demanded that slavery stop immediately. British newspapers from Midlothian to London, Sussex to Wiltshire, reported on antislavery meetings, and these dispatches from home circulated widely throughout the empire.

Driving this tactical shift was a dynamic woman who saw matters more clearly than most: Elizabeth Heyrick, the daughter of a well-to-do manufacturer of stockings. She had married a controlling and possessive husband who didn't like it when she left the house, though they shared a fiery passion for one another. "How they lived together, I know not," remembered a friend; "it was either my plague or my darling." When her husband died in 1797, Elizabeth resolved to give up "all ungodly lusts." Shortly thereafter, she converted to Quakerism and threw herself into radical social causes—factory conditions, the Irish peasantry, capital punishment, and animal cruelty. Her conspicuous compassion was such that she once intervened in a bullbaiting contest by purchasing the animal on the spot and hiding him in a nearby cottage until the crowd got bored and left.[13]

Heyrick soon dedicated her considerable talents to the antislavery cause, which had already become trendy among English writers, thinkers, and liberal philosophers. The famous lexicographer Samuel Johnson was not joking when he raised his glass in front of some "very grave men at Oxford" and offered the startling toast, "Here's to the next insurrection of the negroes in the West Indies!"[14]

Metropolitan liberals soon made the obvious connection between their growing knowledge of slavery's miseries and the product that lay close to the root: the sugar grown in the Caribbean which had so captivated the English palate. What would happen, they wondered, if people just stopped eating sugar?

The poet Robert Southey took direct aim at a beloved English tradition when he called sugared tea "the blood-sweetened beverage," and his fellow poet William Cowper satirized the half-heartedness of the public in the poem "Pity for Poor Africans":

> I pity then greatly, but I must be mum,
> For how could we do without sugar and rum?
> Especially sugar, so needful we see;
> What give up our desserts, our coffee, and tea!

The romantic poet Samuel Taylor Coleridge also lent his creative support. He had won a medal for a poem decrying slavery when he was a Cambridge undergraduate, and in 1785 he thundered against British hypocrisy in a lecture tour: "If only one-tenth part among you who profess yourself Christians; if one-half only of the petitioners, instead of bustling about with ostentatious sensibilities, were to leave off—not *all* the West Indies commodities—but only Sugar and Rum—the one useless and the other pernicious—all this misery might be stopped." He encouraged listeners to think of their sugared foods as "sweetened with the blood of the murdered."[15]

Though she did not pioneer it, Heyrick seized on the idea of sugar abstinence as a political tool and took it to new levels. She went door-to-door in her hometown, asking her neighbors not to use sugar and the grocers not to stock it; and if they must, at least to make sure that it was sourced from Britain's other colonies in Bengal and Malaya, where life for field laborers was hardly idyllic but at least not technically slavery.

If only one-tenth of the citizenry stopped using sugar, Heyrick said, it would surely crush the West Indian economy and lead to the immediate freeing of the slaves. Her booklets were masterpieces of invective and persuasion. The title of the most famous of them gave a hint as to the verbal cannonade that lay within: *Immediate, Not Gradual, Abolition, or an Inquiry into the Shortest, Safest and Most Effectual Means of Getting Rid of West Indian Slavery.* "Let the produce of slave labor, henceforth and for ever, be regarded as '*the accursed thing*,' and refused admission to our houses," she wrote. "Abstinence from *one single article* of luxury would annihilate the West Indian slavery!!"[16]

Heyrick and her allies anticipated the language and methods of twenty-first-century crusades against luxury goods like diamonds, coffee, fur, and gold, which conceal manifest cruelties within their supply chains. The point was to instill in the reader's mind the intrinsic connection between the product and the suffering, using visceral images to make the invisible now unavoidable. Heyrick's fellow Quaker William Fox remarked that with every pound of sugar imported into Britain "we may be considered as consuming two ounces of human flesh."[17]

Gruesome imagery and the links to citizen complicity ran throughout the Blood Sugar movement. "As he sweetens his tea, let him reflect on the bitterness at the bottom of his cup," wrote a pamphleteer with the *nom d'plume* of Anthropos. The author further invited the tea drinker to think of groaning people, "a bloody stroke" with the whip, and death from exhaustion that was happening half a world away in the Caribbean. "And then let him swallow his beverage with what appetite he may."[18]

The tactic worked—at least in persuading a good segment of the public to quit sugar. Thomas Clarkson tried to count heads on his journeys and calculated that at least 300,000 people across England had joined the private revolt. Other estimates put the number of boy-cotters at closer to a half million; and some of them were reputed to be members of the royal family, though this remains undocumented. "There was no town, through which I passed, in which there was not some one individual who had left off the use of sugar," Clarkson wrote, adding that the boycotters "were of all ranks and parties. Rich and poor, churchmen and dissenters." An irate correspondent to the *Leicester Journal* complained that virtually every house in Birmingham had been blanketed with pamphlets proclaiming "it is absolutely con-sidered a crime" to buy anything—especially sugar—from the Ca-ribbean. Sugar from Britain's colonies in the East Indies sold at ten times its usual volume. Some radical households featured bowls of ceramic or silver advertising the contents as "Not Made by Slaves." If such crockery were ever found on the docks at Kingston, one es-tate manger predicted, it would be smashed to bits within minutes. By 1830, at least seventy abolitionist "Ladies Associations" had formed in cities and towns all over Britain, dedicated to humanitarian agita-tion on the local level.[19]

Heyrick had no patience for male abolitionists like Clarkson and Wilberforce who had counseled a gradual change in the status of the enslaved West Indian people. While they thought on thirty-year time-tables, she thought instead in terms of thirty days. Heyrick wrote with sledgehammer force and dripping sarcasm against those who would let the planters have their way, and she rallied the consciences of the half-hearted who made the same private objections against citizen ac-tion that had always been made: *What good would it even do?* And *How can one person make a difference?* "Let him reflect," wrote Heyrick, "that greater victories have been achieved by the combined expression of *individual opinion* than by fleets and armies; that greater moral revolu-tions have been accomplished by the combined exertions of *individual resolution* than were ever effected by acts of Parliament."[20]

Women's antislavery groups generally aligned themselves with Heyrick's "immediate" view and distanced themselves from the gradualist philosophy; as one association in Wiltshire noted, "we must not talk of gradually abolishing murder, licentiousness, cruelty, tyranny." Heyrick's views were also welcomed among slavery opponents in the United States. But her pamphlets were disparaged by leading British abolitionists, who tended to put their faith in working the levers of male-dominated government rather than tapping into the power of consumer choice. Wilberforce, in particular, was cautious about stirring up popular resentment against the West Indians, whom he wanted to charm rather than arm-twist into abolition.[21]

Elizabeth Heyrick died, dejected, in 1831 without seeing abolition come to pass. While a friend praised her as having seen clearly that "the modern grinding system" was a "truly anti-Christian practice," her passing went unmentioned by most of the British press.[22]

Heyrick could not have known that an enslaved church deacon in Jamaica named Samuel Sharpe was—at that very time—reading about the antislavery movement she had done so much to fuel from below and was busy formulating a version of liberation theology that would soon make her call for "immediacy" much more than a fringe fantasy.[23]

THREE

KING SUGAR

As SHE GREW OLDER, Queen Elizabeth I of England rarely smiled with open lips, and some of her visitors reported they found it difficult to hear what she was saying because she spoke in a mumble. A traveler from Germany, Paul Hentzner, was permitted to watch her greet visitors in 1598, and he took note of one alarming detail. He described her thus: "Her nose a little hooked, her lips narrow, and her teeth black; (a defect the English seem subject to, from their too great use of sugar)."[1]

Tooth decay plagued Elizabeth for most of her life. At times it affected her ability to make coherent decisions. "By the reason of her indisposition, being continually troubled by the pain in her face, there hath as yet been no consultation for the Low Country causes," wrote a distressed Sir Francis Walsingham in 1578, when the queen was forty-five years old. By her sixties her teeth had worn down to blackened stumps. At one point the Bishop of London was called in to comfort her before surgeons pulled one of her ruined teeth but she "was very adverse, as afraid of all the acute pain that accompanied it." The bishop assured her that all would be well, and, gallantly, ordered the surgeons to pull out one of his own remaining teeth as a demonstration that the discomfort could be endured. She then assented to the operation. In her last years, she took to stuffing her cheeks with handkerchiefs to fill out her facial contours.[2]

During Elizabeth's long reign in the sixteenth century, the nobility learned to love refined sugar—usually imported from the

Mediterranean region—that delivered a taste and a kick far stronger than honey or fruit. Those who could afford it began adding sugar to their wine like a spice. Sugar imagery began to show up in literature, and the word itself became a synonym for flattery and pleasant words. In *Richard II,* the exiled Northumberland tells a companion, "And yet your fair discourse hath been as sugar, making the hard way sweet and delectable." At St. John's College at Oxford University, students sprinkled sugar on their pork suppers, and the chefs of Richard II served him fried rabbit with a sauce of ginger, salt, red wine, and sugar. An average serving of sugar had the cost-weight equivalent of caviar; some wealthy households kept their supply in lockboxes to prevent servants from stealing even a pinch.[3]

The British elite far outpaced their European peers in their love of sugar, a subject of frequent comment by continental visitors. A group of visiting Spaniards in 1603 noted that the British "eat nothing but what is sweetened with sugar, drinking it commonly with their wine and mixing it with their meat." As more West Indian plantations opened up, and more slaves were abducted from Africa to do the excruciating work of planting, harvesting, and condensing, the price of sugar declined on London markets and demand boomed. Sugar became not just the opium of the better classes but the fuel and delight of everyone.[4]

The health writer James Hart noted that it had become the indispensible condiment of Britain by the middle of the seventeenth century: "Sugar hath now exceeded honie, and is become of farre high esteem, and is far more pleasing to the palat, and is therefore everywhere in frequent use." The bland, starch-based diet of the nation was on the edge of transformation. Market customers hankered for West Indian sugar—especially that which had been refined from its dark molasses state to whiteness to falsely advertise purity. This preference may also reflect a color consciousness about the true source of the product, or perhaps a literal whitewashing of its origins.[5]

By the middle of the eighteenth century, as the Jamaican plantation system was flowering and the slave ships were traversing the Atlantic in unprecedented numbers, the English had developed a collective full-blown sugar addiction reaching across the class system in a way never seen before.[6]

In a smash-hit cookbook of 1747, *The Art of Cookery Made Plain and Easy,* a housewife named Hannah Glasse became a celebrity advocate for working-class indulgence in upmarket gastronomy. "If I have not wrote in the high polite style, I hope I shall be forgiven, for my intention is to instruct the lower sort and therefore must treat them in their way," she wrote in the introduction. Sugar dominated Glasse's menu. Her list of recipes included such sticky delicacies as lemon tarts, apple fritters, German puffs, pink-colored pancakes, raspberry dumplings, butter pudding, macaroons, pound cake, cheesecakes, gooseberry wafers, sugar of pearl, ice cream, syrup of peach blossom, and a thick beverage called whipt syllabub that required "half a pound of double-refined sugar."[7]

Other English cookbooks gave instructions for rendering candy into the shapes of animals, people, houses, and castles. Anticipating bachelor and bachelorette parties of a much later era, it was a widely accepted joke to design hard candies in the shape of male and female genitalia. At some lavish upper-class parties, hosts set the table with wineglasses, plates, and silverware all cast from sugar; they were meant to be sucked and crunched as dessert after the meal. Sugar meant power and class, and all who could afford it were dumping it into soups, sauces, glazes, roasts, breads, puddings, frostings, and especially tea.[8]

When a lump of cane sugar from the West Indies enlivened the Briton's favorite brew, the teacup transformed into something different altogether: a bringer of quick calories; a clarifier of thought; a mood lightener; an appetite suppressant; a pleasant mingling of bitter and sweet; and a small ritual of friendship, hospitality, and cultural pretense that anybody with a few pence could enact in their homes.

Tea with sugar was the soft drug that brought a moment of peace and the resolve to keep laboring. A Manchester industrial worker in the nineteenth century typically breakfasted on oatmeal porridge, buttered bread, and lots of sweetened tea, which was also quaffed during the cherished ritual of the work break. It worked its way into even the smallest villages as a balm to offset the English chill and gloom. Soon the poor were buying more pounds of sugar per capita than the rich.[9]

The Royal Navy provided a valuable subsidy to the island colonies. All of its sailors were granted a daily ration of two ounces of sugar, plus doses of rum diluted with water and lime juice, dispensed from a large wooden barrel into tin cups in a twice-daily ritual on the top deck that was like a nautical version of teatime. Puddings, teas, rum, candies, syllabubs: from the time of Elizabeth's toothaches up until the year 1800, the British consumption of sugar increased by an estimated 2,500 percent, and nearly 250,000 tons of it—mainly from the sugar islands of the West Indies—saturated the world markets each year. A shocking percentage of that total went down English gullets. The average Briton was consuming twenty pounds of sugar per year, compared to two pounds per resident of France.[10]

All of this consumption of sugar boosted the wealth of the plantation owners, and the phrase "rich as a West Indian planter" entered the lexicon. A popular play of 1771, *The West Indian*, featured an opening scene in which servants were bustling to prepare a party for a sugar tycoon. "He's very rich," commented a character, "and that's sufficient. They say he has rum and sugar enough belonging to him to make all the water in the Thames into punch." This reputation followed them to the American colonies, where the impression of loose Jamaican largesse was so strong that the new president of New Jersey's Princeton College published a fund-raising appeal for circulation throughout the West Indies in 1772. He sought to secure donations and to convince the tycoons to send their sons to

Princeton, where the weather and the morals were far better than at Oxford, and prejudice against slave owners' sons would be absent. In England, schoolboys hailing from the West Indies sometimes heard taunts such as, "Don't you come from where they make sugar and boil it down in black man's blood?" and "How many slaves did your father flog to death every year?"[11]

The nouveau riche of Jamaica living back in London endured the insults with a shrug. They formed the Planter's Club in 1740, which morphed into the powerful Society of West Indian Planters and Merchants. Its headquarters were near the fashionable St. James Square, where neighbors complained about the gold-plated coaches taking up room on the street. But it was unlikely that the planters cared; two-thirds of the members of their top committee held seats in Parliament, and they controlled an average of fifty votes in the House of Commons at any given time, enough to block a "no confidence" vote against a prime minister. This did not give them absolute control over legislation, but it did make them power brokers.[12]

The West Indian Interest, as it was called, relied on curious arithmetic. The Caribbean islands had no formal representation in Parliament, but they exerted imperial clout far above their actual population because the planters simply bought their way into empty seats representing rural British districts. Though they usually voted with the conservative Tories, they did not always act in concert—except in defending the pillars of sugar and slavery on which the tropical economy rested. In 1799 this influential bloc got Parliament to approve the construction of an elaborate set of docks on the Isle of Dogs in West London to receive the constant shipments of Caribbean sugar coming up the Thames.

Armed guards watched over the rectangular basins and the three-story warehouses at all hours. When wealthy visitors came from Jamaica, they made Ibbetson's Hotel on Vere Street their clubhouse. Among the most prominent members of the absentee sugar elite were the Beckfords, said to be the richest nonroyal family in Europe.

William Beckford was twice the lord mayor of London, and was mocked for his Latin mispronunciations. His eccentric son, ostracized by British society, lived alone in a small bedroom in a massive Gothic mansion named Fonthill Abbey. Surrounded by a six-foot wall to keep out hunters, the house had the proportions of a major cathedral and could be seen for miles around the countryside before its hastily built tower collapsed.[13]

The primary achievement of the West Indians, however, was a scheme to ensure a permanent market for their product. In the early nineteenth century, import duties were assessed in a three-tier structure: sugar from the West Indies was charged the lowest rate; sugar grown in the East Indian colonies of India and Malaysia was assessed higher; and the most exorbitant rates were charged for foreign sugar, especially that from Brazil—thus guaranteeing the British Caribbean a near monopoly over England's favorite addictive substance.[14]

When King George III was vacationing at his favorite seaside resort in Weymouth, he spotted a well-dressed man whose coach and livery were even grander and more pretentious than his own. He asked his companion, Prime Minister William Pitt, how the man had made all that money and was told the man was a West Indian planter who had grown rich in the sugar business.

"Sugar, sugar," said the king. "Eh? All *that* sugar!"[15]

All that sugar eaten by the British was of the refined variety, sucrose ($C_{12}H_{22}O_{11}$), which is a molecule of the carbohydrate glucose bound to another carbohydrate, fructose.

When sucrose hits the tongue, it makes contact with the tiny raised bumps known as fungiform papillae, which contain a multitude of taste buds. The average person possesses between two thousand and eight thousand taste buds; those who are said to have more sensitive palates simply have more of them, crowded closer together. Maps of the tongue that supposedly divide it into regions of sweet, salty, sour, and bitter are erroneous; the essence of sweetness can be detected anywhere on the tongue with the aid of two common protein molecules, T_1R_2 and T_1R_3, that bind with sucrose and send neurotransmitters bolting into the brain through a complex set of conduits that neurobiologists call "the hedonic pathway." This is also the seat of the reproductive urge and the desire to consume food: both vital to the perpetuation of the species.[16]

Upon anticipation of a pleasurable sensation such as a blast of sugar, a region of the brain called the ventral tegmental area sends a signal to the nucleus accumbens to release a burst of the neurotransmitter dopamine, which then travels across a synapse and binds to a similar receptor. This brings about a brief sensation of fullness. Repeated bursts of dopamine, however, erode the reward sensation. The binding capacity of dopamine gets diminished, leaving the user wanting more of the triggering element to replicate the earlier feelings of contentment. This is the mechanical root of addiction.[17]

The flow of sugar into England, which soon became a flood, brought confusing new sicknesses to its consumers, particularly to those who overindulged. Diabetes was first noticed in the 1670s, just as average British sugar consumption was approaching four pounds per year, leaving physicians baffled but suspecting sugar as a culprit. A founding member of the Royal Society, a doctor named Thomas Willis, described the malady as "the Pissing evil, a disease that causeth the party troubled therewith almost continually to piss, and in a great quantity a clear and sweetish water." In imitation of the chemists in the age of scientific discovery, who were known to occasionally touch their tongues to the substances in their labs as part of their investigatory process, Willis tasted the urine of a diabetic patient and reported it "wonderfully sweet, as if it were imbued with honey or sugar."[18]

As many later food scientists noted, sugar is ultimately deceptive. No correlation exists between sugar and nutritional benefit.

Its presence in food assures the tongue that energy and protein reside within, but sweet foods deliver a benign-tasting venom. A crowning irony of the sugar-slave symbiosis was that it was not fatal just to Africans; it could also be fatal to their masters.

The whole of Jamaican society was built on supplying this craving, and its basic unit of production was the estate—that private spread of fertile acreage claimed by a white Englishman through inheritance, purchase, or a corrupt grant from the governor. The more expensive land was on the coastal plain, where the loam and clay were more fertile, the roads were closer to the docks, sunlight could pour onto the land without interference from jungle canopy, and guests at the master's great house could enjoy a view of the sea. The governor's wife, Lady Nugent, described a typical vista in 1802:

> In front you see a rich vale, full of sugar estates, the works of which look like so many villages, and the soft-bright green of the canes, from this height, look like velvet. The guinea-corn fields make a variety in the green, and the canes that are cut are of a brownish hue; which, with the cocoa-nut and other trees, make a delightfully varied carpet.[19]

One of these was Greenwood Estate, in St. James Parish on the north shore; it was one of the few truly grand structures ever built in the colonial era of Jamaica: a fifteen-room Georgian-style mansion owned by the sugar baron Richard Barrett, who served as the magistrate of St. James Parish. He and his cousin Elizabeth Barrett Browning shared a mutual dislike for each other; Elizabeth confided in a letter to a friend that there was "no love" between them. Richard was, she wrote, "a man of talent & violence & some malice."

She went on to compare him, dryly, to "honest honest Iago," the character from Shakespeare who convinces others to do evil for his own purposes. He was, she allowed, "a handsome man . . . after a fashion!—good features & the short upper lip, full, in his case, of expression. The perpetual scowl spoilt it—and the smile was worse."[20]

Richard Barrett, Speaker of the Jamaica Assembly and one of the most powerful
men in the country. *(Greenwood Great House)*

Others thought Richard's chiseled face more attractive. A visitor
to one of his townhouses in Spanish Town thought him "one of the
handsomest and most agreeable men I ever saw." His charisma helped
his political career, as did his status as one of the island's few gradu-
ates of Oxford. For a time he ran a newspaper, the *Jamaica Journal,*

and used it to attack his rivals. Family tradition held him to be one of the island's many alcoholics, and he was also likely a lothario among his enslaved women. The *Trifler* newspaper once accused him of being "a man of immorality, plunged in lustful sensuality" who had virtually abandoned his wife Betsy, another of his cousins.

Richard Barrett was domineering and sharp; a family biographer described him as one who "neither followed nor gave advice." He sued two of his cousins over some land he believed was his, and the case dragged on for years. He also could be self-pitying in his arguments about money with his family in England, claiming a kind of martyrdom. "I am the only one of the family that has had to labour, I may say, for a subsistence," he told his mother. "Your income is much better than mine, which costs me hard bodily labour, & on which I have many calls."[21]

Barrett took a stab at poetry, but he was considerably less accomplished than his cousin Elizabeth. In the May 3, 1823, edition of the *Kingston Chronicle,* he published a long poem about the execution of an enslaved woman named Mary Russell, full of pretentious references to Greek philosophers, Lord Byron, and the actress Nell Gwyn. But it still made the brutality of island life plain, and even managed to threaten British officials who dared to challenge the institution of slavery. The last stanza read,

> Stay in Jamaica—here bad men,
> Hang only every now and then,
>   Especially if white;
> But when you've crossed the Atlantic big,
> Dancing in middle air, a jig,
>   Is quite a common sight[22]

Barrett had a cruel streak, but he was known as a relative liberal when it came to the treatment of his own enslaved people. As the Speaker of the Assembly, he fought for a ban on the use of the cart whip, which he called "odious, horrid, detestable" and which was far more damaging than the cat-o'-nine-tails in general use. He recalled watching his great-grandfather bear down on enslaved people with a whip "like a divinity" but he never used it himself, and didn't even punish anyone for running away when he was gone himself. As he later told a friend, "It is their only protection against the overseers, some of whom treat the people brutally." He also allowed his enslaved people to be taught to read and write.[23]

Yet Barrett's tolerant position concealed a wily political mind. In 1830 he had been one of the movers behind an assembly bill to put the free colored citizens of Jamaica on an equal footing with the whites—a measure that seemed designed for no greater purpose than to bring free colored slave owners tighter into the coalition of old-line settlers defending slavery against its enemies back home. He rarely spoke during debates, preferring others to do his bidding while he concealed his influence behind an iron smile. A governor of Jamaica once described him as "the incarnation of pride."[24]

As the heir to a vast fortune and the Speaker of the Jamaica Assembly, Barrett commanded significant prestige. The assembly voted to name a major road in the capital of Spanish Town for him, and his magnificent house at Greenwood could be seen from miles across the cane fields and even from the deck of a faraway ship approaching the shore. The splendid view from his veranda—extending a full 180 degrees out to the horizon of the Caribbean Sea toward Cuba—was said to be so broad as to demonstrate the curvature of the earth.[25]

The less opulent "planting estates" owned by families considerably more hardscrabble than the Barretts were up in the mountains, far from markets and typically with rocky soil and lots of trees that had to be cut down to ensure a steady level of sunlight. These estates, scattered all over Jamaica (there are ownership records for more than ten thousand of them), typically looked awful. A particularly ignorant or disinterested planter, especially one who had only recently arrived, might know little about the craft of agriculture and simply rely on the physical exertions of the enslaved people to conquer na-ture and make everything right, driving them harder and harder to make a rate of return. Fields were drained of nutrients past their point of fecundity and were rarely permitted a period of fallowness to recover. Professional farmer Benjamin McMahon was aghast at what he saw: "Large cane fields are planted without manure; weeds are seen luxuriating in the midst of the cane and all classes, old and young, are out at work, under the scourge of the lash, from four in the morning until after dark at night."[26]

Sugar cultivation required immense amounts of labor, but it was a phenomenally simple enterprise. Field slaves dug trenches or holes in the soil, laid down the cuttings of old pieces of cane about nine inches deep, and covered them back up with the soil. The "cane hole digging" was monotonous and backbreaking; the average enslaved worker was expected to plant at least 120 canes a day during the planting season, and then spend the next fourteen months hoeing away weeds until the bamboo-like rods had grown to a luxuriant eight feet tall, with leaves the color of light teal and edges that felt like unsharpened knives.[27]

The interior of a cane field in summer, which breezes could rarely reach, was oven-hot, claustrophobic, and maddening. Thousands of rats scurried among the green reeds, making a rustling sound when-ever footsteps approached. The gnawing of the rats left yellowish-green tooth marks at the bases they chewed. One out of every twenty cane stalks was ruined this way. A harvest was always made in a rush because the cane had to be crushed to juice in short order or its lode of sugar would ferment and turn to acid. An army of field hands made up the primary "great gang," most wearing the simple fabric called Osnaburgh cloth, slashing their way through the sugar forest using a three-stroke move with a machete to cut down the canes—a repetitive motion that enervated the tendons and sent fire up the back.[28]

A gang boss called the driver spurred them on. He was usually an older slave—in his thirties or forties—in a position of trust who was authorized to whip if he felt it necessary. Some were well liked; others were tyrants. The driver also watched over a second crew made up of both men and women who split the canes into yard-long sticks and hustled them in bundles over to the millworks, a series of upright wooden spools whose teeth squeezed out the dark brown cane juice. If anyone got a finger caught in one of the spools, they were liable to be pulled into the gears up to the shoulder, which meant almost certain death from the amputation and infection that followed. Power came from windmills, a waterwheel fixed in a nearby stream, or teams of cattle walking in endless circles as the spools groaned out sweet ooze.[29]

The spent cane—a waste product known as bagasse—was taken to a separate storage shed, usually called a trash house. Every slave knew these leavings were extremely flammable after they dried out, and the whole structure could go up like a bomb if exposed to an open flame. "The firmer the trash is packed, the stronger will be the fuel," wrote planter Thomas Roughley. No pipe smoking or any kind of open flame was allowed nearby.[30]

This vegetable garbage made excellent kindling with which to boil the fresh cane juice inside "the works," a series of four copper kettles of descending size as the sugar lost its moisture and grew more concentrated. The job of head boiler was at once the most prestigious and most difficult, as the works were satanically hot in an already torrid climate, and liquefied sugar clung to human skin like napalm. A careless spill could cost a slave a hand, an arm, or—more likely—his or her life. Flames licking under the kettles had to be fed constantly with dried cane leaves; the oozing river of liquor had to be carefully skimmed and ladled through the cascade of kettles until it "struck"—that is, transformed from liquid into solid crystals. Any mistakes in this choreography resulted in expensive waste—and a vigorous lashing. The hardened remains—a coarse brown product called muscovado—were cured, reboiled, dried, and packed into reinforced barrels called hogsheads that looked like kegs of wine and could hold about 1,500 pounds, which were then loaded on wagons and taken to the nearest wharf. The task specialization in a Jamaican sugar works anticipated the industrial assembly line by at least two centuries.[31]

But it was not a complete production. One of the many ironies of Jamaica was that it had almost no manufacturing capacity. Kingston had two small sugar refining houses, but they were constantly overworked, so most planters sent muscovado to England for finishing and only received a portion for their dining tables after it had crossed the Atlantic Ocean twice.[32]

Just as the London sugar markets acted as a tuning fork to Jamaican society, the island began to absorb some of the religious fervor in Britain as missionaries like William Knibb began to trickle into sugar country through the 1820s. Knibb's own Baptist Church was both the most striking and the most influential, tracing its roots to the beginning of the seventeenth century, when an Anglican priest named John Smyth gradually became convinced that new believers should be totally immersed in a body of water instead of merely being sprinkled, to symbolize burial and resurrection and to make an outward proclamation of their newfound inner grace. Smyth believed in a more spontaneous form of worship than that permitted by the Anglicans, who lived by the rote liturgy outlined in the Book of Common Prayer. The Baptists thought salvation was an urgent matter that deserved the whole world's attention, and they took great interest in the places across the globe that Christ's Gospel had not reached.

A disgruntled Anglican priest of a later generation inspired the founding of another dissenting sect—the Methodist Church—that would come to have a powerfully disruptive influence on the Jamaican social order. During his student days at Oxford, John Wesley had formed a club with his brother Charles and a few others that focused on the right aspects of holy living. Fellow students poked fun at their methodical ways by calling them Methodists. Wesley took ordination in the Anglican Church and accepted an invitation to minister to Indians and settlers in the frontier colonial town of Savannah, Georgia. His tenure there was short and disastrous. The congregation thought him aloof and rigid, and he further alienated himself by refusing to serve communion to Sophia Williamson, a woman with whom he had secretly fallen in love but who had married another man after he broke off their friendship. He was brought up on charges of defamation, and decided it would be best for all if he fled the colony. Back home in England, Wesley found his "heart strangely warmed" at a prayer meeting among immigrant Germans in 1738 and felt for the first time in his life that he trusted Christ alone for his salvation. This was the spiritual beginning of his mission to share the Gospel with the poor and forgotten of Britain in down-to-earth language, under trees and inside coal mines when necessary.

Wesley became the prototypical circuit rider of his era, establishing a pattern for later imitators by traveling more than a quarter million miles on horseback throughout England, Scotland, and Wales. His admirers claimed he preached forty thousand different sermons, to whichever groups would hear him. Though he never formally broke away from the established church, his followers founded the Methodist Church by his example, putting emphasis on the day-to-day joys of Christian living and infusing divine love into every moment. The success of this movement was a large part of what lit Wesley's enthusiasm to spread the mission field to a wider world, starting with the Caribbean. He had seen the brutality of slavery up close in Savannah and chosen then to remain silent. But later in life he condemned slave owners as "men buyers" and "men stealers" and encouraged a partner named Thomas Coke to go on a pioneering mission to the West Indies in 1784 to make the radical step of preaching the Gospel to enslaved people—a group who had not figured heavily in previous calculations of the size of God's family.

One enterprising evangelist had already beaten the white Britons to Jamaica by two years. The freed American slave George Liele, a self-taught preacher, migrated to Kingston with retreating British troops after the Revolutionary War in 1782 and preached to the enslaved people when he wasn't farming. Though he had to have the words of all his prayers and sermons preapproved by the authorities, Liele gained a following. "At Kingston I baptize in the sea, at Spanish Town in the river and at convenient places in the country," he wrote in a letter. "We have nigh three hundred and fifty members; a few white people among them." At one point in 1794, he drew large crowds by preaching in the open at the Kingston Race Course. But in all his writings and public utterances, he took care never to complain about slavery as an institution.[33]

Even so, the majority of sugar bosses remained actively hostile to this effort to Christianize their enslaved property, fearing the spread of dangerous ideas of individual agency and dignity. Others were wary of lost work hours to such unprofitable activities as praying or singing. Though the white missionaries streaming into Jamaica had been warned to scrupulously avoid the subject of politics and stick to religion only, their very presence posed a threat to the existing power structures. Their abstinent habits, social organization, and increasing concern for the welfare of the poor was reflective of a changing world back home. Most of them had been born into the lower middle classes of rural England, Ireland, and Scotland—the same station as many of the young men of earlier generations who had come to Jamaica to get rich from sugar, have sex with an endless stream of young black women, and return home as conquering tycoons.

Jamaica's famous irreligiosity contributed to the hostility shown to anyone who threatened to get in the way of slavery, including missionaries of all stripes. "A religious man is a most unfit person to manage a slave estate," observed the lawyer William Taylor in 1833. "The fact is, cruelty is the mainspring of the present system; so long as slavery exists, and the whip is the compeller of labor, it is folly to talk of humanity." Those who allowed Anglican priests to conduct mass baptisms of their slaves usually did so as a way to promote good behavior. The priest tended to treat it like a business proposition, saying a few words and scattering a few drops of water over a lineup of enslaved people in exchange for a half crown per head. "It was like driving cattle to a pond," noted a disapproving Hope Masterton Waddell, quoting a confused recipient of the mass baptism.[34]

For his part, William Knibb tried to avoid having anything to do the white employees of sugar estates. Nearly all of them, he said, were "living in fornication" with enslaved women, and he did not want any rumors to start that he might also be indulging in Jamaica's favorite vice. Still the missionaries came to the island by the hundreds, driven by devotional zeal and facing a nearly impossible task.[35]

Missionaries had tried to explain the basic precepts of Christianity in the most universal language they could muster, but they fought constant theological skirmishes with their converts: against parables about Anansi, the West African spider-god; against playing drums; against having sex without being married; against the wild excesses of the Christmas holiday; and against stealing, fighting, and drinking. The enslaved people readily understood monotheism, as most West African cosmologies also held up one creator-god. But the maker of the universe was said to take no interest in lowly human affairs and was too far distant to hazard a relationship. A pantheon of lesser deities received their worship instead. Dreams were considered prophecy, and when a particularly vivid one came, they called it the *convince.*[36]

The only free day for the enslaved people was Sunday, which should have been convenient for church, but most were busy tending to their provision grounds or making the long trudge to and from regional markets. So missionaries had to be savvy. Rev. Thomas Cooper said he applied to an average of ten sugar estates before he was allowed to preach at even one of them. If enslaved people wanted to skip the market and attend Sunday chapel as novice believers—what the missionaries called "inquirers"—they had to prove they had good character. They would then be issued paper tickets giving them right of passage on the roads. Intolerant masters could still be fooled: several women made a show of going to Sunday market with a bowl full of goods on their heads that covered up their best dresses for attending chapel services. Those overseers who weren't opposed to missionary work were merely indifferent. Matthew Lewis said he thought the minister's visits would do as much good "as if a man were to sow a field with horse-hair and expect a crop of colts."[37]

Another planter with a relaxed attitude was none other than Richard Barrett, who served as the *custos*—an antique Latin term for magistrate—of St. James Parish. The missionary Hope Masterton Waddell showed up at his estate one day in 1830 to present the required credentials for holding chapel services in a private home. Barrett seemed easygoing about granting the license, and even said he would let Waddell come onto his properties to give religious instruction to his own enslaved people.

Then the two had a revealing exchange.

"But I must in candor own that I am not influenced by religious principles myself in this matter, but simply by self-interest," Barrett told the minister. "I have a bad set of people: they steal enormously, they run away, get drunk, fight, and neglect their duty in every way, while women take no care of their children and there is no increase on the property. Now if you can bring them to a fear of God, or a judgment to come, or something of that sort, you may be doing both them and me a service."

"Well, Mr. Barrett, you certainly are very candid and will allow me to be equally so," rejoined Waddell. "I must say that I have higher objects in mind than those you mention. I wish to make them know

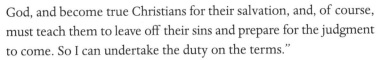

God, and become true Christians for their salvation, and, of course, must teach them to leave off their sins and prepare for the judgment to come. So I can undertake the duty on the terms."

"Very good," said Barrett. "Now when will you begin?"

"Tomorrow and every following Wednesday at shell-blow, and you will allow the people extra time that they should not lose their dinner by coming to me."

Barrett agreed, and then asked, "By the way, what would you think to begin by christening them? It is long since the clergyman of the parish were here for the purpose and I have got a good many people since. It might have a good effect."

Waddell demurred on this tricky point, explaining that enslaved converts should first comprehend the message of Jesus before they made a commitment. This was an important theological concept of which Barrett had no apparent knowledge. But he only laughed good-naturedly. "Ah well! I dare say you are right; you must know your own business best."[38]

By granting a missionary access to his own enslaved population, as well as permission to use the overseer's house as a temporary chapel, Barrett was giving Waddell far more privilege than most estate owners did, and the gesture immediately raised the preacher's stature in northwestern Jamaica. Barrett also promised not to make anyone work on the Sabbath, though on the condition that "no man be obliged to spend the whole day in prayers." He could not have known it at the time, but he was letting a new wind into Jamaica that would leave dozens of sugar estates in ashes, upend his island society, and force a reckoning that would reverberate around the globe.

FOUR

THE DOOR OF NO RETURN

THE JAMAICAN SUGAR BARONS expected to squeeze only a few years of work out of enslaved people before their purchases died of disease, malnutrition, or exhaustion. Letting them raise children was generally not a planter's first choice; it was cheaper to simply acquire new humans. "Buy rather than breed" went a local saying, under the logic that ordinary reproduction would bring added costs, including those of food, clothing, and the loss of the mother's labor while she nursed. This investment in human capital would also not mature until the child would be ready for real fieldwork around the age of fourteen. By contrast, a healthy African adult could be purchased off a ship for approximately fifty British pounds and be ready immediately for work.[1]

Up until 1807, when international slave trafficking was banned for good in the British Empire, the transoceanic stream of kidnapped Africans was a robust and integral component of the Jamaican economy. And it had been around a long time.

On the shore of the Bight of Benin in 1472, the Portuguese made first contact with representatives of the Kingdom of Beny, whose capital was a magnificent walled city ringed by a moat. Their craftsmen were masters of bronze sculpture, and the kingdom's military was feared through the region. King John II of Portugal dispatched an ambassador and respectfully corresponded with Ozolua, the king of Beny, as a fellow monarch. And an international trade developed: manila, jewelry, and firearms in exchange for palm oil, peppers, ivory, and human captives.

The Portuguese knew about slavery; they had taken forced-labor prisoners of their own on previous expeditions. Vatican support for capture of "Saracens," a name for Muslims of Arab descent, was written into canon law by Pope Gregory IX in 1226 and reaffirmed in a series of papal bulls at the beginning of the era of exploration. As the Portuguese ventured farther and farther down the coast of West Africa, Pope Nicolas V had written the *Dum Diversas* giving the adventurers permission to capture Saracens and "reduce their persons into perpetual servitude." Many of the Africans first encountered were not Muslim, but that seems not to have mattered.

In the Akan kingdoms to the west of Beny, in present-day Ghana, indigenous slavery was primarily a household affair. Captured humans—or those who had been born into the role of slaves—were treated as small-scale field laborers, fishermen, gold miners, soldiers, hunters, or household servants. They were typically accepted as part of the family structure, allowed to marry and amass private wealth. Sometimes they could free themselves through a series of ceremonies and payments. While individual situations differed according to the attitudes of masters, more than one visitor remarked on the generally familial treatment they received.[2]

European traders with oceangoing vessels, however, recognized a global opportunity: a commodity that could be further debased, numerically scaled up, and transported across the ocean to work in New World fields much larger than those of small family farms. They made alliances with coastal chiefs and went together on inland raids, destroying villages as they went and creating streams of war refugees who could be captured and sold. The British adventurer John Hawkins reported of one trip in 1567, "I went myself, and with the help of the king of our side, assaulted the town, both by land and sea, and very hardly with fire (their houses being covered with dry palm leaves) obtained the town, put the inhabitants to flight, where we took 250 persons, men, women & children." He had been licensed to the task by no less an authority than Queen Elizabeth I.[3]

But the first dealers in commodity-level slavery did not target the Africans merely because they had darker skin. As the historian Eric Williams has argued, the first European traders were merely envisioning a commercial opportunity no different in structure from the burgeoning trade in gold or guns. "The reason was economic," wrote Williams, "not racial; it had to do not with the color of the laborer, but the cheapness of the labor." Harvesting cash crops in a tropical climate could only be possible by treating humans as biped livestock, which created a permanent underclass. Racial prejudice didn't create slavery, Williams argued, but slavery invariably created bigotry.[4]

By 1791 a British traveler to Africa named John Matthews could rationalize the trade this way—using the term *Cafre* to mean African, which was a derivative of the old Arabic insult *Kaffir*. He wrote, "Trace the manners of the natives, the whole extent of Africa from Cape Cantin to the Cape of Good Hope, and you find a constant and almost regular gradation in the scale of understanding, till the wretched Cafre links nearly below the Ouran Outang."[5]

Seeing as Africans could be viewed as virtual primates, not even human, they could therefore be traded like artifacts or cattle. A group of British operators formed an outfit they named the Royal African Company, with a charter that was originally supposed to be binding for a thousand years. A section of West Africa comprising the modern nations of Benin, Ghana, Togo, and parts of Nigeria soon became known as the Slave Coast: a permanent hunting ground. The Royal African Company would go on to haul away more black bodies than any other institution in history, and give the British nearly three quarters of the market share. The British avatar of individual freedoms, John Locke, was an investor.[6]

For young British men looking for an adventure, or for those less willing who were pressed into service, the Slave Coast was like a giant mining boomtown: a place to work hard, live wild, start trouble, and make money. The adventurers paid tributes and fees known as *dashee* to African leaders in the form of tea, biscuits, silk garments, muskets, jewelry, and a disgusting rum beverage everyone called washmouth.[7]

The Scottish explorer Mungo Park ventured up the Niger River in 1795 and witnessed people being captured. He described the scene in a book entitled *Travels in the Interior Districts of Africa.* "The poor sufferer, urged on by the feelings of domestic or paternal attachment, and the ardor of revenge, conceals himself among the bushes, until some young or unarmed person passes by," wrote Park. "He then, tiger-like, springs up his prey; drags his victim into thicket; and in the night carries him off as a slave." Being kidnapped was not the only way in which Africans found themselves in ropes and chains. People could be sold to ward off starvation; be taken as payment for a debt; or be falsely accused of murder, adultery or witchcraft. Still others were simply born into slavery.[8]

The worst fate was to be marched to the Atlantic coast for a one-way journey to the Americas. Men and women could be roped together by the neck and put in a miserable line called a coffle that shuffled barefoot across the ground for miles at a time under the burning sun. Some of the larger processions, accompanied by "the noise of drums, horns and gongs," were led to fairs next to trading routes where the captured could be auctioned off to Africans, but more often to whites for a bigger profit.[9]

Many terrified captives had never before seen white skin, and assumed the alien visitors were cannibals, for they had heard stories of others being led away in such a coffle, never to return. The neophyte slave "imagines the white man buys him either as a sacrifice to his God or to devour him as food," reported John Matthews. Ominous tales had spread from escapees who had seen the white men at their suppers; it was commonly assumed that their red wine was African blood. Some traders tried to reassure them that they were not being taken for consumption, though the more ruthless among them fed the terror by amputating the arms or legs of would-be runaways as a warning to the others to keep docile. When not marched directly to the muggy littoral regions where ships lay waiting at anchor, they were led to makeshift jails in the bush where they were fed scraps, forced to sit in squalor, and "evacuate nature where they lie" for potentially as long as six months before they could be bartered to a European broker in exchange for brass kettles, gunpowder, or the seashell currency called cowrie.[10]

The European mercantile powers built a heavily armed chain of castles along the coast, painted bright white, with filthy dungeons below called barracoons, and light and airy quarters above for the governor and his staff, the cool breezes and magnificent views of the ocean on the terrace far removed from the sweltering misery below in the darkened cells. They appeared, wrote one observer, like "chalk mountains, especially when the sun shines directly on them." At Cape Coast Castle, the headquarters of the Royal African Company in what is now Ghana, British engineers designed a barracoon carved out of a cliff face that was said to contain space for up to a thousand captives if they were packed in tight enough. Vaulted brick ceilings sheltered a single tiny window twenty feet above the floor, where small trenches were carved to accommodate feces and urine. Newcomers were branded with the letters DY, for Duke of York, the nominal head of the company. During their first few hours in such a place many comprehended their terrible fate. Those who misbehaved were thrown into a more secure chamber behind three locked doors and starved to death.[11]

Frightened, malnourished, and separated from home and family, with their extremities often bleeding and infected from the incisions of iron manacles, the enslaved people tended to fall into a state of catatonia, described by Matthews as a "torpid insensibility," even as they watched others being herded down a ramp through a seaward portal called "the door of no return" which led to the gangplanks of any of the dozens of slave vessels awaiting for new cargo. This would be their final look at Africa and, for many, the onset of their deaths, for the two-month journey across the sea was even worse than their imprisonment on land. Here was also a chance for a ship's captain to give a final inspection of his human cargo. Those who didn't pass a visual test—either because of their physique, age, disposition, or for any other reason—could be subject to execution on the spot. The surgeon Alexander Falconbridge saw this happen at New Calabar during the 1780s. "Instances have happened at that place," he wrote, "that the traders, when any of their negroes have been objected to, have dropped their canoes under the stern of the vessel and instantly beheaded them, in sight of the captain."[12]

The typical British slave ship—called a Guineaman—was essentially a traveling jail; it weighed about two hundred tons, with square rigging and a copper-sheathed hull to guard against the wood rot of the tropics. As many as forty crew members would be on board, with pigtails and wearing checkered shirts and black kerchiefs. Nearly all carried whips. Many of them had been kidnapped themselves from English port cities and forcibly pressed into service; an average of three out of four crew members would be dead within two years from disease, violence, or suicide.[13]

The belowdecks—which were more like crawlspaces, with a height of about four feet—were fitted with manacles and waste tubs to accommodate between one hundred and seven hundred enslaved people who were packed in, each with as much individual space as an average coffin might allow. This essentially created a stench-filled sauna; one trader said his shirt was soaked after he spent ten minutes in the hold. Weak sunlight came in through narrow slats. The miserable passengers were typically taken to the top deck each day for "exercise" while the deck floors were washed with a vinegar solution; the exercise involved being made to dance or jump up and down for the amusement of the crew. Nets were fixed below the gunwales to prevent escapees from committing suicide by jumping overboard; as it was, many tried to starve themselves on the journey by refusing to eat the dribs of mashed corn, yams, or horse beans or the disgusting paste of palm oil, water, flour, and pepper called slabber sauce that provided barely enough calories to stay alive.[14]

Hunger strikes were answered with whippings, or with hot coals to sear the lips. Others had their mouths forced open by a metal vise known as a *speculum oris*. Some grew so desperate they smashed their heads against the bulkheads until they bled to death; some tried to slash their throats with their fingernails. Revolts broke out on one of every eight transatlantic voyages, occasionally aided by one or two members of a disgruntled crew who had their own reasons to mutiny. Africans from rival nations, and even those speaking different languages, found themselves working together for the first time. Those who survived the Atlantic journey together called each other shipmates, and this was considered a bond almost as strong as blood.[15]

The mortality rate on an average voyage ranged anywhere from 3 to 30 percent, aggravated by the enslaved people's willingness to sacrifice themselves in revolts or suicides. "When we found ourselves at last taken away," wrote a captive named Ottobah Cugoano many years after his ordeal, "death was more preferable than life, and a plan was concerted among us, that we might burn and blow up the ship, and to perish all together in the flames." It was not uncommon for an enslaved person to wake up next to a companion who had died in his manacles from dysentery or malnutrition; in those cases, the body was thrown overboard. The Dutch trader Willem Bosman observed "not without horror" a cluster of sharks attack the pitiful jettison, and "before you can tell twenty have sometimes divided the Body amongst them so nicely that not the least Particle is left."[16]

The prisoners who survived the voyage might have been struck with awe at their first sight of Jamaica's southern shore: a massive harbor ringed by hills coated with jungle steaming in the tropical sunlight, with the summits of the Blue Mountains fringed with clouds. Their slopes were covered with "trees of every name, the mahogany, the boxwood, the rosewood, the cedar, the palm, the fern, the bamboos, the cocoa, the breadfruit, the mango, the almond, all grow in wild confusion, interwoven with a dense tangled undergrowth." The scene was bright, exotic, and horrifying at the same time, a vista "as to convince the traveler of his having entered into a new world," thought twenty-four-year-old traveler Theodore Foulks.[17]

Immediately before them was the city of Kingston, with a fort overlooking the wharves and barrels of sugar stacked amid the cotton bales, mahogany bundles, kegs of nails, and bags of pimento, with hundreds of enslaved porters clattering and scrambling, carrying parcels and bundles of every description. Beyond the din of Harbour Street was a hodgepodge of commercial townhouses laid out on sandy streets choked with oxen and jabbering merchants, a dusty parade ground, a cemetery with sepulchers that blazed white in the sun, the spire of an Anglican church steeple poking upward, a synagogue down a side street, tobacco stores, cobblers, guesthouses, and rum shops, all nestled at the basin of a broad earthen tureen. Above the dismal urban scene were the wealthier districts, fringed with painted homes decked with the vertical blinds called jalousies and encircled with piazzas laced with honeysuckle, jasmine, and darting hummingbirds. These homes were perched atop masonry foundations bearing a few arrowslits on each side, through which guns could be fired outward. The owner of a country house had two primary objectives: "stability against the shock of hurricanes, and security in the event of an insurrection of the slaves." Kingston was a dichotomy of residential bunkers and low-grade chaos on the muddy streets below.[18]

At his first sight of the West Indies, Olaudah Equiano was convinced that he had stumbled into a country of magical horrors. He had never before seen brick houses or men on horseback; it had only been two months since he had witnessed the novelty of men with white skin, the ocean, and tall ships with billowing sails that floated atop the great waters like clouds.[19]

The arrival of a slave ship was typically heralded with an advertisement in the newspaper, such as the one that ran in the *Kingston*

Daily Advertiser on June 4, 1796, next to announcements of the arrival of hogsheads of salt, crates of shoes, kegs of olives and Yorkshire hams, and barrels of brown sugar and sweet cider:

FOR SALE

610 CONGO NEGROES

Imported in the ships Crescent and Thomas

The captives for sale generally looked like zombies after their hellish passage, so before they were led to the auction blocks, the traders greased them down with beeswax and palm oil to make them look healthier and shaved off any gray hairs that might have betrayed anything less than youthful vigor. Little could be done, however, for the grossly emaciated, who had had so much sagging flesh rubbed away by manacles and the tossing of the wooden deck that the whiteness of bones was visible inside the suppurating wounds on their wrists and shoulder blades.[20]

Buyers from the sugar estates waited inside holding pens in a mad selling ritual called a scramble. The new arrivals were ordered to jump up and down to display their fitness and expose their genitals for signs of venereal disease. The proceedings struck many observers as nothing so much as a livestock auction. Captain Thomas Lloyd of the Royal Navy remarked that enslaved people were "considered as black cattle, and very often treated as post horses." The disgusted Anglican rector Richard Bickell went even further: what was once an autonomous human being had been reduced, he said, to "a mere machine, impelled by the whip." Prior to the 1790s, Jamaican buyers generally purchased twice as many men as women—the former primarily for the blistering job of field labor, the latter also for the fields and for housework, cooking, and recreational sex.[21] But pecuniary interest in women would grow in the early nineteenth century, as planters took more interest in expanding their labor force through childbirth.[22]

Some of those buyers at the scramble were landless brokers who intended to resell their human acquisitions in the United States or other British colonies. About a quarter of the prisoners who landed in Jamaica were then dispatched again on another ocean voyage in a cramped, stinking hold. And an unlucky few would experience the worst emotional cruelty of the commerce: the splitting up of families. The bonds of friendship and shared experience that had formed on the transatlantic voyage would also be severed. "Relatives were separated as sheep and lambs were separated by the butcher," recalled the repentant slave captain John Newton.[23]

Another captain, Clement Noble, would defend the practice, but admitted that he heard "grievous outcries" from slaves upon their landing in the New World because they "think they are going to be parted from their husbands, wives, mothers, children, etc." Such forced partings were all too common because entire village populations had often been captured and transported en masse across the Atlantic, only to be broken apart forever—family bonds and all. Planters encouraged upset onlookers not to think of the wailing slaves as fully human, but as lesser entities in a kind of Aristotelian chain of being. The colonial administrator and sugar grower Edward Long, who viewed Africans as brutish apes, described black and white as "two tinctures which nature has disassociated, like oil and vinegar." He also borrowed unrelated verses from Alexander Pope's *Essay on Man* to explain the island's racial hierarchy:

> The general order, since the whole world began
> Is kept in nature, and is kept in man
> Order is heaven's first law; and, this confest
> Some are, and must be, greater than the rest[24]

But racial theory alone did not justify this cleaving at the docks. Cold-blooded military logic lay behind peeling off a slave from those he knew: social bonds could make it easier for groups to band together and rise up in rebellion. If loyalties could be scrambled and debased, it meant more security for the plantocracy. Splitting up those people who happened to speak the same African language was considered especially important; they would be less likely to develop secret patterns of speech that could conceal a plot from their masters.[25]

As they were led away in a coffle through the sandy streets, the enslaved people would have seen firsthand what kind of life awaited them. On his first day in Kingston, Dr. George Pinckard looked with astonishment at sixteen to eighteen men yoked together in a harness who "were drawing an immense trunk of mahogany, conducted by a driver with a cart-whip, who went whistling at their side and flogging them on, precisely as an English carter does his horses."[26]

This was only the beginning of their new existence as human livestock; the beginning of a series of psychic shocks that drove even the strongest into a state of deep depression and catatonia. At their plantation homes, the enslaved people would be branded on the shoulder with a heated silver tong bearing their master's initial and given a new name on the spot. Some were effused with classical gallantry like Achilles, Caesar, Plato, or Pompey, which only seemed more insulting. Other common plantation names included Cudjoe, Cuffie, Dick, Empress, Hamlet, Hector, Jenny, Jug-Betty, Neptune, Quashee, Sam, Sappho, and Whore. Then came the slow process of learning enough English to communicate, often through a mix of words from West African tongues that settled into a distinct patois. "If you can learn a new Negro to count twenty, he will learn to pronounce most English words very well," wrote Thomas Thistlewood in his diary. Among the first of the new terms they relearned was *buckra,* which meant "white person" in the Efik language of western Nigeria. In Jamaica, it meant "master."[27]

The first three years were called the "seasoning," which was essentially a test of whether the slave would die from the work or from any of the bouquet of diseases that flourished in the island. Two out of every seven died quickly. Suicides were common, often managed with pilfered lengths of rope to hang themselves. Others driven to the brink of malnutrition ate handful after handful of reddish dirt until they fell unconscious. Plantation masters wrongly assumed that this desperate attempt to ingest calcium and other essential minerals was a crude attempt at suicide. A Jamaican planter named William Fitzmaurice complained of his capital loss by this practice, though not without a tinge of sympathy: "I lost in one year a dozen new Negroes by dirt eating though I fed them well—when I remonstrated with them, they constantly told me, they preferred dying to living; and a great proportion of the new Negroes who go upon sugar plantations die in this manner."[28]

While these atrocious conditions were largely tolerated or ignored by Britons back home, one group never condoned the practice. The Christian offshoot group known as the Religious Society of Friends had been founded in the 1640s by a disgruntled Anglican named George Fox, who thought it should be possible for a believer to have a direct experience with Christ without a church in the way. A sarcastic magistrate told Fox he seemed to be coaxing his followers to "tremble at the name of the Lord," lending the sect the nickname Quakers. They emphasized simplicity in their lifestyles, spontaneity of expression mingled with periods of quiet they called "holy conversation," strict nonviolence, and the dignity of each individual. As far back as 1671, long before other dissenting sects took an interest in the subject, Fox had looked at the slave trade and found it repulsive; he encouraged his coreligionists to stop owning human beings.[29]

Almost no subject had more power to drive an average Jamaican planter into an angry rant than the specter of distant London philanthropists working behind the scenes to free the enslaved people. What one newspaper labeled "a whole tribe of canters and hypocrites" were generally those regarded as villains, traitors, fanatics, or dangerous idiots who didn't understand basic economics. Without kidnapped labor, the West Indies would collapse and Britain's financial vitality would vanish. The Quakers and their moralism were no match for this discourse. Daniel Defoe—author of *Robinson Crusoe* and *A Journal of the Plague Year*—had argued in 1713 that slavery was central to global hegemony: "No African trade, no negroes; no negroes no sugars, gingers, indicoes etc; no sugars etc no islands, no islands no continent; no continent no trade."[30]

Though some outsiders wrote romantically about the noble-savage origins of the enslaved, Jamaican planters had only a crude understanding of the African societies from which they had acquired their laborers. A matrix of racist stereotypes as detailed as any chart of animal breeds took hold as a convenient way for estate officials to understand their purchases. Knowledge of the various ethnicities also came in handy when putting advertisements in the paper for runaway slaves, who could be identified by their racial characteristics, as well as the brands on their shoulders or the number of lash marks on their backs.

The most coveted workers on the island were the Coromantee, a name referring to the Akan and Ga-Andangme people who had been kidnapped from what is present-day Ghana. Even though they played a central role in some of the minor mutinies that had convulsed Jamaica over the previous two hundred years, they were valued for their strong work ethic. A planter named Stewart said they were "fierce, violent, and revengeful under injury and provocation; but hardy, laborious, and manageable under mild and just treatment." They were preferred over the Ibo people from what is now Benin and western Nigeria, who were thought "crafty, artful, disputative in driving a bargain." The lesser groups included the Mandingo, from Senegambia, who had been Muslims and sometimes knew how to write Arabic characters. They were judged more peaceful and made natural gang foremen, but were not to be counted on for heavy labor. To call anyone "an Angolan Negro" was Jamaican slang that everyone understood to mean "worthless." To put an Angolan to work in the sugar works, commented one scornful planter "is throwing away money."[31]

Favored ethnic groups looked down on the others, and the haughty feelings were returned. Those who had been born into slavery in Jamaica sometimes evinced a curious pride at their life bondage, calling themselves Creoles and looking with disapproval at the newly arrived "Guinea-birds" or "salt-water Negroes" with their Old World languages, strange religions, and teeth sharpened to points. The children that came from sexual liaisons with whites occupied a complicated set of classifications as mulattoes, Sambos, quadroons, octoroons, mustefinos, quintroons, and even more exotically named fractional categories that baffled outsiders. In the byzantine genealogies of sexually loose Jamaica, however, these categories were a matter of intense importance for those on the color scale, for the further an individual could travel from "black," the more prestige could accrue. Those who were only one-eighth black, for instance, were often treated as close to coequals with whites. The libidinal economic theory of the Caribbean placed a high value on the hard currency of skin color: a family was said to be able to journey from black to white within three generations if they only conceived with buckra. Rev. John Barry testified back in England that he knew mothers who would rather "put out their daughters in concubinage with white men than allow them to marry with men of their own color."[32]

Job hierarchies also interfered with what could have been more unity among the enslaved people. The head boiler was a man who always commanded respect, and then there were drivers, governing either through charm or fear. The head cattleman had command of the livestock and an easier job than most. Those who worked serving food or cleaning rooms in the great house typically enjoyed greater prestige than field hands, though they constantly worried about offending the master's family and being sent to the cane rows. Lowest of all were those on "jobbing gangs" which belonged to a white contractor without any land of his own who would hire out his blacks for temporary work. They were often assigned the worst and most dangerous tasks and were whipped the hardest, being considered expendable property of no higher status than farm implements. "I consider that the most miserable life that a slave can lead," said a lawyer named James Beckford Wildman; "they go from place to place, put up a little hut but with leaves of trees, and are out for weeks at a time."[33]

Whatever their differences over work and ethnicity, all of these groups could mingle with one another in the row of huts and shacks known on every estate as the negro village. Though they lived there at the master's pleasure, they still took pride in their hand-built homes; many contained furniture and crockery they had been able to purchase, as well as at least one good ladies' dress hanging from a beam and a decanter of wine or rum on a side table. Another space of limited autonomy was the Sunday Market—an island-wide ritual in which the enslaved people were allowed to walk to the nearest town to buy and sell farm produce and other goods, as long as they had a paper ticket of passage from their master proving they had permission to be away from the plantation. This was an opportunity for enterprising workers to wheedle and bargain—to "higgle," in the local parlance—and keep socking away coins in the hopes of one day buying their freedom from their masters. Though they dealt in tiny prices that lay far beneath the commodity-level transactions of their masters, the Sunday Market was nonetheless a venue for significant economic activity. Enslaved people held about 20 percent of the circulating silver coin on the island, and some were such legendarily tough negotiators that their masters trusted them to make large-scale deals at the Kingston docks.[34]

Some enslaved people walked as far as twenty-five miles in a day just to be at the markets, staying up all Saturday night if necessary, balancing baskets of produce on their heads as they walked. On those days it seemed to visitors that the entire slave population of the island was in motion. The market was also a rare chance for enslaved people from different estates to see each other, exchange gossip, and tell stories.[35]

One white onlooker, Theodore Foulks, described "a rainbow throng" of enslaved people going to market with ribbons, lace, corn, salted fish, pigs, chickens, fruit, bonnets, and stockings to sell. He wrote a colorful account of the conversations that ensued, partly rendered in island patois and soaked in the racial stereotypes of the era: "*Chantoba will tell Cooba how Quaw teifed her fattest hog: how Mumba's John left his old wife Venus to attach himself to Pussy;* while the younger ladies in closely knotted clusters, some laughing, some with serio-comic countenances, relate how *Jupiter lub Jelina for tru'; or how Soger Buckra handsome for too much.*"[36]

In times of adequate rainfall, the enslaved people could sell the excess food they grew on their provision ground, which was typically a rocky half acre deemed useless for sugar cultivation but on which yams, corn, plantains and other staple crops might grow. This tiny concession of "ownership" from the masters had the curious psychological effect of bonding the enslaved to the land on which they were imprisoned. Tending even a stony garden brought a sense of pride in a home, even in an alien place, and the provision ground became a rare place of liberty where a person could make management decisions about what crops to plant, which to sell at the market, and which to eat themselves. The estate manager William Taylor observed that an enslaved man "who has his house and his ground will not run away unless he receives very bad treatment." And they would care for their own crops like they never would for buckra's sugar. "A negro will lift a load for himself that it would require a severe flogging to make him lift for his master," wrote Taylor. Meals from the gardens in good times were sometimes garnished with a bit of salt pork or fish. Some considered cane-field rats a special treat, though others shunned them as disgusting.[37]

The animated higgle for garden food at the Sunday Market had nothing on the Christmas holiday, which was one time of unabridged joy in the calendar. Skies were typically cloudless in late December and the heat close to ninety degrees Fahrenheit; white newcomers to Jamaica during this season often expressed wonder that Christmas could be celebrated in such broiling weather. Enslaved people across the island were given three days off, December 25–27, for a festival known as John Canoe, or Junkanoo, which was also the name of a character—typically played by a male slave known for his dancing abilities—who carried a wooden sword, sported a long false beard of animal hair, and wore ox horns, or sometimes a pasteboard toy house stuffed full of satirical rag puppets, on his head.[38]

He would gyrate in exaggerated ways in the middle of a circle of clapping spectators, aiming to inspire laughter. Often he would imitate various white masters through certain gestures and mimicry that everyone understood. The supporting players in the pageant wore masks; others tapped on goatskin drums, scraped animal bones together, played fiddle-like instruments, drank, and sang, while spectators laughingly called out "Junkanoo!" as freely as any sports chant.

This was the only time of the year that wine and rum flowed freely; enslaved people tried to dress in whatever fine clothes they happened to have acquired, and white overseers typically made themselves scarce—though some lenient masters went so far as to invite field slaves into the great house for a drink, and their wives lent the women their jewelry, which would have been a breach of manners at any other time of year. On December 25, 1774, Thomas Thistlewood—he of the frequent lashings and coerced sexual encounters—made the following notation in his diary: "Christmas Day. Served my Negroes 18 herrings each, likewise gave Lincoln, Dick and Abba each a bottle of rum, Cudjoe and Solon a bottle between them, Caesar and Pompey ditto, Chub and Strap ditto, Fanny Damsel and Bess ditto. Rest of the women 2 bottles among them." Later that day, he had sex with a woman called Little Doll in the garden shed.[39]

The skeptical planter John Stewart complained of the "three successive days of unbounded dissipation, and of the danger, at such a time of unrestrained licentiousness, of riots and disorder." But he also acknowledged the beneficial role that Junkanoo had on the collective psychology of a beaten-down people. "Pleasure throws a temporary oblivion over their cares and their toils; they seem a people without the consciousness of inferiority or suffering."[40]

The cultural origins of Junkanoo remain murky, but the name is probably derivative of the Ewe word for "sorcerer." Secret societies known as Mmo—which means "knowing the masquerade"—designed elaborate coverings for the face and invoked various gods for their blessings as they danced, keeping their identities concealed through their highly stylized masks. Women were supposed to pretend not to recognize their male lovers in one of these masks, for it was intended to represent the mortal's elevation into a powerful spirit to allow communication with ancestors.[41]

The Dionysian release offered by Junkanoo arrived every December in an intense expression of feeling across the island, and militias were typically put on a state of heightened readiness—even extending into declarations of martial law—in case the exuberance should take a sudden turn into violence. Junkanoo was about ritualized fun, but it also was about masks, subversion, and secrecy among elite slaves. Most whites dreaded its coming and expressed private relief when it was over.[42]

The terroristic methods that white Jamaicans employed to keep themselves from being ripped apart by their own enslaved people—the chains, the whippings, the casual rapes, the torture, the citizen militia, and the final backstop of the British Army—were efforts to stave off a pending eruption everyone could sense was in the offing. The overwhelming numerical strength of the enslaved, their pent-up rage, their easy access to torches and sharp hand tools, and their ability to pass secrets among themselves created a combustible atmosphere that hung over every discussion of Jamaican public affairs.

Edward Trelawny had seen the situation clearly in 1746 and feared an eventual bloodstained uprising that would be "plainly owning to the too great Number of Negroes in proportion to white Persons, being at least ten to one, and the too little Care that is taken to manage those Negroes."[43]

Even planters who agreed with his dire assessment didn't care if the enslaved people picked up weapons, as long as the planters themselves weren't around to be attacked. In Jamaica, the point was always to acquire fast money and go home soon, not to waste time on collective projects or planning for the future. "Many see symptom of a country approaching to its ruin," fumed Trelawny, "but they fancy it may last their time, and they may sell out and get home first, and what comes afterwards they care not." Slave uprisings had passed through Jamaica like tropical storms about once every five years—there had been nineteen of them during the eighteenth century—and the ruling class had learned to live with them as another cost of doing business. The fabric of revolt had already been woven into the island before the British even wrestled it from the Spanish in 1655. Some of the first enslaved people brought there by the Spanish had run away from their plantations, built fortifications in the wilderness, and formed their own renegade society.[44]

They were called *cimarrones*—the Spanish word for "the untamed" or "the unbroken"—which the British corrupted to Maroons. Despite numerous campaigns to flush them out, they proved a fierce and gallant enemy. The colonial government finally tired of the backcountry war and signed a peace treaty with the Maroons in 1739, which granted them the right to live as free people in exchange for their help at capturing and returning runaway slaves, as well as their military assistance in quashing rebellions. Maroons founded several towns of their own, lived peacefully with British neighbors, and had their own courts and justice systems. They also displayed little sympathy for their fellow blacks still in bondage.[45]

Forced laborers in Jamaica had tried to rip off their chains as far back as 1673, when a band of slaves seized the firearms of their master and murdered him. Insurrections such as this were usually contained to a small area and decisively crushed within a week. But in 1760 a more serious challenge to white rule emerged. An enslaved man named Tacky began holding secret meetings in a cave with a band of friends, and in the early morning hours of Easter Sunday, April 7, 1760, he and his followers—mainly speakers of the Akan language that the planters called the Coromantee—marched on a garrison named Fort Haldane, murdered a guard and gained access to forty rifles and four barrels of gunpowder.[46]

Using fishing weights for bullets, Tacky's improvised platoon attacked two neighboring plantations and convinced more than a thousand enslaved people to join them. Governor Henry Moore declared martial law and called up the militia, which—though slow and incompetent—pursued the slave forces into the mountainous slopes of St. Mary's Parish, where a Maroon sharpshooter killed Tacky with a shot to the head. The remainder of his allies fought a two-month guerilla war before committing mass suicide in a cave, symbolically ending their cause underground just as it had begun. All of them had shaved their heads as a show of solidarity with each other. By the time the militia and regular troops put down the scattered uprisings that Tacky's bravado had inspired, sixty whites and approximately four hundred enslaved people were dead and much of a sugar harvest was lost.[47]

White leaders tried to make a public example by burning one of the suspects to death. "The wretch that was burnt was made to sit on the ground," wrote Bryan Edwards, "and his body being chained to an iron stake, the fire was applied to his feet. He uttered not a groan, and saw his legs reduced to ashes with the utmost firmness and composure; after one of his arms by some means getting loose, he snatched a brand from the fire that was consuming him, and flung it at the face of his executioner." Through what must have been extraordinary pain, the nameless rebel demonstrated not only a final act of physical defiance but also the characteristic Jamaican slave practice, so unnerving to the whites, of going into death with remarkable composure.[48]

Five years later another group of Coromantee met in secret in St. Mary's Parish to swear an oath of loyalty to each other, drinking from a cup that contained a mixture of gunpowder, rum, graveyard dirt, and blood drawn from all those in attendance. They aimed to take Tacky's revolt further and establish an independent black nation in Jamaica. And they would do it under the cover of the Christmas holiday.[49]

A man named Blackwall had developed a network of confidants on seventeen estates. But he lost control before it even began: there was "impatience of some among them to do the work" and at a plantation named Whitehall they set the trash house on fire on November 29 as a signal that the insurrection was afoot nearly a month before it was supposed to begin. The plotters killed two white men in the great house, and then approached a neighboring estate, Ballard's Valley, aiming to burn it down by hoisting a bundle of flaming sugarcane trash up to the roof. But a white defender hiding behind the stone fortification of the ground floor got off a lucky shot, killing one of the leaders, and the rest scattered into the woods. Thirteen enslaved people were rounded up and executed. "The plan for the rising appears to have been well-laid," commented a churchman one hundred years later, "but this premature action frustrated it."[50]

While less competent and not as bloody as Tacky's Rebellion, the details of the 1765 plot nevertheless made an impression on the white planter class. The secret society, the blood oath, the assumed plan to found an independent nation of blacks, the cover of the Christmas celebration, the awesome sight of a plantation on fire as a signal for a general uprising, the sudden explosion of murderous anger from those who had previously been so cowed, the reminder that there were far more of *them* than *us*: there was something primal and horrifying about all of it. As it was, enslaved people in Jamaica found ways to protest their bondage almost on a daily basis that were far less obvious. They stole animals, pretended to be sick, worked in the cane fields at an agonizingly slow pace, lingered in the boiling houses, ruined the sugar production, and deliberately injured themselves. Then the nightmare of a successful revolution actually came to fruition—in stutters and half steps, and in gradual and increasingly violent fashion—on the neighboring French slaveholding island of Saint-Domingue. Inspired by the enlightenment ideals of *liberté, égalité, fraternité* emerging from the French Revolution, a group of free blacks called for the right to vote in 1781—a suffrage movement that soon reached the ears of the enslaved inhabitants, who conducted a vodou ceremony in a thunderstorm on the night of August 21 and then rose up in coordinated attacks. They executed planters in their beds and set fire to sugar works and fields, sending what C. L. R. James described as a "rain of burning cane straw" over a wide region. Before long, the rebels—touting the ideals held up by French revolutionaries an ocean away—controlled a third of the island. A charismatic and literate slave named Toussaint Breda drilled the free men in European-style military tactics, taking for himself the nom de guerre of Toussaint Louverture, his surname meaning "the opening." When France declared war on Britain in 1793 for unrelated reasons, the terrified white planters of Saint-Domingue invited the British to seize their island and help them regain control.[51]

Worried that Louverture's example would spread revolution all over the West Indies, Prime Minister William Pitt dispatched British troops, but they held on to only a few coastal settlements. Nearly 90 percent of the invasion force died of yellow fever. At one point the Jamaican colonial government mustered a regiment composed entirely of enslaved people to help put down the rebellion, but then grew so afraid that they would be radicalized by what they had seen in Saint-Domingue that they were not permitted to return. The overwhelmed British commander, Colonel Thomas Maitland, signed a secret agreement with Louverture on August 31, 1792, stating that British troops could withdraw without fear of attack if Louverture promised not to foment revolts in Jamaica, which lay just ninety-three miles away. Here was a remarkable admission of Jamaican weakness, as well as a revealing disclosure that the sugar gentry were as afraid of an idea as they were of knives. Napoleon Bonaparte tried and failed to pacify the island with fresh troops, though he succeeded in capturing Louverture, who died in a French prison before he could see the 1804 declaration creating the independent republic of Haiti. The new nation was crippled by debt and smeared with blood, but it was governed by those who had recently been in shackles.[52]

Refugees both white and black had poured into Jamaica telling stories of what they had seen, and enslaved people everywhere heard about it from their coworkers who served at the masters' dinner table. Saint-Domingue had been a major competitor on the world sugar market, and prices soared as its plantations burned. But white Jamaica's glee was tempered with distress about possibly suffering the same bloody fate.

"Jamaicans cannot be too much on their guard," warned Robert Charles Dallas. Ships and small boats had "swarmed like bees" between the two colonies for decades; many of them had enslaved crews aboard with sharp ears and discreet ways of passing on the information that was far more up-to-date than what little appeared in Kingston's carefully self-censored newspapers. The militia began drilling furiously in plain sight, the cavalry was dispatched to the interior, and Jamaican slaves were prohibited from traveling as deckhands on vessels bound for Haiti. But none of these conspicuous intimidations could cut off the flow of information. The British military commander lamented that the enslaved people were "immediately informed of every kind of news that arrives" and had already learned "perfectly well every transaction at Cape Francois."[53]

Nothing made the Jamaican gentry more paranoid than the thought that an uprising might arise in their midst. In St. James Parish, where the chatter was especially heavy and where the governor feared "mischief," the Committee of Secrecy and Safety took on the job of deporting foreign sailors and French- and Spanish-speaking blacks. Rumors spread that slaves were making cutlasses in the blacksmiths' shops and secretly buying gunpowder at the Sunday Market. Even white evacuees from Haiti—fellow petty aristocrats—were regarded with more suspicion then pity. "Their presence, and especially that of their slave, was declared to be dangerous," wrote W. J. Gardner. The fears grew even more inflamed when a Portuguese radical named Issac Sasportas showed up in Kingston and tried to make contact with the Maroons to spark a second Caribbean revolution. Louverture tipped off the Jamaican governor, and Sasportas was led to the gallows on December 23, 1799, shouting "Vive la liberté, vive la Republique!"[54]

Some planters in Jamaica heard song lyrics celebrating liberty drifting over from their slave villages at night, and shared the dread of Thomas Jefferson in faraway Virginia, who wrote in a letter to James Monroe in 1793, "I am becoming daily more convinced that all the West Indies will remain in the hands of people of color, and a total expulsion of whites sooner or later take place." The Royal Navy, in partnership with the US Navy, enforced a policy of quarantine against ships coming from the independent black republic in the name of "preventing the dissemination of dangerous principles among the slaves of their respective countries."[55]

Three years before the start of the Haitian Revolution, a French coffee planter named Nicolas Lejeune had tortured two women to death by burning their legs with a torch and then locking them in a jail cell to die of their wounds. His was one of the rare cases of a white man to stand trial for killing his own black enslaved people under the widely ignored Negro Code, which forbade such abuses. After a time on the run, he surrendered and then made a speech defending himself before the fourteen-member Superior Council of Le Cap in 1788. In its own way, his reasoning was every bit as coldly empathetic as Trelawny's warning about the sorry state of the Jamaican militia.[56]

"The unhappy condition of the negro leads him naturally to detest us," Lejeune said. "It is only force and violence that restrains him; he is bound to harbor an implacable hatred in his heart, and if he does not visit upon us all the hurt of which he is capable it is only because his readiness to do so is chained down by terror. . . . I dare to say that our negroes lack only sufficient courage or resolution to buy their freedom with the blood of their masters. Just one step can enlighten them about what they have the power to undertake."[57]

The council acquitted Lejeune and he was set free. His fellow planters insisted that his enslaved people be given fifty lashes each for having dared to speak publicly about what they had seen.[58]

FIVE

THE PLOT

THE MOST REACTIONARY of the Jamaican sugar planters did not just fear the Christianity spread by the missionaries. They feared the education that many of them wanted to bring to the island.

More than price depressions or war with the French, more than even machetes or guns, the sugar elite of Jamaica was most afraid of an idea: the consciousness spreading among the enslaved people that they deserved freedom and that it was within their power to achieve it. Literacy could not only give a slave a higher sense of worth and a new sense of self-awareness. It could bring imaginative access to the broader world, an ability to communicate beyond the boundaries of the plantation, and perhaps the means to spread a conspiracy across long distances. What possible good could come from book-reading slaves?

Literacy was just the goal the missionaries desired, for the Protestant road to the divine leads through the words of the Bible. One flatly said it would be "impossible" to communicate any meaningful religious knowledge without first teaching an enslaved person to read. William Knibb's ministry, therefore, was centered on perpetuating the work of the school his brother founded; others made the early rounds of plantations for 6:00 A.M. lessons in Bible reading before the workday began. While some enslaved people were indifferent to the meanings of sentences on the page, most could not get enough and pleaded for the ministers not to leave the estate until they had learned just one more word. Hope Masterton Waddell thought it was splendid to watch the most enthusiastic lay their tools aside in the evening only to "run and take up the quill and wield it so well." Enslaved people who had a knack for reading could earn extra pocket money giving lessons on the sly with any sheet of printed material they might scrounge up. It became common for enslaved people to carry torn scraps of British newspapers. Some used them as wrapping for the cherished tickets that would allow them to leave the plantation for Sunday services—a material metaphor for the blending of the message of Christianity and the newfound awareness of a bigger political world. After eight years of work in Jamaica, Knibb estimated that most of his congregation of three thousand had some level of literacy.[1]

The growth of literacy had sparked an awakening—welcome to some, dreadful to others—across the slave empire of Jamaica. Reading seemed to ignite a hidden store of fuel within an enslaved person. "The slave submits to his condition in consequence of a degraded state," the missionary Thomas Cooper told a committee of inquiry. "If you instruct him and bring him acquainted with the Christian religion, and teach him to read, he at once discovers that he is a man, a reasonable being; and he asks, how is it that he should be placed in such a situation?"[2]

One who was undoubtedly asking this question was Samuel Sharpe, as he mingled his reading of current affairs back in England along with his religious texts. In his private teachings to his fellow enslaved people, Sharpe emphasized those passages of the Bible explicitly dealing with freedom.

Four passages in particular drew his attention: "No man can serve two masters" (Matt. 6:24); "If the Son therefore shall make you free, you shall be free indeed" (John 8:36); "Ye are bought with a price: be ye not servants of men" (1 Cor. 7:23); "There is neither Jew nor Greek, there is neither bond nor free, there is nether male nor female; for ye are all one in Christ" (Gal. 3:28). He appears to have neglected all those that seemed to justify slavery or harped upon obedience—the favorite localized theology of the established church. When fused with rumors of abolitionist sentiment and sugar boycotts back in Britain, the kerygma could become electric.

The slave Robert Gardiner said of Sharpe, approvingly, "He can read and used to read the newspapers and hear the people talk at the Bay; he would then bring up all the news and spread it among the negroes; sometimes he would bring the newspapers up from the Bay, and read them to the negroes." There can be no telling, of course, which articles Sharpe chose to read, and which he omitted, and what kind of commentary he may have appended or what he may have fabricated on the spot. There can be little doubt, however, that the overall narrative was proliberty and highly invigorating because Sharpe mixed the overseas news with the same dangerous passages of scripture that the white missionaries had been ordered to censor from their own messages.[3]

Because Sharpe was a pastor and a "daddy" of the Native Baptists, his message also carried the imprimatur of the church, and, hazily, God's plan. A close associate, Thomas Dove, said the enslaved people trusted Sharpe's word implicitly because of his dramatic presentation and magnetism, and, no doubt, because they were hungering to believe that freedom really was coming their way, just as it had for free colored citizens. As the local saying went, "Brown already free, black soon." Sharpe had also spent most of his time circulating around the cosmopolitan town of Montego Bay and therefore had access to the gossip from the sailors just off the ships from England. He became an important link in the underground network of information that circulated in the Caribbean in the period of late slavery—what the historian Julius Scott has termed "revolutionary currents"—aided by literacy, newspapers, and the passages of the Bible that promised personal liberation.[4]

"The negroes believed all that Samuel Sharpe said to them," recalled Dove, "because he being born and brought up on the Bay, was intelligent and could read, and besides was head leader at the Baptist church, and always attended there; and the negroes considered that what Sharpe told them when he came to the mountains must be true, as it came from the church." A slave named Bingham agreed. The white repression could last only so long as the secret of liberty was concealed: "The Baptists all believe that they are to be freed; they say the Lord and the King have given them free, but the white gentlemen in Jamaica keep it back."[5]

As it happened, this new underground teaching was swirling as the once fantastic profits of the Caribbean were drying up, partly in response to Elizabeth Heyrick's sugar boycott but also because of larger economic forces. In the last decade of the eighteenth century, for example, it was considered normal to get a 14 percent annual rate of profit on even a marginal estate. But new fields were opening up throughout the Caribbean and Asia, causing stiff competition and reckless oversupply of sugar. The expected annual rate of return on an estate had plunged to 5 percent, which made the island much less attractive to the high-risk personalities suited to thrive in its lawless atmosphere. In some of the hard-farmed areas of Trelawny Parish, where soil exhaustion was rampant, approximately one-third of the plantations shut down or were sold to faraway investors at a deep discount. Ten went bankrupt in 1831 alone. Within one bad decade, the white population had declined from approximately thirty thousand to fifteen thousand, with enslaved people now encircling them in even more lopsided proportions.[6]

Freedom was coming, said Sharpe, and it was coming soon. Both the newspapers and the word of God said it was so—no matter how much the earthly master might try to deny it.

Caribbean planters, of course, had different ideas about resistance. In his prescient 1788 speech to exonerate himself for burning two women to death, the Saint-Domingue planter Nicholas Lejeune had claimed that whips, beatings, and intimidation were not enough to keep slaves from rebelling. To keep them docile, they had to be stripped of their humanity at every opportunity and kept unaware of their own agency. "It is not the fear and equity of the law that forbids the slave from stabbing his master, it is the consciousness of absolute power that he has over his person," he said. "Remove this bit, he will dare everything."[7]

The audacious self-liberation movement dreaded by Lejeune and the Jamaican planters was well underway. Many on both sides of the racial divide knew was it coming.

Samuel Sharpe made another step toward insurrection by cultivating a set of insiders who would be let in on the grand design. And at every planation they could reach, they would in turn cultivate a select group to help carry a message outward in concentric circles.

Sharpe chose fellow conspirators who, like him, were a part of the "slave elite": the talented craftsmen, the drivers, and the head boilers, who were sometimes literate themselves and held in a position of trust by their masters. He may have chosen them for their credibility, the respect they enjoyed among the field hands, or perhaps because their relative freedom of movement allowed them to be better organizers of an underground movement.[8]

A committee of the Jamaica Assembly later expressed astonishment at this cellular structure, noting that "it has been a remarkable and unprecedented feature in this rebellion, that many of the chief conspirators and ringleaders were to be found amongst those enslaved people who, from their situations as head-people or confidential servants were the least worked, were the best clothed, and received the most indulgence." A reader can almost hear the bafflement over how the plot emerged from what amounted to a slave aristocracy—in a similar way that modern Western governments have been surprised by revolutionaries or terrorists who come not from the poorest quarters of society but the layers of the educated bourgeoisie.[9]

Even more remarkable was the speed by which messages could be passed among enslaved people connected in social networks across

a wide stretch of territory. A north shore planter named John Whittaker had expressed amazement in 1791 after one of his workers told
him about an event in Montego Bay that had happened less than a
day earlier, even before a rider on horseback could arrive with the
news. In other cases, enslaved people seemed to know precise details
of militia maneuvers. Whittaker surmised that there must be "some
unknown mode of conveying intelligence among Negroes." The
verbal webs of underground communication that stretched across
Jamaica relied on a combination of those who were permitted travel
outside the estates: higglers at the market, trusted negotiators, sympathetic free colored people, and traveling Baptist deacons like
Sharpe.[10]

One example of this network in action came when a slave named
Edward Hylton said he received a message from Sharpe to come to
a prayer meeting at the house of a slave named Johnson who worked
at Retrieve Estate. After the meeting, and when most had left, Sharpe
told Hylton to stay behind. Other black men whom Hylton did not
recognize "stealthily and with extreme caution made their way into
the house." It seemed to Hylton that Sharpe had been expecting
these visitors, and that the meeting was serious business.[11]

Sharpe began to speak in "a low, soft tone," seemingly out of concern that somebody might hear him through the thin walls of the
slave cabin. The clergyman Henry Bleby, who heard the story directly
from Hylton, told what happened next:

> He then proceeded with his address to those around him,
> speaking for a long time on various topics relating to the great
> subject he had at heart, and with an eloquence which, from
> Hylton's account, kept all his hearers fascinated and spell-bound
> from the beginning to the end of his speech. He referred to the
> manifold evils and injustice of slavery; asserted the natural
> equality of man with regard to freedom; and referring to the
> holy Scriptures as his authority, denied that the white man had

any more right to hold the blacks in bondage than the blacks had to enslave the whites.

Sharpe then told the group astonishing—and untrue—news that went far beyond rumors of a sugar boycott: that, back in England, King William IV had made them free and the white slaveholders were keeping it a secret. They were plotting to kill all the black men, saving the women as their playthings and sparing the children to grow into a new generation of slaves. And "if the black men did not stand up for themselves, and take their freedom, the whites would put them out at the muzzles of their guns, and shoot them like pigeons."[12]

The week before Christmas, Sharpe held a meeting at Retrieve Estate, where a slave named Joseph Martin said that Sharpe's simple message was that they should not agree to work after Christmas and "he said nothing else." Another slave who heard the same speech, Robert Rose, testified of an overtly peaceful method to the upcoming work stoppage. "He said we must all agree to set down after Xmas," Rose said of Sharpe. "We must not trouble any body and raise no Rebellion. We must set quite peaceable. . . . We did not swear to burn any where or to fight."[13]

Did Samuel Sharpe, like Toussaint Louverture, harbor ambitions of founding an independent republic? Nowhere in the fragments of his recorded speech does he mention Haiti, and any writings that he might have made have been lost. But he was literate and well informed, with a powerful curiosity for international affairs. It would have been impossible for him not to have heard of it given that he was reading British newspapers and listening in on the nervous conversations of whites. From a jail cell six months later, and under intense pressure to make a confession, Gardiner noted that "Samuel Sharpe swore every man all around" that "every man should fight, and do his utmost to drive the white and free people from Jamaica; if they succeeded, a governor was to be appointed to each parish."[14]

If the testimony of Edward Hylton is to be believed, Sharpe's plan contained an option for violent overthrow which would be triggered only if the initial stage should fail. The two-stage plan might be summarized as, first try a peaceful strike, then go to a fighting phase. Sharpe appears to have arrived at this strategy after a lengthy talk with other members of his committee, as Hylton relates through Bleby's summary:

> Further discussion ensued, and their deliberations were carried on far into the night; when all scruples being set at rest, and the plan of operations more fully detailed by Sharpe, the whole party bound themselves by oath not to work after Christmas as slaves, but to assert their claim to freedom, and to be faithful to each other. If "Buckra" would pay them, they would work as before; but if any attempt was made to force them to work as slaves, then they would fight for their freedom.[15]

Sharpe's exact attitude toward armed overthrow was never recorded, though the first stage of the plan—the refusal to work—was indisputably his. There is a small bit of evidence, however, that he may have been forced to concede to a fighting plan in deference to his companions' arguments. The only other participant in the meeting that Hylton identifies by name is the slave Johnson, who would later call himself a colonel and lead one of the only successful military strikes against the Jamaican militia in the early days of the fighting. His aggression was such that he would be killed in that battle.[16]

As the house belonged to Johnson, he may have been the one who suggested the meeting and he likely would have had an elevated role in the discussion. Johnson's skepticism about peaceful resistance actually working may have contributed to the formulation of a battle strategy. But for his part, Sharpe insisted that violence was never a part of his ideology. Bleby recorded his own thoughts thus: "He did not wish to destroy the estates, nor did he desire that any person should be injured: his only object was to obtain freedom."[17]

A major problem in recounting slave experiences from colonial Jamaica, as with any slaveholding society, is that enslaved people almost never got to record their true feelings in writing. They had no unrestricted access to pen or paper. Their thoughts usually died with them, or were passed on in oral form to their friends and family, where they invariably were forgotten by later generations.

What few fragments survive from the revolt come in the form of court testimony—often given under duress—to a white interrogator who tended to record only what would be relevant in front of a judge who aimed to hang the slaves, or in the memoirs and propaganda of abolitionists, who were infinitely more sympathetic to them but also filtered their words through a political lens and for maximum pathos to their reading audience. The British legal and publishing apparatus thus served as a flawed mouthpiece for the slaves, and much authenticity has doubtless been lost. Having been greatly condensed and distorted by the prejudices and political aims of these interlocutors, the testimony of the slaves is highly compromised in quality and cannot entirely be trusted. Yet it is also an indispensable part of Afro-Caribbean history as the only available record of the voices of the slaves themselves.[18]

One of the white middlemen was Rev. John McIntyre, a white Anglican priest who interrogated many of the captured rebels in jail cells in the early winter of 1832. He came to the conclusion that there was indeed a two-stage plan to the Christmas Uprising: to first try a peaceful work stoppage, and then go to blunt force. And after that Rubicon was crossed, the next logical step would be to strive for an independent republic of freed slaves. "They all stated that their leaders had told them they must be free after Christmas, but this was the work God gave them to do; they must be ready to fight for it; if their masters kept it from them, they must be prepared to take it themselves," McIntyre told an official inquiry, quoting the slaves he had debriefed. "'The white people made bad laws for them; when they were free the country would belong to themselves and, and they could make laws for themselves.'"[19]

Sharpe undoubtedly exaggerated the facts, and he could not himself have been deluded about the true state of the abolition bill in Parliament, which was still stalled as of December 1831. The newspapers he read had covered this thoroughly. But this ran contrary to his message. "I know we are free," he kept telling people. "I have read it in the English papers."[20]

This was not the first time in the British Caribbean that Bible preaching had mingled with rumors that a king in faraway London had made a decree of freedom: when taken together, they fulfilled a deep craving for "good news." In 1816, word of a parliamentary debate about creating a slave registry arrived in Barbados and quickly became interpreted through the estate grapevines as a prelude to certain emancipation, which the local whites would certainly resist. A driver named Bussa tried to speed matters along with a plot to revolt. Signal fires were lit on Easter Sunday, and the resulting three-day revolt claimed approximately a thousand slave lives and a quarter of the sugar crop.[21]

Seven years later, in the British colony of Demerara on the coast of South America, similar rumors flew when news of slavery amelioration laws reached the colony via British newspapers. A slave named Jack Gladstone told a personal servant of the governor of the prevailing rumor that the "king had sent orders to the governor to free the slaves," as well as the scripture reading from the previous Sunday, Romans 8:28: "And we know that all things work together for good to them that love God, to them who are the called according to his purpose." As rumors and bits of information flew, Gladstone's father, Quamina, assumed a lead role in a plot to seize freedom by force. The chapels for Sunday services became venues to marshal support and swear oaths for what became an almost entirely nonviolent act of mass resistance that lasted from August 18 to August 20, 1823. Plantation owners were locked inside their houses for their own safety, even as the militia fired on crowds of enslaved people. Though upward of 250 blacks lost their lives, they killed no more than two or three white people in a remarkable show of restraint.[22]

Whether Samuel Sharpe had heard of these previous defeats is unknown, though given the range of his contacts and the extent of the Jamaican slave network, it seems likely that he had. Either way, it did not seem to dampen his confidence. For his part, Henry Bleby thought Sharpe was trying to take advantage of an upcoming window in which the Christmas holiday would provide cover for organizing, as well as the trip away from the island on the part of his spiritual mentor, Thomas Burchell, who had the authority to debunk the wildfire rumor about King William IV.

"Sharpe was not deceived himself concerning the slavery question," wrote Bleby. "He was, I believe, too intelligent not to be aware of the true state of the case." But he created the belief among his friends "that they had actually been made free by the king, and putting himself at their head, to commence a struggle for freedom."[23]

As slaves grew increasingly excited by the talk of abolition schemes far across the Atlantic, counterrumors of a planned insurrection were coursing through moderate white society and eventually reached the ears of Somerset Lowry-Corry, known formally as Lord Belmore, the governor of Jamaica.

Belmore had been appointed to the governorship in 1828, after a career representing an Irish borough in the House of Commons and also a stint as a yachtsman. An injury suffered when he was sixteen years old had given him a permanent limp and the nickname the Lame Earl in his hometown in Northern Ireland, but he made up for his handicap with strong willpower, a fierce tongue, and a taste for world travel. Lord Belmore had purchased an American schooner, USRC *James Madison*, which had been captured by the British in the War of 1812, and had it refitted for cruising with his family around the eastern Mediterranean. While there, he hunted for antiquities and developed the unusual habit of climbing to the top of the larger Egyptian relics and carving his own name into them. He etched the name

BELMORE, in all capital letters, into the Temple of Dendur, the Great Pyramid at Giza, and the tomb of Ramses II.[24]

In Jamaica he presented himself as an ally of the sugar grandees and the bearer of news from the colonial secretary, but little more. A clergyman would later characterize Belmore's tenure as one of "amiable weakness." Even so, he made few personal friends except for his own male secretary and later an Anglican rector named George W. Bridges, who would eventually prove to be a dangerous companion. The two of them gazed at the stars through a telescope at night, and Bridges shared his own view of the Jamaican situation: the enslaved people were ruthless savages, little better than animals, who needed the constant threat of violence to keep them from murdering their owners. Belmore seemed to have absorbed the lessons. He began to tell overseas dignitaries the story of an emancipated slave who begged for reenslavement to a kind master because the weight of freedom was too much for him to bear.[25]

When Belmore acted in the interests of enslaved people, it was only with the greatest reluctance and only regarding their status as property. When a woman named Eleanor James went to a neighboring estate to collect a hog she was owed, the owner had her whipped two hundred times and her wounds washed with brine, causing permanent disfigurement. "I could not then speak," she said, "in consequence of having bawled so much." When the magistrate John McLeod refused to hear her case, she walked and crawled thirty miles to another one. News of the incident reached the ears of the colonial secretary, Frederick John Robinson, also known as Viscount Goderich, who fired McLeod and castigated Belmore for his plodding response. This was the beginning of a growing mistrust between Goderich and Belmore that would soon burst open.[26]

Samuel Sharpe's plan of resistance received another boost from an unexpected quarter: the defenders of slavery and the newspapers they consumed. Jamaican planters began to talk openly of secession from Britain throughout the summer of 1831, seeking to become the twenty-fifth state of the United States of America.

At public meetings in every city except Kingston, they adopted resolutions whose language at times seemed to mirror that of the US Declaration of Independence. A group in St. Mary's Parish called on British officials to either return all agricultural profits to Jamaica or "leave us to our own resources, by absolving us from our allegiance." In St. Ann's Parish, the language grew apocalyptic: "When we see ourselves scorned, betrayed, devoted to ruin and slaughter, delivered over to the enemies of our country, we consider that we are bound be every principle, human and divine, TO RESIST." One of the planters told a departing Royal Navy vice admiral that when he returned to Jamaica, it would no longer be British territory.[27]

Though the missionaries thought this idea was "perfectly childish and disgusting," the enslaved people quietly spread the news that their island was about to leave the king's grasp. Some of the most trusted and elite servants on the plantation had accompanied their masters to these meetings as attendants and carriage drivers; the household staff had heard secession discussed around the dinner table. Nearly all of them were revolted by the idea of joining the United States. Through the networks of transatlantic slave traffic, Jamaica received a share of people who had first been forced to work in the United States and had witnessed the prejudiced treatment meted out there to free people of color. As a result, explained Rev. Peter Duncan, "their hatred for America is just as deep and deadly as their attachment to the British Constitution is warm and devoted." The American flag was equally reviled among free colored people and enslaved people alike, in a fervor that matched or even exceeded the planters' desire to make an overture to Washington, DC. "I have heard colored gentlemen say that they would spill the last drop of their blood before a Yankee should set his foot on the shore," remarked William Knibb. Even Richard Barrett—no great champion of civil liberties—had been unnerved during his 1816 trip to New York state at the poor treatment of free people of color. "When we are despised by others," he noted in a moment of empathy, "we soon lose all respect for ourselves."[28]

Though the plantation workers had been enslaved under the Crown and would never lay eyes on the faraway sovereign, the king of England held a nearly mystical place in their mind. "I have seen in a thousand instances," reported Duncan, "that His Majesty has not more loyal subjects through the wide extend of his dominions, than the religious slaves are in the island of Jamaica; they will do anything for the King, they revere the very name of the King."[29]

Distanced from the true situation on the sugar estates and lacking a sound pipeline of information, Lord Belmore assured his boss back in London that the enslaved population was "sound and well-disposed." But a mistrustful Goderich insisted that Belmore put out a proclamation under the name of the enslaved people's beloved King William IV—which Goderich likely wrote himself—denying all the rumors of emancipation and declaring that the misinformation "has excited our highest displeasure." For reasons that remain murky, Belmore delayed issuing this order for several critical days while the misinformation spread. Copies of the royal notice were finally tacked up in public places on December 22, 1831—too late to get to the underground network. One militia lieutenant colonel reported "evident contempt" on enslaved people's faces when the king's words were read to them. The enslaved people seemed to believe they were being told yet another lie by their masters, and that the proclamation was not really that of King William but of some sort of puppet.[30]

They might have been surprised at the true nature of the man on whom they had placed their hopes, as his views on slavery were almost identical to that of Jamaican sugar planters. He was also one of England's more incompetent monarchs.

William IV was an accidental king who ascended the throne after his brother George IV died unexpectedly on June 26, 1830, without leaving heirs. Since William's father, King George III, had never expected his third son to rule Britain, he had allowed him to join the Royal Navy as an ordinary teenage midshipman, where he slept in a hammock; washed the dinner dishes in the galley; and picked up the sailor's vices of drinking, cursing, and fighting. During a night of tavern crawling in Gibraltar, William took part in a brawl and got arrested; the admiral had to intervene with local authorities to get him released. Moreover, William knew where to find the brothels in various world ports and was said to "whet his carnal appetites by watching the women engage in lesbian exhibitions." Such were the liberties a prince could take if he never expected to be king.[31]

On the day William was crowned, he raced his royal carriage through the streets, stopping frequently to get out and doff his hat to ordinary citizens. He also was known to spit out the window and to offer lifts to random Britons, who found themselves shocked to be riding to work or home alongside the monarch. Once, while out walking, he saw a girl dressed as a Quaker gazing at an expensive basket in a shop window. Meaning to tease her, he said, "So I see thou art not above the vanities of the world." This upset her, and a mortified William went into the store, purchased the basket, and insisted she take it as a gift.[32]

William retained more than a touch of Royal Navy style: he had an encyclopedic knowledge of dirty jokes, a boisterous dancing style (his favorite tune was "Country Bumpkins"), the intestinal capacity for multiple bottles of wine at a sitting, an insistence that others should drink alcohol with him, a puffy crimson face on a head that was shaped, in the eyes of an observer, "like a pineapple," and a bluff manner of speaking that left some thinking he was refreshingly honest but others feeling that he was a boor. One acquaintance described William's worst social tendencies as a "rudeness even to brutality."[33]

Once he hosted the visiting King Leopold of Belgium for dinner and inquired what beverage his guest was drinking in his goblet.

"Water, sir," Leopold answered.

"Goddamn it!" yelled the king. "Why don't you drink wine? I never allow anyone to drink water at my table."

Leopold remained silent, finished his dinner, and left as soon as he could. "All of this is very miserable and disgraceful," the head of the privy council, Charles Greville, noted in his diary.[34]

William had also been to Jamaica and had loved every minute of it. In command of HMS *Andromeda* in 1788, he sailed to Kingston and was invited by the colonial authorities to attend debates in the assembly about the conditions of the slaves. While there, he apparently indulged in the hedonism that Jamaica was famous for, even though he had written in a penitent letter before his arrival of having lived a "terrible debauched life, of which I am heartily ashamed and tired" and had resolved to keep himself from his customary excesses in drink and fornication—vows he broke in the tropics. He lodged at the Date Tree Inn on East Street in Kingston, where he enjoyed the evening companionship of local women, and then gave an address to the assembly in Spanish Town without breaking stride. He proved such amiable company that some Jamaican planters considered writing to King George III to ask that William be appointed colonial governor. They settled instead for appropriating one thousand pounds for a bejeweled gift to the sailor-prince: a star encrusted with diamonds "as a humble testimony to the very high respect and esteem the island entertained for his eminent virtues."[35]

William's Jamaican sojourn was to make a lasting impression on him. Slaves were key to the economic health of the British Empire, he thought, and their emancipation would also be a foreign policy disaster. His beliefs were so solid that he had once served as an unofficial envoy to relay messages between the slave-trading elite and Buckingham Palace. William had been a fierce opponent of the 1807 measure to ban the overseas slave trade, not only because it ensured a goodly annual production of sugar but also because a well-staffed slaving fleet was a useful annex to the Royal Navy and a training ground for the king's future sailors.

During his carefully curated trip to Jamaica, he said had seen slaves "in a state of humble happiness" who had been kidnapped from Africa—for their own benefit, he deemed—so they would be saved from "gross barbarism." He found them charming and harmless; quite different from the description of them promoted by abolitionists. While in Kingston, the future monarch had been "awakened and disturbed in the morning at an early hour by the joyous festivity, songs and dances of those very slaves, who are described as such miserable wretches."[36]

The writer Zachary Macaulay was introduced to the forty-two-year-old William when he was making the case for slavery with these recollections from Jamaica. Macaulay had been appalled at William's proslavery zealotry: "It is shocking that so young a man, under no bias of interest, should be so earnest for the continuance of the Slave Trade, and especially now [that] its horrors are confessed by all."[37]

Not every Jamaican planter succumbed to the fervor of possible secession from Britain. Those who held government posts, for example, felt obliged to keep themselves aloof. For his part, Richard Barrett never displayed public sympathy with the movement to join the United States, having taken an extended trip through New York state when he was twenty-seven years old. He was, at heart, a monarchist with a distaste for the messy ways of democracy, writing of American politicians,

> Their power is dearer to them than their country. They depend on chance to extricate themselves from their embarrassments & they depend still more on the suspicion & hatred in which one part of the citizens hold the other. In fact so violent is the

party spirit in these states that if any measure is proposed on one side, it is sure to be reviled on the other; the Editors of newspapers and ruling pamphleteers are enlisted, disputes grow warmer, till at last the measure is forgotten in personal altercation.[38]

The dialogue in Jamaica began to take on a sort of American-style passion—enough for Belmore to notify the Colonial Office of the "violent and intemperate" meetings in which some of the wealthiest men on the island were calling for separation from the Crown. Physical threats began filtering down to the enslaved people. A white bookkeeper at Flamstad Estate told his assistant that "when the war broke out between the whites and the blacks, he, the pen-keeper, should be the first that he would shoot."[39]

The Baptist preacher Henry Bleby, who found that statement in court records at Montego Bay, also related a conversation that allegedly took place in the same city in that summer of mounting unease:

MASTER: "I am sorry that I shall have to kill you, James."

SLAVE: "What I do, massa?"

MASTER: "Nothing, But if you buy a boy, James, and any one come to take him away, won't you think hard of it?"

SLAVE: "Yes."

MASTER: "Well, don't you think it is hard that, after I have taken my money and bought you, you are to be taken away from me? . . . *The King says you are to be free, but you will all be killed.*"

SLAVE: "What are we to be killed for? If the King says we are to be free, that is not our fault."

MASTER: "*We can't help it; you will all be killed,* and probably *you will be the first I shall have to shoot myself.*"[40]

Conversations like this were fueled by dire predictions in the *Jamaica Courant*, whose columns never failed to be entertaining, eloquent, and fierce; it was a favorite juicy read of the most conservative plantocracy. Most of the articles had been written by Lord Belmore's stargazing companion, the firebrand Anglican rector George W. Bridges. By the summer of 1831 he had become more distant from the British government and become one of the main propagandists for the ultraconservative planters and the "true patriots" of Jamaica who should rise up to correct an errant government—even by violent or treasonous means.

Bridges was the son of a successful grain dealer from Essex, and his matriculation at Oxford University to study history helped confirm his identity as an upper-class gentleman, a status he would later flaunt in the tropics. Bridges developed affinities for existing hierarchies, and deplored the revolutions in France and Haiti. Abrupt change horrified him. After he secured a post in Jamaica as an Anglican rector in 1814, he told his new neighbors that if slavery had to die out, it should do so as a slow economic withering, and not in the instant freedom demanded by abolitionists, whom he disparaged as "false philanthropists."[41]

That was the same year, in fact, that Bridges experienced what many other whites landing in Jamaica had experienced before him: a profound shift in values after being exposed to the daily reality of slavery. He remembered years later that before he arrived he was "biased by as great an abhorrence of the very name of slavery" but that he had come to see its manifest virtues. Within ten years Bridges was one of the loudest proslavery voices on the island, and an owner of humans himself from a magnificent house in St. Ann's he named the Cloisters. In his study there he authored a two-volume history of Jamaica throughout which the colonists were painted as brave and altruistic pioneers and their enslaved people as filthy animals. In one of his typical passages, he wrote of black laborers, "whatever they see, they covet; their desires are insatiate, and their sole industry is the hand of violence and rapine." Copies of his *Annals of Jamaica* were hard to find, however, because colonial authorities considered passages to be libelous and they banned its sale.[42]

Not surprisingly, Bridges treated his own enslaved people in accordance with his new beliefs. When a housemaid named Kitty Hylton misunderstood his instructions not to slaughter a turkey, he punched her in the face, repeatedly kicked her, and had her flogged until her back was "one mess of lacerated flesh and gore." Bridges then threw her in a cell without medical treatment. This would have passed without any notice whatsoever had Kitty Hylton not been determined to seek justice under an 1816 slave law which, though widely flouted, offered at least nominal protection against maltreatment. In an echo of the Eleanor James incident, Hylton crawled her way toward a sympathetic magistrate, and Bridges became one of the few white men in Jamaica to be brought up on charges of abuse. He was acquitted, but the evidence against him was disturbing enough to cause his removal as the magistrate for St. Ann's Parish. Even his old friend Lord Belmore reported it to the Colonial Office as a case of "unmanly and disgraceful cruelty." Domestic violence was almost never mentioned at high levels, and it seems likely that Bridges had begun to irritate the government, as well as Belmore personally. His astringent personality may have also played a role; a later scholar who chronicled Bridges's life flatly called him "not a nice person."[43]

Bridges's fear-mongering grew hotter as summer wore on. Writing under the pen name Dorcas in the *Jamaica Courant* on August 15, 1832, he warned of an approaching "storm" of probable slave insurrections if the planters did not wake up: "If you would not have it rush upon you unsheltered, unprepared, and scattered,—if you would not have *your blazing canefields* to be your watchfires, *the shrieks of your wives and children* your alarm bell, and *your burning houses* for your beacons— attend to the warning voice of DORCAS."[44]

In between attacks on faraway influences like the Anti-Slavery Society—whose supposed goal was "strife confusion, blood and massacre"—the proslavery newspapers spread a conspiracy theory that would become influential in the months to come: the idea that the British military was secretly in league with the enslaved people. As one letter writer to the *Courant* asserted on August 11, 1831, "It must be alarming when whispered that our brethren, THE BRITISH SOL-DIERS—who have been ostensibly stationed for our protection, who are liberally paid by us, the expense of whom forms the chief drain on our exchequer—HAVE RECEIVED SECRET ORDERS TO REMAIN NUETRAL, OR TO ACT AGAINST US, IN THE EVENT OF A DISTURBANCE."[45]

Enslaved people who worked in the planters' houses and heard the angry table talk passed the word on to those in the fields: the British across the ocean want to make us free, and the redcoat soldiers are secretly our friends; the *Courant* is saying so.

Samuel Sharpe had almost certainly known that what he had been telling his followers was more hope than reality. But this turn of events might have convinced him that the insubstantial dream was indeed close at hand, and needed only to be seized.

SIX

SWEAR TO ME

THE CONSPIRATORS USED a particular code term to describe their plan of resistance. They called it "the business."[1]

"There are a great many people concerned in this business," said a slave named Linton in March of 1832, after it was all over and he was sentenced to hang. "If I chose, I could tell a great deal of this business but as I am going to die, let it all go with me."[2]

Samuel Sharpe conceived of a way to seal the loyalties of those he brought into his conspiracy: he would make them swear an oath on a Bible that they would not work after Christmas and that they would not give witness against their coconspirators. Some slaves were asked to kiss the Bible. Sharpe himself claimed to be the first initiate, and he did it in a private meeting with a copy of the King James Bible as a prop. "I was the first man who took the Oath," he said later. "We had the Bible brought. I got up before them and took the Book in my right hand, and I said—If I ever witness against my brothers and sisters connected with this matter, may hell be my portion."[3]

A slave named Edward Barrett—who was apparently owned by Richard Barrett's brother Samuel—said the oath was both simple and pledged to the cause of nonviolent resistance. It also had a specific economic aim: the demand to be paid 50 percent of what a free laborer would normally earn for the same work. "Sharpe said we must sit down," Barrett later told a white prosecutor. "We are free. Must not work again unless we got half pay. He took a Bible out of his pocket. Made me swear that I would not work again until I got half pay."[4]

Swearing an oath served multiple purposes. It appeared to give the illicit activity the sanction of God. It helped lift up slaves with the implicit suggestion that they were persons of value whose word was trustworthy. Once they had taken an oath, slaves could be said to have committed the capital crime of rebellion, and it left them feeling like they now had nothing left to lose. An oath also gave Samuel Sharpe some psychological leverage over reluctant participants and those who had divergent ideas regarding strategy.

Thomas Dove, for instance, was unsure if Christmas was the right time to be disobedient, and he said so in a meeting. Sharpe rebuked him. Dove later paraphrased what he was told: "This oath obliges them to rebel and not to flinch until they had succeeded in getting their freedom."[5]

Sharpe's fellow conspirators fanned out among the various plantations and repeated the swearing ritual among new recruits. If postinsurrection testimony is to be believed, not all of them did it gracefully. A slave named Donald Malcolm described a rough experience with one of Sharpe's disciples: "We were sworn in at Haughton Grove Gate Pasture, Richard Trail was there from Shuttlewood, he had a gun and said if we did not take the oath he would shoot us." Another initiate claimed he was made to lie flat on the ground while two men swung machetes over his neck and threatened to kill him on the spot if he didn't promise to burn down his master's property at the appointed time.[6]

The network relied on people who were in elite positions; Thomas Dove, Robert Gardiner, and Samuel Sharpe were favored by their masters and had the respect—or at least the fear—of the lower-ranked slaves on their respective plantations. Once sworn to secrecy and loyalty, the leader of a "cell" could bring others into the plan on a selective basis.

It doubtless helped Sharpe's cause that these Christian-flavored rituals had some crossover with traditional West African spiritual practices, which even unchurched slaves would have recognized. Even across lines of language and ethnicity, the Africans had believed in one supreme being whose ways were mysterious to humanity. Fetishes and oaths also played a strong role in worship. The kissing of the Bible—when presented as a sacred object—would not have seemed incongruent.

Every slave was familiar with the spirit practice called obeah, whose practitioners kept themselves secret from the whites and were widely feared among the slaves. To be an obeah priest was to have knowledge of the unseen world of spirits. Many drivers and head boilers doubled as obeah priests and used their status as a part of their motivating power. White masters feared the practice of obeah not because they believed in its magic but because they worried that a charismatic obeah figure would convince others to start a rebellion, as the slave Tacky was said to have done in 1760. Slaves who wanted to pledge loyalty to one another drank a mixture of gunpowder, rum, grave dirt, and their own comingled blood; this had been a signal of serious intent in the 1765 Coromantee uprising in St. Mary's Parish. The ritual was called "taking the swear."[7]

The practice also contained a powerful metaphor in which enslaved people might have drawn some mordant meaning. Obeah and the Haitian practice of vodou shared the belief that corpses could be made animate, but in obeah the spirits of the dead were known as duppies and typically dwelled in the woods. They were shambling shells, half-alive mockeries of humans, not unlike how slaves saw themselves after a few weeks under the relentless heat and whips of Caribbean slavery.[8]

In obeah, as in other traditional West African religions, death was just a passageway to another existence and nothing to be overly feared. Many believed they would return to Africa in the next life, which would be considerably easier. Souls of the dead were said to be in constant communication with the living; the world was full of voices of those who had passed from one essence to another. As the Akan proverb went, "Nyame nwu na mawu" (God does not die, so I cannot die). The willingness of so many neophyte slaves to commit suicide by jumping over the gunwales of a ship or hanging themselves with their chains offers powerful testimony to the firmness of this belief. The urge to be free was stronger than the fear of death, and this made it easy to extract a promise to fight.[9]

The taking of oaths and the cell building lasted for several months, and before it was over, Sharpe's influence had extended over six hundred square miles; his Christmas work stoppage plan was known to approximately twenty thousand slaves on more than one hundred plantations. With such a broad reach, and with such imperfect and clandestine ways to communicate with each other, eventual misunderstandings were inevitable.[10]

Samuel Sharpe could not have known it, but at the same time that he was planning his labor strike another enslaved Baptist pastor was laying the ground for a freedom movement in Southampton County, Virginia.

Nat Turner had almost died in his infancy at the hand of his mother, who was reported to have wished him dead rather than to have to endure a life of slavery. He took easily to reading the Bible and writing, and decided that since he was destined for greatness, he must appear as such to others and therefore "wrapped myself in mystery, devoting my time to fasting and praying." Like Sharpe, he became fascinated with biblical verses that pointed to freedom and liberation and, also like Sharpe, he was allowed to travel between plantations to preach and became well known for his charisma and rhetorical gifts. Turner's local travels exposed him to the tangle of dirt roads around Southampton County, as well as the complex web of social relationships among the enslaved.[11]

On the morning of August 13, 1831, when Turner saw the sun rise with an unusual bluish-greenish tint and a dark spot on its surface, he took it as a sign from heaven. Eight days later he gathered a small group of conspirators over a dinner of pork and brandy and told them they would soon be on "a march of destruction." They moved among the plantations on which Turner had preached, slaughtering whites, stealing guns and horses, and trying to enlist other enslaved people to their cause. Alarmed whites quickly mustered into militia companies and fought back, potentially killing approximately thirty black people, many of whom had nothing to do with the uprising. Turner successfully dodged the law for two months, even as his associates were captured and hanged, but was eventually discovered hiding in a hole in the woods that was covered by a fallen tree.[12]

Before he went to the gallows, Turner dictated a lengthy "confession" to the solicitor Thomas Gray in which he admitted killing a woman named Margaret Whitehead with a few blows from a fence post. He was never precise about his goals, but acknowledged that he wanted to "carry terror and devastation wherever we went." Gray reported that Turner had told him this story in a matter-of-fact tone as he was chained to a jailhouse chair, his clothes still stained with blood, "yet daring to raise his manacled hands to heaven, with a spirit soaring above the attributes of man; I looked on him and my blood curdled in my veins." Gray's later publication of *The Confessions of Nat Turner* created a sensation.[13]

While the Turner conspiracy was tiny when compared to the slave population of the whole American South, and Southampton County was a swampy backwater in a remote corner of the Mid-Atlantic region, the revolt nevertheless terrified the ruling class. Slaveholding families wondered if another Nat Turner might be lurking on their properties. The governor of Virginia, John Floyd, was convinced that the violence meant that forced black labor was unsustainable; he confided in his diary, "I will not rest until slavery is abolished in Virginia." Within four months the Virginia Legislature took the extraordinary step of debating the gradual abolition of slavery, a discussion many in Virginia had never before dreamed could happen. "Nat Turner, and the blood of his innocent victims have conquered the silence of fifty years," editorialized the *Richmond Whig*. Prominent residents in the mountainous western sections of Virginia—portions of which would later secede from the state entirely—argued that further bloodshed was likely if blacks were not quickly repatriated to Africa, and that the state's economy was hamstrung by large plantations and their idle owners. But a resolution calling for abolition failed by a vote of 73–58. Instead the Virginia legislature instituted crackdowns against black literacy, religious meetings, and preaching—measures which were widely duplicated by other Southern states.[14]

The revolt made big news in Britain, which received its first reports three weeks after the conclusion of the violence. The American brig *Manchester* arrived in Liverpool and the packet ship *Ontario* arrived in Portsmouth in the third week of September 1831 with bundles of American newspapers. The proslavery *Morning Post* of London initially cited false reports that three white men were in the marauding party and concluded that the violence was "surely to be traced to the notions instilled into the minds of the Negroes by that hypocritical and detestable set calling themselves philanthropists and Christians, who are exerting themselves by similar means to effect the ruin of our own West India Colonies."[15]

Newspapers all over Britain repeated the "melancholy narrative" of Nat Turner, as the *Liverpool Albion* put it, and the story received further life in December when British papers reported on the publication of Gray's edition of Turner's lurid *Confessions*. "It appears that all originated with Nat, who in a religious frenzy deemed himself commissioned by Heaven to perform some great work," reported London's *Morning Advertiser*.[16]

News of the Turner rebellion hit Jamaican newspapers at the zenith of the planter's secessionist frenzy. The *Royal Gazette* devoted three entire columns of its front page for October 1, 1831—an enormous amount of space—to the cataclysmic bloodshed of Nat Turner, including descriptions of "horribly mangled" bodies. The more liberal *Watchman and Jamaica Free Press* ran multiple stories over two issues and quoted a Virginia newspaper predicting that another insurrection was likely on the way and that planters would use it as an excuse for more extrajudicial killings of enslaved people—in effect, "putting the whole race to the sword."[17]

But it remains unclear what influence the Nat Turner rebellion may have had on "the business" that Samuel Sharpe and his ring of conspirators had already been planning. While it seems probable that at least some of the literate enslaved people, including Sharpe himself, had gleaned the news from the British papers that arrived at the docks that autumn, as well as from the lurid reports in the Jamaican papers in their masters' houses, none of the plotters ever mentioned these as inspirations. Nor did any of the king's troops or volunteer militiamen note it in their reports.

Edward Jordon of *The Watchman and Jamaica Free Press* nevertheless saw Nat Turner as an omen for Jamaica. Such violent uprisings should be seen as "a natural result of the state of things in our country," he wrote on October 15, 1831. "It is one of the necessary consequences of slavery and it is perfectly idle to attempt to conceal it."[18]

As it happened, Sharpe's rebellion almost started by accident, twelve days ahead of schedule. On December 15, a widely disliked lawyer, William Grignon—who had earned the nickname Little Breeches among those he enslaved—was walking through his estate, Salt Spring, when he spotted a woman taking a small amount of sugarcane from the fields. This was not uncommon, as enslaved people made abundant use of the fresh condiment in their food; they also chewed the pulp for energy. But for some reason, Grignon lost his volcanic temper and beat the woman on the spot. Then he marched her over to the slave quarters to have her stripped naked and flogged by the driver. The man protested; the woman was his wife, and he could not bear to do it.[19]

Other enslaved people then made a conspicuous refusal to obey Grignon's order that *somebody* should come forward to lash the woman. An outraged Grignon went to Montego Bay, fetched several police officers to back him up, and returned to find the mood even worse—the laborers were brandishing their machetes and threatening to throw Grignon into a vat of boiling sugar. A number of them ran off into the woods and refused to return, which was a serious embarrassment to Grignon.[20]

In the sympathetic view of a fellow planter, Grignon was "a gentleman of mild temper" in his late middle age who became a victim of "the most scandalous and exaggerated aggravation" of the basic story, which nevertheless went viral throughout northwestern Jamaica: it was said he had ordered a slave whipped and that instead his slaves almost killed him. Nobody was punished for this flagrant show of defiance. The Christmas holiday drew near with a mounting sense—flashing through the invisible network of information—that the enslaved people might be able to make a stand if they held together in unity.[21]

The chief conspirators held a final meeting on Christmas Day at the hut of George Guthrie, a slave who belonged to Grignon. More than a dozen of them quietly ate lunch and went over their plans one last time. Four men would assume leadership in the hilly interior: Campbell, Thomas Dove, Robert Gardiner, and Johnson. Somebody had brought a bottle of wine, and they drank a toast to the success of their project.[22]

Guthrie mentioned that William "Little Breeches" Grignon was sleeping at a nearby barracks with the Western Interior Regiment of the militia. He was quartered there along with dozens of other plantation whites, who were likely unhappy to have been called away for the holiday and perhaps frightened by the talk of rebellion.

"I hope we shall overcome Little Breeches," said Guthrie, recalling that his master had told him he would lose every drop of his blood before he would tolerate a free Jamaica. Guthrie then snapped his fingers expressively and used a nineteenth-century slang word for a bullet: "Though I am his slave, I'll give him a pill as I follow him."[23]

Whatever Samuel Sharpe might have said in response went unrecorded.

A few white Baptist missionaries tried to shout back the waves of revolutionary sentiment even to the last minute.

Hope Masterton Waddell told his black friends he thought freedom was probably on the way for the enslaved people but "assured them it could come to them only in a peaceable and lawful way." Any violence from the slaves, he warned, would only "insure their own destruction."[24]

As Christmas Day and the first night of ritual Junkanoo dancing passed, a few white planters let themselves believe that it had been a false alarm. Perhaps the warnings of a general strike were another Jamaican rumor, part of the tissue of myth and half-truths that justified the quasimilitary footing of the whole island. But there is evidence that the militia had learned the names of the conspiracy leaders and even laid a trap for Samuel Sharpe ahead of time. His name had been furnished—probably via an enslaved informant—to Colonel George Lawson, who told William Grignon of how they had been watching Sharpe's movements and planning to make an arrest.

"The negro, Samuel Sharpe, is at Croydon, as he was at Easthams on Saturday week, without having called on his master in his way either coming or going," Lawson wrote in a communiqué to Grignon, who was then barracked with his regiment at Belvidere Estate. The militia was planning to send in a relative of Sharpe's master to find him with a request to carry some packages, Lawson explained. If Sharpe refused, that would be considered proof he was involved in a strike of conscience. His master's relative had then been given instructions to "prevent him from doing any mischief, in a summary way, by securing him" before the day of the strike, which they already knew was supposed to be December 28. "I hope therefore, that we shall not be found napping," concluded Lawson. But Sharpe failed to materialize.[25]

On the last night of peace, December 26, as enslaved people were still enjoying the Christmas Junkanoo festival and clapping along with the traditional figure wearing ox horns, William Knibb answered a knock at the door from a Presbyterian minister named Blyth who told him that trouble was imminent and that they needed to vigorously counteract the false reports that King William IV had issued a "free paper." But Knibb had an appointment: he was leaving that night to dedicate a new chapel at Salter's Hill in the countryside above Montego Bay.[26]

This settlement, up a rutted road, was a bit removed from the underground currents of information flowing through Montego Bay, but Knibb still spent the entire day of December 27 mingling with the religious slaves who had foresworn the usual Christmas bacchanalia and shown up for the resistance. By his own description, he spent the morning "begging them to go to their work on the morrow, and not to be led away into sin and violence."

Knibb then preached a sermon entirely consumed with the approaching disaster. God, he claimed, was commanding the enslaved people to be obedient, not violent. "Hear me; I love your souls," he told them. "I would not tell you a lie for the world. What you have been told is false—false as hell can make it." Though he had heard that the resistance was supposed to be nonviolent, he even threatened to excommunicate anyone who refused to work after Christmas. Though he likely did not know at that point that the Baptist deacon Samuel Sharpe was behind the conspiracy, he denounced "wicked men" for spreading rumors. The more he talked, the more sullen the audience became, and it dawned on Knibb that "the idea of freedom had so intoxicated their minds as to nullify all I said."[27]

The enslaved people were, in fact, quite angry with Knibb for the first time since he had arrived to minister to them seven years earlier.

Many believed that he had been bribed to tell them a lie—just like the estate masters who had been secretly repressing the freedom news. "Minister never said a word about freedom before," one wondered; "why does he come to talk to us about freedom today?" Knibb's impassioned denial at Salter's Hill thus confirmed what many had suspected all along: the king's free paper *did* exist, and there was a local white conspiracy to conceal it. Now it included even the missionaries.[28]

Dejected and apprehensive, Knibb rode his horse down the hill in the late afternoon of December 27 and back into the town of Montego Bay, where he complained about his troubles to a few friends. They told him he was overreacting. But after the sun went down, Knibb went outside to clear his thoughts and spotted several fires blossoming in the mountains that encircled the city.[29]

SEVEN

THE FIRES

EVERY PLANTATION HOUSED the equivalent of a firebomb. Leaves of old sugarcane were stored in the wooden structures called trash houses, where the flammable material was used as fuel for the boilers for the next season, and they burned at an average temperature of three thousand degrees Fahrenheit.

The first fire, at Kensington Estate—on a hilltop 1,660 feet above sea level and visible for miles around—was soon accompanied by flames roaring to life at the nearby plantations Argyle, Lapland, Montpelier, and Retrieve, accompanied by noises of riotous celebration; the enslaved could barely have conceived of such a Dionysian vision in a society where the most minute slight against the ruling order was answered with a severe beating or flogging. "The conch shell was heard to blow in every quarter, accompanied by huzzas and shouts from the infatuated slaves," reported a witness. Later, a few could only say "the devil got into their heads." Heat, liquor, mad joy, and bright orange luminescence ruled the next several hours, blotting out the half-moon.[1]

At some plantations, the enslaved people brought burning sticks and touched them to the driest portions of the cane fields themselves. Soon the hills were on fire, each spiky leaf of sugar like a small torch or match head. Millions of yellow, flaming pinpricks spread in all directions in the velvety Caribbean night. "Whole fields, each perhaps containing twenty, thirty, forty acres or upwards were thus ignited and the atmosphere appeared one solid mass of flame," reported one horrified militiaman.[2]

The Presbyterian minister Hope Masterton Waddell ran into the slave quarters of the estate where he was staying, and was told in a panicked voice, "Palmyra on fire!" That property was perched on the coastal slope eight miles from the first fire at Kensington, and it was an important visual link in the chain of manor homes that lay across the green knobs of the northern shore. Whether through calculation or by accident, the emerging rebels had burned those estates, most likely to invoke terror among both slaves and their owners. Waddell spotted an even more ominous pattern: it seemed to him that the first mansions to go aflame had belonged to those masters who were well known for their cruelty. But the fires soon blended together into common destruction.[3] "Soon the reflections were in clusters," he wrote; "then the sky became a sheet of flame, as if the whole country had become a vast furnace."

Waddell could nevertheless perceive a small measure of divine justice in the conflagration he was witnessing, which seemed like a display of Old Testament wrath. The necklace of destruction was, to him, "a terrible vengeance which the patient drudges had at length taken on those sugar estates, the causes and scenes of their lifelong toils and degradation, tears and blood." He stayed awake the whole night, dreading the sound of the conch shell and the shouting that might mean slaves were coming to kill him, even though he was their ally.[4]

Henry Bleby could not help but think of the fires as the original sin and foundational mistake of the uprising, which was supposed to have been a peaceful demonstration. He trusted the word of Samuel Sharpe that "life was not to be sacrificed, except in self defense." But the sight of the first fire at Kensington—orgiastic and ungovernable—seemed to him to be the first sign of events turning in a darker direction.

"The devastation of the property on that estate was the work of a few ungovernable spirits, who, having broken into and plundered the rum-store, had become infuriated with liquor," Bleby would later write. "The example, once set, was rapidly and extensively followed; and incendiary fire broke out on plantation after plantation, till one of the fairest portions of this beautiful island was laid in ruins."[5]

Despite the visceral chain of destruction, none of the white aristocracy died that night. At least a few slaves had taken the trouble to warn their masters of the impending violence. On the night the rebellion began, John Henry Morris, the planter who owned Kensington, said he received a letter from one of his slaves "apprising me that that my house was to be burnt and my family destroyed as of that evening."

An alarmed Morris galloped to an army post six miles away to report this news, and was stunned at the indifference he received. Morris said he was told "we were a parcel of alarmists" and that the army was satisfied nothing would happen. Morris then protested to the commander, Major John Lysaght Pennefather, that the wife of one of the army officers was staying at his house and would be in danger. "He did not care a damn," reported a disgusted Morris. "If she was burnt there, there would be one woman less in the garrison."[6]

With no other options, Morris decided to evacuate his family and travel by carriage to the nearby town of Montego Bay. They had not gotten down the road more than ten minutes when he looked back and saw his house go up in flames. It was approximately 7:00 P.M. on December 27, 1831. Before the night was over, Bleby, Morris, and thousands of others watched awestruck as new fires spread on neighboring plantations, in an unstoppable chain, as if the universe itself was answering the first call of flames and setting free some beautiful and terrifying spirit that could not be called back.

When the sun came up on the morning of December 28 at a plantation named New Forest in faraway Manchester Parish, a white woman sat on the sofa doing needlework.

Her husband had just been called up for militia duty to help quell what looked like a minor disturbance about seventy miles away, and she gave it no special thought. As she worked the needles, she heard the door open and she listened to the footsteps of the head driver approaching. He wore a red jacket and a hat with a feather stuck into it: clothes for a party. The lady assumed the Christmas holiday for the slaves had been extended one more day.

"Well, driver," she said as a joke. "I see you're a soldier today."

"Oh, yes ma'am," he said. "We all be soldiers now."

"I don't understand you, driver," she said.

"I'm telling you the plain truth," he said, and then sat down on the sofa next to her. By the mannered standards of Jamaica, this was a severe mark of impudence on the part of the slave to sit without invitation.

"You are not my missus now," he said, using the term for female master. "The star has come to the corner of the moon, just as the Baptist parson told us. When Christmas came, he said we shouldn't work or we would never get free. We are obliged to burn everything and get free. All the burning is going on well. They will soon be here, and then we will burn this house and all the works on the property, too. You never heard what was going on in St. James?"[7]

"Why, driver, you astonish me, but it cannot be true," she said, and then added with a note of genteel threat, "However, I shall soon know because I expect your master here at any moment."

"True, ma'am, all true," he said, getting up from the sofa. "Every estate in St. James has been burnt down, and nigger fight buckra two, three times. Some are killed and a great many shot, ma'am. We're sure to win, but I'll come to see you, by and by."

The driver had migrated to the door by this point, but turned to give her a meaningful look and a shake of the head before he departed. It was this gaze, more than anything, which convinced the woman to flee.[8]

Among the earliest of confused rumors was that the magnificent house on the hill belonging to Richard Barrett had been torched. But as the *Watchman and Jamaica Free Press* explained, "little credit can be attached to this report, Mr. Barrett is reputed one of the most humane slave owners in the island." This explicit linkage between slave violence and the assumed cruelty—or lack thereof—on the part of the owner is testament to the knowledge of mounting retribution that most of the aristocracy had been feeling in their bones for years.[9]

Most of the rebelling slaves took Sharpe's peaceful idealism seriously. At an estate named Zion Hill, some of the slaves "refused to turn out" to work but stayed pacifistic. There were reports from Portland of slaves on three estates who had refused to work, but the disobedience "had not proceeded to any acts of violence." A militia chased them into the woods and forced most of them to return to chopping cane in the fields; only seven managed to escape. As the senior custos of Trelawny Parish reported on December 28, "Nine-tenths of the whole slave population have this morning refused to turn out and work."[10]

On another planation on the north shore, an elderly planter was sitting down to dinner on the third night of the rebellion when some of the slaves came into the dining room and told him simply, "Massa had better go away." The rebellious slaves on the neighboring estates were planning to come by that night and burn down everything. The planter tried to protest, but his slaves, holding accurate information of what was to come, insisted to him that "the sooner massa go away, the better." He asked them to help him load some valuables down to the wharf on the ocean, but they told him—as Samuel Sharpe had instructed—that they would do no more work without pay. He boarded the boat with only the clothes on his back, and watched from the water as his entire property went up in flames. He lost his fortune, but his enslaved workers had likely saved his life.[11]

Hope Waddell visited Carlton Estate, where the headman assured him that everyone had stayed in their homes the previous night and would not be vandalizing anything. All the same, the headman was determined "that he would never hoe again as a slave, though he would never burn nor kill. He would keep his house, work for himself, and pray to God."[12]

The following night brought even less reason for hope. Waddell went to see Richard Barrett's cousin, Samuel Moulton Barrett, and the two tried to encourage the striking slaves on a neighboring estate that they should go back to work and resume a life of bondage. Instead, they got a vigorous argument: "We have worked enough already, and will work no more. The life we live is too bad; it is the life of a dog. We won't be slaves no more; we won't lift hoe no more; we won't take flog no more." Barrett and Waddell gave up and went to sleep in the great house. At midnight, they were awakened by an angry and excited voice coming from the slave quarters, apparently that of a rebellious slave from another plantation.[13]

"No watchman now! No watchman now!" he screamed. "Nigger man, nigger man, burn the house—burn buckra house! Brimstone come, brimstone come! Bring fire and burn master's house!"[14]

Barrett and Waddell hustled out of their beds, got on their horses, and rode to a place of safety in the brush where they spent an anxious night. But they saw no flames: Barrett's slaves would not count themselves among the violent resistance. Rather than stick around to see whether that would last, the two men left for a white refugee camp in the town of Falmouth. A few black headmen carrying cutlasses rode alongside to protect them from, as they said, "the wild people in the bush," though this was a confusing sight in colonial Jamaica. As Michael Craton observed, "to outside viewers it might have looked as if the Englishmen were being politely ushered out of the way by armed elite slaves."[15]

Unpredictable alliances and rivalries arose all over the burned territories in those first hours. One slave at Wiltshire Estate risked his life to show a militia party where some of his colleagues were hiding out in "the romantic high grounds" above the fields, even as the slave women of the estate were "breathing vengeance" against him. "This man deserves well of the country," said the *Royal Gazette,* withholding his name, "and we trust he will not be forgotten."[16]

Slave-on-slave resentments culminated in murder at Hampton Estate, where Lawrence Tharp and James Gordon Tharp broke down the door of the great house two nights after Christmas and set fire to a bowl of rum set out on the table—the liquor was potent enough to burn like kerosene, and spilling it was apparently enough to doom the house. Then they set fire to the trash house, and—with the uncompromising statement "Whites must go"—they threatened to chop off the heads of any fellow slaves who did not join them. Two slaves named Dick and Robert Brown apparently objected to the destruction and were promptly slain with machetes. Tharp later said he had never been whipped by his masters, and that he had no good explanation for why he went after his fellow enslaved people. It would not be the last case of spontaneous slave-on-slave violence during the uprising.[17]

Rushed into the field with his militia unit, Bernard Senior noticed an ominous detail as he inspected the wreckage of the plantation houses: in all cases, the blacksmith's shops had been spared. He suspected this was done with an eye toward the forging of improvised pikes, lances, and cutlasses if the slaves needed more weaponry. At these ghostly wastes where houses and sugar factories once stood, not a soul could be seen "excepting the old, disabled, sick or children."[18]

Senior hoped that one night of fire would end the uprising, but he was dismayed the following evening at sunset when "all was blaze again, and such buildings and fields as had escaped the preceding night were then sacrificed without delay." Such burning was easy to accomplish because most attorneys and bookkeepers had been hustled into militia service and weren't around to stop it. They would come to view the terrifying orgy of flames as the signature symbol of the uprising, and a mark of impulsivity. But there was likely some calculation to the burning. In destroying sugar works and lighting the sugar crop on fire, the slaves were not only creating signals to other estates but taking aim at the means of production of their owners. If they could remove the economic modes of their bondage, they might succeed in making themselves economically irrelevant to their masters, even if their protest failed in the end. It might have been a crude expression of freedom, and certainly a long shot, but it was a chance the enslaved people clearly felt was worth taking to attain their liberty. There must have been great satisfaction for many, in any case, to watch the ecstatic destruction of the hated sugar works, where so many thousands of hours had passed in dreary and dangerous misery. Furthermore, it created maximum psychological impact with little effort. "The destruction of an estate, by fire, is generally an easy task; as the roofs of the buildings are usually made of wood," wrote militiaman Theodore Foulks. "The canes, too, when ripe, are soon ignited and quickly extend the conflagration over large fields, while sugar and rum are near at hand to feed and increase the flames."[19]

On December 28, Samuel Sharpe traveled to the Ginger Hill plantation overlooking the plains of St. Elizabeth; there he made a speech convincing the slaves to make a prisoner of overseer William Annand, but not to hurt him. Sharpe then gave an extended soliloquy to a captive Annand to the effect that Sharpe "had begun to know much of religion, but that now he knew, and I knew as well, that freedom was their right and freedom they would have." Sharpe added that he "did not wish to take away the life of any person who did not stand between him and his rights." A listener acquainted with Sharpe's prior commitment to nonviolence might have heard a note of growing compromise inside the qualification that people "who did not stand" in opposition would not be hurt.[20]

The rebels with Sharpe pointed their guns at Annand and swung muskets over his head, then locked him inside his own house with a little food to sustain him. It was unclear if Sharpe stuck around after this was accomplished, but before the day was out, most of the estate was put to the torch and Annand was moved to an improvised jail cell inside the cabin of one of the slaves with little food or water. Annand told a rescuing militia unit he thought his captors were trying to work around Sharpe's command to "shed no blood" by starving him to death. He also testified that Sharpe unquestionably had command over this roving military-style band.[21]

When news of the uprising reached the capital of Spanish Town late on December 28, two companies of the king's grenadier troops hastily replaced the "inefficient" soldiers standing guard at the courthouse, and two ships in the Kingston harbor were ordered to turn toward the city and aim their guns at the approaching roads. By 3:00 P.M. the next day, as dire reports continued to stream in, the troops were ordered into the Kingston Parish Church and told they would be put aboard two ships—HMS *Blanche* and HMS *Sparrowhawk*—bound for the center of the action. A land journey would have been inefficient; even a fast rider on horseback could not reach Montego Bay in less than thirty hours. Before marching to the docks, the brigade yelled out three cheers, which were lustily echoed back "by the numerous spectators who assembled to watch the novel occurrence." Other ships carrying British troops were sent to Savanna-la-Mar and Lucea.[22]

But if the panicked white Jamaicans were looking to the British Army as a magical deterrent against the rebels, they would be disappointed. The king's troops were not in top condition. They were fed an unhealthy diet of salted meat and rum, and forced to wear heavy scarlet uniforms in the noon sun, while their officers were often clad in foppish lace-fringed jackets with large feathers emanating from their hats. The troops' quarters were cramped and filthy, often located near mosquito-infested marshes. The wretched experience in Saint-Domingue—fighting against a powerful slave army and dying for nothing—was still in recent memory. The typical Jamaican diseases of cholera and yellow fever took down many new recruits as soon as they arrived; at some West Indian military posts, the commander suspended the traditional military funerals because there were so many dead. Being sent to the Caribbean was seen almost as a death sentence for British soldiers; those who survived had a monotonous life relieved only, said a lieutenant colonel, with "cold punch, sangaree, cigar-smoking, musquito bites, and every now and then a friend swept off by yellow fever."[23]

The British troops were also on bad terms with the local militia, whom they considered sloppy and unprofessional. This opinion was not controversial; one disgruntled militia private thought so poorly of his own colleagues that he believed just twelve well-trained men could easily kill a hundred of "these braggart militiamen." The visiting soldiers' habit of attempting to seduce local white women also did little to improve relations with the civilians.[24]

At the seat of government, in the mansion named King's House on the central square in Spanish Town, Lord Belmore declared martial law and ordered every able-bodied man to find his militia unit "at the pain of our highest displeasure." Troops hoisted the royal standard on the flagpole, giving everybody the sign that the island was officially in a state of war. The planter Theodore Foulks reported for duty in the capital and witnessed frenetic activity:

> An unusually large assemblage of persons was observed in the area of the square;—military, as well as civil, officers were hurrying to and fro;—the Council Chamber presented an animated scene; and it was apparent to all that something extraordinary had taken place. . . . A lawyer might then be seen standing sentry at the arsenal. A physician would visit his patients in a scarlet jacket. A quiet citizen was converted into an active voltigeur or bold dragoon.[25]

Rumors flew that enslaved people planned to burn down the capital; guards were posted everywhere to keep a nervous watch. When a military officer was spotted leaving Saint Catherine's Parish Church in a hurry after being handed a note, the rest of the congregation went into a near panic. As terror melted into boredom later in the evening, many crept back into the church rather than sleep exposed in their own homes. Some got drunk and danced amid the pews. They served liquor on the communion table and sang what Foulks described as "loud bacchanalian songs" well into the night. They caroused atop grave markers laid into the church's floor, right above the decomposed bodies of many of British Jamaica's most esteemed families, dating back two centuries. Under those stones lay Thomas Modyford, the governor who had handed out corrupt land grants to his friends; the Earl of Effingham, who had resigned his commission rather than fight in the American Revolution; and Richard Barrett's rough-edged ancestor, Hersey Barrett, who had helped conquer the island and claimed to have personally beheaded Charles I before his exile to the tropics.[26]

Behind this riotous merriment at Saint Catherine's Church lurked an awareness of cold racial arithmetic. Blacks outnumbered whites by more than ten to one. The only real weakness of the enslaved people was their inability to band together under a shared ideal. If they feared no reprisals, their power would be matchless and the militias would be of no help. Edward Trelawny had pointed it out as far back as 1749, and the cruel French planter Nicolas Lejeune had perfectly echoed the dread in the Jamaican subconscious when he said that white island society was doomed once a black man stopped being convinced of his own weakness: "Remove this bit, and he will dare everything." Foulks ruminated on this disquieting notion as he lay crouched in the church in Spanish Town amid drunken revelry and muskets firing impotently in the air:

> It had generally be considered, that the power of the white people over the negroes rested on opinion; as the latter were supposed to be ignorant of their own strength. It had been

argued that the negro population of Jamaica, amounting to three hundred thousand slaves, if they should arise en masse, would easily overmaster the comparatively small force of eighteen thousand militia-men, supported by only three thousand regular troops.[27]

Most of northwestern Jamaica was into its third night of flames by the time professional British soldiers sailed for Montego Bay. A cluster of white refugees took refuge in the town of Falmouth, where they lived miserably from day to day under the doubtful protection of a militia garrison. Among them were Samuel Moulton Barrett and his minister friend, Hope Waddell. The two men watched "the scene of confusion" on the town square and listened to the "incessant babble" as militia companies marched uselessly back and forth. Falmouth also filled with black prisoners, most of them facing imminent execution on thin evidence. Sharpe's conspiracy had come as a surprise to many of them. Waddell looked with pathos at "the men, sturdy and sullen, handcuffed; the women, burdened with infants on their sides, and baskets of household things on their heads; and children running besides their mothers, crying bitterly. Arrived at the court-house, they squatted huddled together on the ground-floor, in pitiable plight, for the night, to await the issue of court martial on the morrow."[28]

And the fires continued, night after night, encompassing the hills in an eerie glow. Almost fifteen new fires appeared at every sunset. As a Methodist minister wrote to his superiors, "On the night of New Year's Day, we counted distinctly fourteen properties blazing at one time—the whole atmosphere appeared to be illuminated. Surrounding the Bay at various distances the fires burned with terrific fury and had a most appalling appearance. Indeed the whole country seemed given up to destruction." Almost nobody who recorded their experiences during the rebellion that first week of January failed to mention the profound visual impression of the fires, which contained a note of near suicidal glory.[29]

"The whole surrounding country was completely illuminated, and presented a terrible appearance, even at noon-day," recalled Foulks. "When, however, the shades of night descended, and the buildings on the side of those beautiful mountains, which form the splendid panorama around Montego Bay, were burning, the spectacle was awfully grand."[30]

On December 30, the whites almost lost the crucial port city of Montego Bay, tenuously held by the St. James Militia but surrounded on three sides by forests teeming with rebels and enslaved people of undecided loyalties. On the fourth side was the Caribbean Sea. Most residents figured an attack was inevitable and rowed out into the harbor to take refuge on one of the dozen or so merchant vessels at anchor.

Their suspicions were correct. A group under the command of leader Charles McLenan—with no apparent connection to the Baptist ring led by Samuel Sharpe—was eager to come down from the hills and "burn the Bay," which would have given the group access to a huge amount of money, food, and captured weapons. It joined up with another column, headed by enslaved leader Captain Williams, and marched past the ruins of Montpelier Old Works Estate, which had been ordered torched a few nights earlier by another slave named Williams who had put a stolen gun to the heads of two fellow slaves and ordered them to do it. These combined forces headed toward the coast, but were stopped at a barricade barely four miles from their goal.[31]

The slave in charge of the checkpoint, John Tharp, was personally closer to Samuel Sharpe and not in agreement with McLenan's idea to ransack the town of Montego Bay so early in the proceedings.

If anybody was going to do this, it was going to be Tharp himself. McLenan replied that he was a "general" and clearly outranked Tharp.

"I'm the king of St. James!" Tharp insisted. "Who made you a general? I've already cut off two white men's heads at McGalloway's Estate and I'm not a general, so what right do you have to call yourself a general?"

A brawl between these two groups of rebels nearly broke out, but McLenan eventually got discouraged with the argument and told his friends they should just return to the village of Springfield because Tharp's group was clearly not serious about this revolution.

"Everybody was sitting down, and would not fight for [freedom]," McLenan complained. He announced his own intentions to "go home and sit down." This may not have been the only arm of the plot to fail at the time. A newspaper in the capital of Spanish Town would later report that an unnamed enslaved woman was caught holding "a quantity of gunpowder and other combustibles which was intended to be used in destroying the town of Montego Bay." With its cluster of wooden artisanal shops and townhouses built adjacent to one another, a catastrophic urban fire would not have been hard to start.[32]

That bungled encounter was the last chance the enslaved people had to take Montego Bay, for on New Year's Day 1832 the commander of the king's forces in Jamaica, Sir Willoughby Cotton, arrived at the docks aboard HMS *Sparrowhawk,* accompanied by two hundred soldiers of the Seventy-Seventh Regiment and four field artillery guns. Close behind them was HMS *Blanche,* also carrying British troops and commanded by Commodore Arthur Farquhar, who had the power to deputize the merchant fleet in the harbor into the service of the Royal Navy.

When sailors went ashore they found the militia in a disorganized mess. The volunteer soldiers refused orders to march up into the hills and stop the fires. Colonel George Lawson had to be commanded to get his panicked men into some semblance of discipline, and a Royal Navy captain later said that if the gunships had not arrived when they did, "the town of Montego Bay would have been burnt that night" and turned into a spectacular monument to the militia's incompetence.[33]

Sir Willoughby Cotton questioned some captive rebels, learned the names of the leaders, and dispatched their identities to Lord Belmore. Two days later a notice ran in the Kingston newspapers offering a generous reward for the capture or killing of "General Ruler Samuel Sharp [sic], or Tharp, alias, Daddie Ruler Sharp, or Tharp, director of the whole, and styled also Preacher to the rebels, belonging to Croydon Estate." Oddly, his bounty was valued at three hundred US dollars, not in British pounds. This intelligence—which likely misidentified Samuel Sharpe's home plantation—seems to have come from a militia unit that had been scouring the woods in Westmoreland Parish.[34]

Cotton ordered the captives hanged after he questioned them. Before they died, the prisoners told Cotton they believed their freedom was in reach and that they had been instructed not to harm anyone unless they were attacked while sitting down, and that the only property they had agreed to burn was houses, in order to create beacon fires. Sugar works and cane fields were to be left untouched, the prisoners said, for these were essential to the sugar economy and to destroy them would be to eliminate any jobs they might have in the future—a piece of evidence that should have confirmed to him the crucial information that Samuel Sharpe's goal was not to overthrow white rule but only to end the practice of forced labor.

Cotton was a tubby and heavy-jowled product of the British upper class who had earned some early notoriety for helping instigate a juvenile revolt at Rugby School when he was fourteen years old. Bored students were shooting off corks from homemade guns and the headmaster, who heard these improvised missiles rattling on the windows, demanded to know the source of the gunpowder they used.

Students led by Cotton responded by blowing the headmaster's door off its hinge with some of their illicit explosives, then lit their books on fire in further protest. A local militia arrived to restore order and took the unusual step of reading the rowdy students the Riot Act. A few militiamen crept behind them with swords drawn and captured the hyped-up teenagers. Cotton was expelled for the stunt, but, true to upper-class invincibility, it did not hamper his ability to win a lieutenant's commission in 1799. The author of a history of Rugby School called this juvenile incident the "Great Rebellion" and noted dryly that Cotton "showed more skill in his later career as a soldier than he did in this first attempt. Perhaps his experience as a *corpus vile* helped him to put down the rebellion of the slaves in Jamaica."[35]

Before he arrived at his dangerous new assignment in the West Indies, Cotton was at the center of another embarrassing episode as a young officer fighting against Napoleon Bonaparte's army in 1814. The French took his unit prisoner at the Battle of Bayonne, and his captors demanded some payment before they would release him. Cotton had only his watch and a single Spanish dollar to hand over, and they gave him a beating for his paltry offer of ransom. "It really seemed as the though the enemy had made choice of our fattest officers," noted another member of the unit, who apparently had not liked him.[36]

Cotton's official portrait shows him with muttonchop sideburns and a slender white beard, bedecked with various medals—the picture of a "fuss-and-feathers" defender of Britain's far-flung empire. He had recently led combat against the natives during an uprising in Burma, and would later see action in Afghanistan and India and receive the Knight Grand Cross, Order of the Bath, among other baroque decorations. Questioning slaves and insurgents had become one of his subspecialties.

Cotton's basic—and accurate—knowledge of the rebellion's ideology was written into the forceful proclamation from Montego Bay he made on January 2, 1832:

TO THE REBELLIOUS SLAVES

NEGROES, You have taken up arms against your Masters, and
have burnt and plundered their Houses and Buildings. Some
wicked persons have told you that the King has made you free,
and that your Masters withhold your freedom from you. In
the name of the King, I come amongst you, to tell you that
you are misled. I bring with me numerous Forces to punish the
guilty, and all who are found with the Rebels will be put to
death, without Mercy. You cannot resist the King's Troops.
Surrender yourselves, and beg that your crime may be pardoned.
All who yield themselves up at any Military Post *immediately*,
provided they are not principals and chiefs in the burnings that
have been committed, will receive His Majesty's pardon. All
who hold out, will meet with certain death.

WILLOUGHBY COTTON, *Maj. General Command^g.*

GOD SAVE THE KING[37]

Stacks of this proclamation were printed and ordered tacked up
all over the northern shore—on street corners, in slave villages, on
the sides of great houses. When a militia company marched up to
the hilltop estate of Richard Barrett, they found a contingent of loyal
slaves guarding the house. But Cotton's proclamation had been ripped
down from the door of the sugar works—which seemed a grave offense to this amateur band of militia. They lined up the slaves and
threatened to execute them all unless the guilty party came forward.
The head driver then lost his nerve and fingered "a fine handsome
young fellow as the delinquent" who barely had time to call out "O,
Lord, massa, don't kill me" before a private named Watson shot him
point-blank.[38]

Richard Barrett himself wasn't there to stop it. He had taken refuge
in the armed encampment of Montego Bay, where on New Year's
Day he wrote the governor approving words about the courts-martial,

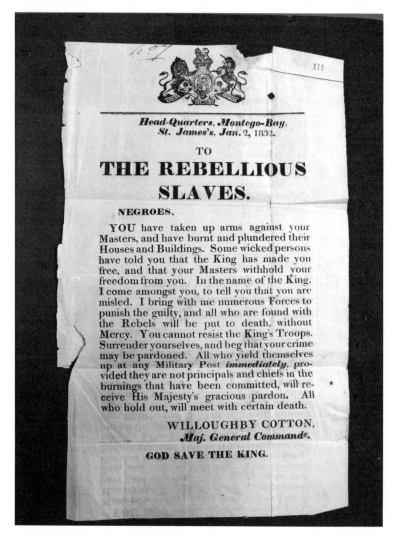

The British Army tried first to win through intimidation. General Willoughby Cotton promised amnesty for those who surrendered, and death to those who held out. *(UK National Archives)*

as well as the military movements of Captain George Gordon, who had done "much mischief" to the rebels by setting fire to the so-called negro villages and huts on all the estates where trouble had been spotted. Many enslaved people had fled into the woods, "where they must soon starve," noted Barrett.

Elizabeth Barrett Browning had always thought her cousin had a ruthless streak about him, and the Machiavellian quality of Richard Barrett's political insight can be glimpsed in what he wrote about Cotton's offer to penitent rebels. It seems possible that Barrett might have had a hand in crafting the offer.

"Sir Willoughby has put forth a proclamation offering pardon to all but principals and chiefs," Barrett wrote. "I have some hopes that, backed by an imposing force and the many losses the rebels have already suffered, this measure will cause them differences and suspicions of each another, if it serves no other purpose—as yet, the insurgents have exhibited the most wretched cowardice."[39]

He would soon be proved wrong.

The brutality of the volunteer militias was matched only by the ineptitude of some of their commanders. One of them was about to commit a major blunder and hand the rebel army an outright victory.

The Western Interior Regiment, led by Colonel William Grignon—the lawyer nicknamed Little Breeches by his own slaves—had been barracked at Belvidere Estate without adequate food or weapons. He had about a hundred men with, as he later said, "defective rifles" and a small amount of gunpowder and bullets. On December 29 he sent an urgent request for five barrels each of beef, pork, and bread, as well as ten gallons of lamp oil, six lamps, and three hundred weight of coffee. That same day, he inexplicably marched his regiment over to the still burning ruins of Montpelier Estate, where he was surprised and attacked by a group of perhaps four

The attack on Montpelier Estate was the high-water mark of the revolt.
Drawing by Adolphe Duperly, January 1832. *(National Library of Jamaica)*

hundred rebels, "advancing in four columns," who seemed to have emerged from the woods.[40]

Channeling what must have been enormous reserves of pent-up frustration and a good deal of adrenaline, the soldiers of the rebel army descended down the meadows with what one eyewitness described as a "regular Indian war whoop" and a tremendous blanketing of musket fire in the last light of the sunset which killed a member of the militia and perforated the hats of two officers without injuring them. One of the columns of rebels crouched behind a stone wall. Some rose up to give covering fire; others remained hidden. The enslaved man Robert Gardiner recalled that Thomas Dove had a pistol; "it was loaded, but he did not fire it; he was frightened at the bullets, and went under the wall."[41]

A confused and overwhelmed Grignon ordered the grasses of the field set on fire in an attempt to disperse the slaves. Then he retreated, after some disorganized shooting that killed only ten of the rebels.

This was likely a source of great satisfaction and amusement for the enslaved people, who got to witness the priceless sight of Little Breeches running away from a fight. The slaves responded by lighting dried sugar leaves on fire inside a still-unburned trash house. By this time it was fully dark, and the light of the blaze allowed the remaining troops of the St. James Regiment to direct their aim into the darkened cane rows. Before they left for the night, a sniper managed to take down a captain named Johnson, described by a militiaman as "a notorious Baptist leader and distinguished incendiary." It was hardly any comfort. The regiment barely slept that night, every man clutching his rifle, and the next morning all of Grignon's officers demanded they leave the area immediately. He agreed.[42]

Grignon later insisted that he ordered this humiliating retreat because he was facing a rebel opposition numbering over ten thousand—a wildly exaggerated figure—and promised that reinforcements hadn't arrived to help him fight "an overwhelming body of negroes" that was "collecting in every quarter around us." While he may have been speaking in defensive hyperbole, he nonetheless got the essentials right. Grignon's defeat represented a terrifying omen for the white minority: given proper organization and armaments, the slaves could well eliminate the landed class if they chose to do so, if only because of their numerical strength.[43]

The events at Montpelier gave an electrifying psychological boost to the rebels, who had just witnessed successful armed resistance against their oppressors, perfectly embodied in the despised Grignon, who had once ordered a husband to whip his own wife. "When they saw the military retreat from place to place and finally disappear from the scene, the negroes had enough sense to believe that the 'buckras' were afraid," concluded the churchman Henry Bleby, using the Jamaican slang for "bosses." The entire county of Cornwall now belonged to the insurgents, and barely any whites could be found there, even in hiding. Roads between major towns were cut off. And slaves who would not have believed that any show of defiance against their masters would have been possible now became convinced of an almost unfathomable outcome—in Bleby's words, "that the whites had abandoned the island and left it in the hands of the blacks." Many of them were persuaded to join the rebellion as a result.[44]

Visual impressions contributed to the euphoria. Fires were already raging just a half mile from Montego Bay, where they could be seen from the headquarters of the British troops who had, ironically enough, made their barracks in the First Baptist Church where Thomas Burchell and Samuel Sharpe had preached. The burning hillsides seemed to make the relentless daylight of Jamaica even sharper and more dazzling, and the visual effect of flames spreading in all directions at night was like nothing anybody had ever seen before, as if the combined anger and desperation of three hundred years had been unleashed on the hills. The white people, it seemed, had been magically dispelled.[45]

In truth, they were in hiding, and some asked their enslaved people to do the fighting for them. A plantation owner in St. James Parish who stood on his own porch and watched his neighbors' houses burn down decided on the spot to give rifles to twenty of his most trusted slaves, asking them to bring in any prisoners they could find. He wrote a friend, "I am assured it will be a war of extermination, for rumours reach us that the insurgents are in large bodies, well-armed."[46]

Willoughby Cotton sent a private note to Lord Belmore on January 2 that reflected a far more pessimistic outlook than the resolute face he was showing to the enslaved people. With only two hundred British troops to contain a rebellious force that perhaps numbered as many as thirty thousand rebels, the military situation was a metaphor for Jamaica: a droplet of white riding atop a brown sea. The entire northwest was held by motivated slaves, save only a few islands of untouched plantations, the ports of Falmouth and Montego Bay, and a few bumpy carriage roads that could be cut off at any moment. Cotton promised the governor that he would try to disrupt the "horrid incendiary system" of plantation burning that had gripped the country, but he was not hopeful because of the "utter impossibility of affording parties of military to every estate." Not even an army of ten thousand British troops could keep that kind of watch, he said. Instead he would try to ascertain where the slaves were gathered en masse and "strike a blow by simultaneous movement that will have a decided effect." Even this would be difficult, because his scouts were telling him the slave gangs were "moving every hour from one place to another."[47]

This assessment was not entirely correct. With several days to consolidate their positions in the wooded hills above the north shore, the slaves, according to one correspondent, "appear to have taken to the interior and other commanding heights, and have communications with the negroes by means of signals." By this he meant that slaves who appeared to be peaceful might really be taking secret orders from the hillsides and rise up to kill at any moment, unexpectedly. Another owner noted that even as trash houses were burned to the ground, the slaves had left the sugarcane fields untouched; he presumed they were saving them as "lurking places" and for sugarcane to eat for energy. He expressed hope that the soldiers would just burn the cane fields themselves and hopefully kill the slaves hiding inside.[48]

On the morning of January 4, a large group of slaves overtook a plantation in the town of Knocklava and burned down the dry works. This only served as a beacon for the militia, who marched toward the conflagration expecting a fight. They got one. A regiment was approaching the burning property when gunshots "were heard in all directions, and in a few moments, rebels appeared in considerable force on the neighboring hills."[49]

Captain John Huggup ordered twenty of his mounted men to advance into the enemy fire. They broke down a gap of passage in a stone wall and made a stand there, facing a large group of rebels standing behind another wall at the opposite end of the meadow. Afraid of having their horses shot out from under them, a few of them tried to flank the rebels on the side, which pulled their attention away from the meadow. At this point Augustus Beaumont screamed "Charge!" and led the majority of the cavalry through the gap in the wall, across the meadow, and toward the main line of the slave army. "The rebels fired on us and then fled in all directions," reported a colonel. "Several were shot and sabered. We might have killed double the number in a direct charge." Beaumont was said to have slain two himself.[50]

Two or three days later, many of the slaves present at this engagement gave themselves up and went back to work. The others remained in the woods to continue the fight as a guerilla conflict. The battle at Knocklava was the second head-to-head infantry clash of the uprising, and it would also be among the last.

EIGHT

ONE COMMON RUIN

ONE MEASURE OF Samuel Sharpe's abundance of idealism—or naïveté—was his attempt to forge an alliance with the Maroons: the dark-skinned descendants of the runaway slaves of the Spanish. Though they shared a common racial heritage with the slaves and had fought their own vicious wars with the British, they had made a lasting peace treaty with the Crown in 1739 and were allowed to claim their own territory in the steep interior hills that were unsuitable for sugar or coffee.

The Maroons were fierce fighters who occasionally helped the militia put down localized revolts; one observer called them "a sort of rural police force." They also had a deal with the planters to return runaway slaves at the price of forty shillings per head as a standard bounty. Their loyalties in past insurrections had almost always been with the British.[1]

Sharpe had reasoned that if he couldn't form an overt alliance with the Maroons, he might at least try to break their nine-decade alliance with the plantocracy and neutralize them as a fighting force. Shortly after Christmas 1831 he sent a comrade named Peter Douglas into the wilderness to make contact with the Accompong Maroons and offer an undisclosed "present" to a high official, Colonel White.

Douglas and a companion, John Williams, made the bad decision to approach the Maroon encampment by "crawling on their hands" through the trees and rocks. Taken by surprise, the Maroons managed to grab the two men and immediately turned them in to the

St. Elizabeth's Regiment—presumably for the usual payment. One of their leaders testified at Williams's court-martial, saying that "he said he came from his general to Maroons to get them to join the negroes against the white people." Both men were executed. That was the end of Sharpe's wartime diplomacy.[2]

The Maroons later joined British troops in helping flush out pockets of rebels, and their local knowledge would prove valuable, for some of the hunted slaves were using backcountry redoubts the Maroons had been using for decades: limestone caves known as cockpits.[3]

Some of the pirates who prowled Caribbean waters had used these caves as dumping grounds for bodies, or as hideaways for stolen freight or money. A few of these forgotten hidden fortresses— sometimes braced with logs and concealed with branches—had been rediscovered by those fugitives participating in the revolt. The densest collection of them between St. James and Trelawny Parishes was known as Cockpit Country.[4]

The slaves took pains to makes their cockpit forts near the top of the roughest, sharpest limestone they could find. This type of "honeycomb rock" was an effective defense against intruders, as noted in the race-generalizing view of Bernard Senior: "The only mode of traversing such districts is by carefully insinuating the body between occasional clefts in the rock, and when compelled to pass over a portion of the honeycomb rock, the tough skin of the negro foot is much more applicable to the duty than the flat or slippery sole of the white man's boot or shoe."[5]

From an isolated cockpit, a team of slaves could conduct the kind of hit-and-run operations familiar to guerilla forces throughout history. The tactics of Samuel Sharpe's slave army in the second phase of the uprising came to resemble those of the Continental Army of George Washington that had fought the British colonial troops a half century earlier, though without the same level of munitions and centralized command and control. They emerged to cut trenches and fell trees across roads, thus making them difficult to travel by mounted cavalry. They also burned down wooden bridges across creeks. For the commander of British forces, Sir Willoughby Cotton, the principal goal was to keep the roads open for troop movements and free of obstructions. The British Army had been trained for direct battlefield engagements against visible and uniformed enemies; it had a much harder time fighting in the hills or peering into cockpits.

That work went mainly to frustrated Jamaican militiamen, who discovered that flushing out desperate slaves was hard and dirty work. After enjoying a lunch of recently slain chicken and pig from Eden Estate, a detachment from the Seventh Regiment tried to follow the trail of rebels up a footpath "barely sufficient for a goat to pass." Near the top of the mountain they found a huge supply of yams, plantains, coconuts, and assorted other produce sufficient to feed several regiments.[6]

The British high command recognized the value of food as a weapon. On New Year's Day, Major General Robertson ordered a command read out loud to his men: "It is my desire that, on the properties you visit, the head people be called up and informed, if any fires take place on the properties, it is the Governor's instructions and my positive orders that every negro house be burnt down, and all their hogs and poultry killed. If any horned cattle belonging to them they are to be killed for the use of the troops; also their provision ground destroyed."[7]

The staggering amount of food gathered up and stashed away by the rebels was a source of frequent remark among British soldiers: they tended to frame it as evidence of the slaves' greed and poor moral character instead of their seriousness of purpose. The size of the rations also might have indicated the length of time the slaves thought it might take to hold out in the caves and in the wilderness fortresses until their freedom papers came through from the king of England. Some food caches might have sustained them for six months or more, and they had sentries posted with rifles on the hills and at the mouths of their cockpits at all hours of the day.[8]

"Master, you do not know what a wood is up there," a slave named William Evans told one of his interrogators. "The white people never will be able to get them there, for they can kill them easy without the white people seeing them. They all say, and I say, too, the dogs only can drive them out."[9]

The prisoners executed at Montego Bay on New Year's Day were only the first victims of a wave of extrajudicial killings and summary executions that swept the island for the next five weeks. The governor had declared martial law, which obviated the usual need for a formal court to render a death sentence. Any prisoners could now be subject to courts-martial, conducted by Jamaican planters furious over the destruction of their homes, that could take as little as sixty seconds each.

These were terrifying affairs for those caught up in them. The "evidence" could be as simple as a slave having been seen in a crowd watching as a building burned down. A soldier would ask a few leading questions, then order the man taken away without further details. Captain George Gordon oversaw the proceedings in Montego Bay without giving any hint of empathy or mercy. An observer gave the following description of one trial:

"A prisoner, sir," said a soldier leading in a captive.

"Where was he taken?" a distracted Gordon asked, his head bent down to his desk.

"In the cane-piece, sir."

"Had he arms?"

"A macheat, sir."

"Take him forth," said Gordon, and the prisoner was prodded away to be hanged without the captain once having looked up from his desk, apparently unconcerned that in a cane field with a machete was exactly where an enslaved person on a sugar estate might expect to be found during the workday.[10]

At another trial, Henry Bleby heard one terrified slave ask the armed men dragging him away, "What are you going to do with me?"

"Oh, you never mind," answered one of the marshals. "You will find out presently what will be done with you."

The slave then saw a few militia members loading their rifles. The panicked slave asked again, as he was being tied between the posts of two gallows, "O captain! What are you going to do with me?"

The officer made no reply, except to pick up the prisoner's jacket from the ground and tie it around the doomed man's head as an improvised hood. Then he gave the order, "Make ready! Present! Fire!" and the man was shot. Afterward he lay tied there, slumped, still suspended above the ground by the ropes, the jacket now torn from his head.

Several of his friends gathered at the spot where an angry and sputtering white man rushed up to them and pointed to one of the bullet holes in the skull.

"You want freedom, do you?" he screamed. "This is the sort of freedom we'll give you, every devil of you! Come here and put your finger where mine is, and see how you like it."[11]

A few of these killings were reported deadpan and with little detail in the Kingston newspapers. Eventually the *Watchman and Jamaica Free Press* created a regular column titled simply "Executions" just to keep score. "During the week, there have been 22 rebels tried and executed, and upwards of 50 have received the punishment of flagellation," read the tally for one week. The *Cornwall Courier* made cryptic reference to multiple "executions on the spot" and noted with satisfaction that they had "the desired effect" of convincing the witnessing slaves to get back to work.[12]

Greater still were the number of reprisal killings made with thin evidence against slaves who were believed—fairly or not—to have threatened white people. "Such acts were not unfrequent," remarked Bernard Senior, "but merely considered '*signs of the times*.'"[13]

These quasiofficial killings took place with little evidence or fanfare, and many slaves were killed on sight if they were discovered not working or even simply walking on the road. The militia soldiers seemed to take glee in the proceedings, as if they were part of a big game hunt. Simply avoiding or running away from a militia was usually taken as a sign that the slave had something to hide. "Their flight was regarded as sufficient proof of guilt, and they were shot at and often shot down," wrote Bleby, appalled at the "sanguinary and callous men who thought the hunting and shooting of negroes excellent sport." The unhappy farmer Benjamin McMahon, forced into militia service, watched as his fellow troops went after a black man on the road who had done nothing but look terrified as they approached him. The doomed man leaped over a wall, bullets flying at him, and "he was struck but rose again, and ran, bleeding; again he fell, rose up again, and several times fell and rose, running a few paces at a time—the militia still firing on him." The captain hacked at the fallen man with his sword, and one of his colleagues finished him off by shooting the slave though the head.[14]

Some planter-soldiers went so far as to call the violence "fine fun," expressing hope that it would continue indefinitely. Robbery of slaves—who had little money to begin with—was also common, as were burning down the so-called negro villages and killing livestock. One colonel averred that "Christianity was abrogated by martial law." McMahon watched with dismay on the morning of January 2, 1832, as his fellow troops opened fire on a group of unarmed slaves outside Golden Grove Estate. A head driver who had been awake all night protecting his master's house was shot in the legs, while one of his men going dutifully to work in the fields was shot in the head. As McMahon wrote, "So wild and ungovernable was the fury of the militia-men in seeking to destroy the poor negroes that, in their haste and confusing in running about the negro houses, firing in all directions, it was a miracle they did not kill one another."[15]

No official count would be made of the spontaneous murders taking place all over northwestern Jamaica. One of the rare descriptions that appeared in the newspapers read only, "Mr. Beaumont, being well-mounted, overtook another armed negro and shot him with his pistol."[16]

Even the generally promilitary *Watchman and Jamaica Free Press* was moved to protest the actions of "subordinate militia officers" and their "condemnable proceedings," which led to "the most extravagant notions of arbitrary power." At least two hundred slaves would be killed through these cryptolegal murders that went unpunished or even unnoticed. One letter writer from Montego Bay gave a sense of the times when he reported, almost offhandedly while relating other doings on January 3, "This day more than ten rebels will be shot, and a party for that purpose are now paraded." Within the span of a week, such public murders—both the state sanctioned and the unofficial—had become a normal part of the Jamaican scenery. They became so common as to become boring, and passersby even began to ignore them.[17]

Willoughby Cotton may have intended some measure of restraint with the proclamation of mercy for the rank and file, as well as his sparing use of "examples," but there is evidence that the militia committed other battlefield atrocities. The *Cornwall Chronicle* reported, for example, that the ears of some of the dead slaves were being cut off and taken as trophies by the Maroon allies of the king who had killed them, anticipating the mutilation practices of American soldiers in the Vietnam War. The Jamaican authorities had been in the habit of paying bounties for the severed ears even before the rebellion, and there is some reason to believe the payments continued throughout the conflict—a way of outsourcing some of the dirty work. An official court account in the *Royal Gazette* reported only that there was a "pursuit of several desperate characters" in a northern town; no details were given.[18]

"This was nothing less than putting a premium upon murder," wrote the clergyman Henry Bleby, "and I have not the slightest doubt that scores of slaves, innocent of all participation in the revolt, were shot by the Maroons for no other purpose than to obtain their ears for sale."[19]

The severed body parts were exhibited around town as a "demonstration" of military strength, wrote the Cornwall Chronicle, adding that "executions of the very basest kind of their leaders" was a daily occurrence in the market place. Many of these were likely innocent slaves caught in the middle of the uprising whom had trusted the promise of immunity upon surrender and received an awful surprise.[20]

The Royal Gazette, the voice of official Jamaica, felt compelled to admonish those performing the killings to at least do so in a dignified fashion and not resort to torture or unusual methods of dispatch: "Death is the most terrific of punishments—it is the acme of suffering, and there is no need for refining upon its mode—the leaden bullet or the hempen line are quiet sufficient."[21]

If the public hangings and severed ears weren't enough to terrorize the insurgents, the severed heads of dozens of slaves were placed on posts near public thoroughfares.

The head of an executed slave named Stothert, who had been accused of murdering a white sergeant major named Mr. Pearce, was stuck on a pole near Welcome Estate as a warning to others. While the militiamen were mounting this gruesome trophy, they encountered another of Pearce's suspected murderers, a man named Patrick Ellis. The rumor circulating among the militia was that Pearce had been stripped down to his socks before he was hacked to death, and so they ripped off Ellis's clothes and slashed him several times with a cutlass.[22]

At this point Ellis made a final display of courage. He begged to be shot, crying: "I am ready. Give me your volley. Fire, for I will never again be a slave." The troops obliged him.[23]

The party also caught sight of a slave named George Brown, whom they summoned over with the intention of inducing him to surrender. He called back, "Jesus Christ has made me free and I will work for no man!"[24] This defiant statement would later become notorious, and the lieutenant who first heard it was outraged. He ordered his troops to ready their weapons and shoot the man who had used Jesus's name. Brown's head was then mounted on another pole a few yards away from Stothert's, and everyone who saw it was cautioned not to disturb the exhibit "under the penalty of having their own substituted in their stead," noted the conservative *Royal Gazette*. "It seemed to have the desired effect on their feelings," wrote the paper's unnamed correspondent, "and it is to be hoped that will operate as a most salutary example to those poor deluded creatures, many of whom, perhaps, scarcely deserved the appellation of deluded."[25]

See what happens said the empty eyes, ragged neck, and dripping blood. This graphic demonstration of the barbarism and ruthlessness of the white authorities had been made only occasionally during previous rebellions, a tropical version of what passersby might have occasionally seen displayed outside the Tower of London in late medieval times. But there was a particularly Caribbean twist to the use of this messaging during a slave revolt. The white ruling class was well aware of the prevalent belief among enslaved people that the dismemberment of a corpse would derail that soul's journey toward an afterlife back in Africa, condemning that person to wander the spirit world as an outcast—a *zumbi*, in the Kikongo language. In this way, the ultimate punishment could reach beyond the grave.[26]

The widespread revival of head mounting in January 1832 was perhaps the truest sign of the anxiety on the island during those weeks.

Jamaican whites wondered how their slaves—formerly so pliable and useful—could have turned into revolutionaries so quickly. A soldier marveled in a letter how the slaves were acting "as though they never knew their master, nor received any kindness at their hands." The gulf of understanding between the slave owners' self-interest and the simple urge for liberty on the part of the enslaved people seemed unbridgeable. Whatever crude understanding there may have been of the slaves' motives was lost in the panic and the confusion of daily events. "The slaves are well-armed, and are firing sugar estates, pens and settlements," noted one letter-writer from Savanna-la-Mar. "They say they are fighting for their freedom, and executing their diabolical schemes with glee. Fires are seen every night."[27]

At the *Watchman and Jamaica Free Press* back in Kingston, editor Edward Jordon was forced to start running a regular section on the front page of his newspaper. Roundups of the latest reports of violence, plantation burnings, and troop movements were all presented under a regular heading, "The Disturbances," that needed no further explanation. This was the biggest breaking news story the startup newspaper had ever seen.[28]

These accounts of violence were usually disorganized and sometimes contradictory, and it was difficult for any reader to draw a total picture of the trauma convulsing the island. Jordon was also in the habit of printing any letters he received from the north shore of the island, and the raw information was impossible to verify. At first he had reported with pride that "no human blood has been spilled by our peasantry" with the exception of a wounded militiaman. In another column he added that the slaves in and around the capital of Kingston "have behaved themselves with the greatest possible propriety." But that early optimism soon gave way to a more serious treatment of the violence.[29]

The dispatches often included precise troop movements into towns and plantations, as in the following lines about various militias on January 11: "Colonel Cadian, Trelawny Regiment, moves on Weston Favel, Spring Vale, and Maroon Town road. Colonel Hilton, St. Ann's

Western Regiment, moves on Falmouth, and Colonel Hamilton Brown occupies Duncans, Mountain Spring and Cambridge."[30]

Some of these updates came directly from Willoughby Cotton's headquarters in Montego Bay. Other fragments of information were gleaned from letters sent by ordinary citizens to Kingston. Jordon knew that some of the leaders of the slave uprising were literate and might therefore make use of the intelligence about military maneuvers from the newspapers they could acquire through raids. How much of the content might have been intentional disinformation is impossible to say. Equally uncertain is how much of it might have been rumors passed on as fact, the falsity of which would only become apparent days later. Letters from the north to the south typically took two days to arrive, by which point the anticipated battles would have been long over. The reading must have been excruciating for white Jamaicans in Kingston who had friends and relatives in the midst of the action, and equally so for free coloreds.

The *Watchman* summed up the feelings of many when it wrote, "We freely confess that when it first began to be rumored that a great number of the slaves on different estates in the parishes of St. James and Trelawny had refused to work, and had proceeded to acts of outrages, we doubted it, from the hitherto peaceable, orderly, and correct demeanor of that class of the population. But the awful truth has burst upon us with tenfold horrors." The fertile shore of St. James had been reduced, said the newspaper, to "one common ruin" of smoldering works and ruined houses. The sickly scent of burnt sugar hung like fog over the hills and the coastal plain, while newly freed slaves who hadn't joined the uprising wandered, unsure of what to do or who to believe. For some of them it was a first trip away from the several hundred acres of land that had been both the focus and the limit of their entire lives.[31]

Those white owners who were not slogging through the country in militia uniforms were either huddled in the impromptu guarded camp at Falmouth or crammed on board a ship anchored in the waters off Montego Bay. The exact state of their property—the only source of their continuing wealth and power—would be a mystery for some weeks. "In common with our fellow-colonists, we deplore the infatuation which has lighted the first torch, which excited the first rebellious act, and had led to scenes of anarchy, turbulence and blood," thundered the *Watchman*. They had reason to be worried: all but four or five of the sugar mansions around Montego Bay had been burned to the ground, and the city itself still remained a possible target of invasion.[32]

The British Navy commodore Arthur Farquhar was alarmed enough to put out a call to the merchant vessels docked in the harbor at Montego Bay asking all captains to "form an association for the purpose of considering how you can best render yourselves and crews efficient in the present crisis." Captain David Paton of the ship *Christian* was named the head of the twelve-ship posse comitatus.[33]

The rebels, meanwhile, were still cutting trenches across roads along the coast in an attempt to prohibit the British Army from moving wagons or artillery into the region. Willoughby Cotton's troops had succeeded in reopening some roads by building makeshift bridges across the trenches and cutting through felled logs, but he was totally incapable of moving his troops anywhere beyond well-traveled areas. His men spent two weeks essentially marching in circles, from Montego Bay to Seven Rivers to Lapland and back to Montego Bay without encountering any hostile forces. The rebels were lurking in the mountains, where he dared not attack.[34]

The closest the two camps came to actual battle during the round-about march was on the morning of January 9, when Willoughby's troops surprised a group of insurgent enslaved people who were eating breakfast near Lapland. The rebels scattered to the woods, leaving their cooking fires still burning. The British troops helped themselves to their abandoned food before trailing the rebels up some mountain slopes to a fortified position across a bridge, where the enslaved people finally started shooting back at their pursuers. "They fired a few shots, and then ran like the devil. The only damage they did was hitting a Trooper's horse," wrote an officer. "They might have played the duce with us if they had courage."[35]

Other vigilantes joined the popular scorn against the enslaved people, heaping the accusation of cowardice on men who had spent their lives in bondage and under constant threat of beatings or death. "Courage among these freebooters (negroes) is out of the question," wrote a soldier of the Seventh Regiment, without apparent self-awareness of the inequality of the fight. He added, "Apathy, cruelty, brutality and ingratitude are their ruling passions."[36] An editor in Cornwall, surveying the charred ruins around him, concluded, "The negro fights badly with the musket: but his conquests with the torch have been fearfully satisfied."[37]

This was not only condescending but false. For enslaved people who had spent their entire lives under the shadow of the whip, without any military training or experience with guns, to one day pick up a firearm or a machete or even a rock and oppose a superior force must have taken an extraordinary level of nerve. The thirst for liberty was powerful enough to overcome even the fear of probable death. Though he was no friend of the slaves, the militiaman Theodore Foulks expressed grudging admiration for his enemy's ingenuity. "During this servile campaign," he wrote, "the negroes manifested a degree of military science that was, in many instances, surprising." They split themselves up into manageable companies of forty or fifty each, and kept time in marching by muttering "War, war, war." The rebels slowed the advances of their British pursuers by tearing down bridges, cutting up roads with trenches, and mounting guerilla-style ambushes from the underbrush, where they could remain concealed and the scarlet uniforms of the approaching British troops were "easily distinguishable at a considerable distance."[38]

Henry Bleby described the only plausible battle strategy the slaves were able to mount in a direct engagement: "They would wait until the soldiers came within range, and then fire upon them from their hiding-place with the few muskets or fowling-pieces which they had amongst them, while others would pour down a shower of stones, and all would then immediately attempt to make their escape."[39]

Yet when rocks hit their marks, it only served to enrage the militia. A company marching through Hanover got ambushed from a cliff over the road shortly after New Year's Day by a few rebels who were have reported to have screamed the unlikely words "You white rascals, we have you now!" and rained down "a volley of musketry and stones." One of the latter missiles struck a Captain Grant in the head, throwing him from his horse. The militia responded with an indiscriminate slaughter. A later witness reported seeing the spot of the ambush teeming with the "putrid remains" of the impudent rebels, their heads and bodies "perforated with bullets."[40]

In several fights the slaves were bold enough to try direct engagements on militia detachments—even against long odds. Many made the assaults without any weapons whatsoever, showing near suicidal levels of bravery.

A party of white men, for example, had been camped at Anchovy Bottom Estate in St. James on or about January 13 when they were set upon by a brigade of slaves led by a leader wearing a red uniform top with black sleeves and blue pantaloons. The militia repelled the attack and chased the rebels into the cane fields, where eight slaves— including the leader—were matter-of-factly slaughtered.[41]

The houses and sugar works of the planation had already been destroyed, perhaps leaving the rebellious slaves feeling like they had little to lose. The blood-stained sugar leaves beneath the ruins of the mansion would lead the *Watchman and Jamaica Free Press* to later contemplate "something majestic and beautiful, though melancholy, even in their destruction."[42]

The dead leader's uniform top—a martial-looking red garment with striped black sleeves—was presented as a trophy to an approving Willoughby Cotton. "The General is satisfied that examples must be made, although no man deprecate the necessity more than himself," reported the *Watchman* correspondent, suggesting that its wearer had been executed in the cane fields after his surrender. "The absolute safety of the island requires it."[43]

The next day, Cotton finally started a real offensive with his Seventh Regiment against the slaves congregating at Montpelier—the site of Colonel William Grignon's shameful retreat. One house had been torched, and the troops arrived in hopes of saving the other house. A soldier related what happened next, in vague terms that left many questions unanswered:

> We were not on the property one hour before the negroes assembled, shouting and blowing their horns in different directions. They then surrounded us, and commenced a fire in three quarters: in the meanwhile, they set one of the trash houses on fire. We pursued them and they gave us battle for upwards of an hour; after several of them had been killed or wounded, they ran into the canes. On Friday we returned to the Bay, as it was thought fit by our commanding officer, and it was lucky we did so, for we scarcely quitted the estate before it was fired and consumed to ashes.[44]

Even an editor as confident as Edward Jordon had to admit his newspaper's limitations as a journal of combat, and said so with a touch of grim humor. "So contradictory, in many instances, are the Bulletins which have appeared since our last, that we are inclined to discredit one-half of their contents," he wrote. "To arrive at the real state of matters, it is necessary to rid the Bulletins of these incongruities, and not allow their ambiguities or their suspicions of Mr. This or That, and Mr. So and So had been informed, that such and such was the case, to have any effect." Some of the letters and military reports he had been receiving were hysterical in nature, he said, but he still went on to complain of nonspecific "atrocities" committed by the rebelling slaves—with no mention of excessive force by the militias or the British Regulars.[45]

He had earlier laid down furious invective for the slaves taking up arms: "What have they gained by their improper conduct? Have they gained freedom? No. The bullet or the bayonet will terminate their existence, while many will be reserved for the more ignominious death of the gallows."[46]

But Jordon was in a complicated position, for he himself was a colored businessman who had only gained his own full civil rights the previous year. He had reason to create some distance between himself and the abolition movement, as he was a member of the black bourgeoisie who had to support the existing slave regime to have any credibility. In his youth he had worked at a liquor store and then found an apprenticeship with a Kingston tailor whose shop happened to be next door to a printer. He struck up a friendship with another young man of color named Robert Osborne who worked there, and the two pooled their resources in 1828 to start the thrice-weekly *Watchman and Jamaica Free Press,* conceived as an alternative to the stodgy *Royal Gazette.* Osborne managed the business side, and Jordon wrote the unsigned articles.[47]

Making a little money with a newspaper in colonial Jamaica involved nonstop work. Paper had to be fashioned from a combination of cloth rags, cornstalks, flax, hemp, sugarcane, or whatever kind of fibrous substance could be turned into crude pulp and run through hand presses. Ink was expensive to buy in bulk from England, and many printers formulated their own version to save money. For Jordan's newspaper it was synthesized from tannic acid and iron sulfate. Leaden type had to be painstakingly set by hand, letter by letter, into a slot called a composing stick that was slid into an iron frame known as a form. But an editor usually filled just a portion of a page while waiting for more news, which usually came through the door via a friend or an employee carrying court documents, lists of ship movements, police reports, items copied from other newspapers, or gossip

Edward Jordon, editor of *The Watchman and Jamaica Free Press*.
(*Jamaica Information Service*)

delivered by politically connected acquaintances who had their own
motivations for drawing attention to certain events. The most en-
gaging news of the week might thereby be in the lower right-hand
corner of the back page: the last tidbit to come in before deadline.
Remarkably, the Jamaican newspapers of the 1830s contained almost
no misspellings. Though the process was often harried, and the news
could be disconnected and dull, the editors—who often set the type
themselves—took special care to form their words correctly.[48]

Paid advertisements for runaway slaves, new bolts of cloth, and lost canoes filled out the three or four columns on the page, which appeared to the reader as a foreboding wall of small type. Each issue was run off a flatbed screw press at the rate of about 250 copies per hour, then delivered to subscribers' houses and sold on street corners around Kingston by young boys. It was not uncommon for a single copy to be passed among several readers.

Though it tepidly defended the institution of slavery and admonished those in bondage to obey their masters, the *Watchman* was liberal for its day. Though Jordon was an Anglican, he unflinching defended the Methodists and the Baptists who were busy evangelizing potential converts and educating slaves on the north side of the island. He had been a cautious proponent of some of the liberalizing measures of the slave laws meant to temper some of the worst tortures inflicted upon slaves by their masters. The *Watchman* was highly sought after among the enslaved people, especially those who were barred by their masters from reading anything. Rev. Peter Duncan said that if he were to give any slave a copy, "he would have a conviction, instantly, that I was his friend." Though William Knibb didn't have much enthusiasm for journalism, he had contributed a few articles in the past.[49]

The *Watchman* switched to a policy of white patriotism and unabashed opposition to Samuel Sharpe's revolt during the heat of the violence, but it did not indulge in the fire-eating tendencies of its most rabid proslavery competitors—most notably, the *Jamaica Courant*, edited by William Bruce, with whom Jordon fought an unceasing (and entertaining) war of printed insults. A taste of Bruce's archconservative leanings may be found in a surviving fragment of his prose, in which he reported on an offer from the Spanish governor of Cuba to lend troops to help put down the insurrection. Lord Belmore declined this entreaty, for it would have meant an awkward alliance with a traditional European foe. But Bruce jumped all over it, with a lavishness that reflects the paranoia of the times:

We say, let the dogs loose, until every slave who continues in the woods with arms in his hands is brought to his senses. We are aware of the hue and cry such a recommendation would create in England: but the people of England must now be told that we shall wholly disregard their opinions. Our lives are in peril, and the necessity which exists to put an end to war, on any terms, will sanctify the means.[50]

At some point Bruce attacked Jordon for being insufficiently committed to the cause of putting the rebellious enslaved people in their place with violence, and Jordon responded in his January 14 issue that he cared about that resentment "about just as much as the man in the moon." He added, "To charge us with sedition is the essence of stupidity; for it will produce no more an effect upon us than the pitiful snarling of an insignificant cur."[51]

Even as Jordon freely and joyfully attacked his white newspaper enemies, he showed unfailing deference to colonial authorities and heaped praise on Lord Belmore. Perhaps also to cement his bona fides as a free black man loyal to the king of England and the practice of slavery, he showed no particular mercy to other free black men who showed sympathy for the insurrection. His approving January 21 coverage of the execution of Joseph Rodrigues stands as an example.

Rodrigues was accused of making his house a "depot of plunder" and giving bullets and gunpowder to the rebels. A plantation owner named Augustus Hamilton testified at the court-martial that he had asked Rodrigues on Christmas Eve if he had heard the slaves talking about anything suspicious, and Rodrigues answered he had heard them "talking in such a way as he had never before heard, and he was afraid there would be some disturbance after Christmas."

Hamilton later spotted a rebel skulking around Rodrigues's house, and after chasing him away, found a load of stolen goods, as well as a quantity of ammunition and weapons. On this evidence Rodrigues was sentenced to die and his oldest son was given three hundred lashes with a whip and sent off to a prison in England. A few minutes after the death order was handed down, Rodrigues was shot by a firing squad. He insisted with his last breath that a chief of the rebels—possibly Thomas Dove or Robert Gardiner—had visited him before Christmas and threatened to kill him if he did not stay at home during the coming war and help them store arms in his house. He said he heard this unnamed preacher say the slaves "would fight to be free."[52]

NINE

LAUNCHED INTO ETERNITY

THE REBELS BUILT their most formidable stronghold on Greenwich Hill, where nearly three thousand emancipated people gathered with large stocks of food and about fifty guns. At the top of the hill they erected a stone wall as an improvised battlement. A few of those who had acquired rifles climbed up into the trees, cut notches into the branches in which to rest their barrels, and positioned themselves as snipers to pick off stray members of the militia who might be seen advancing toward them. Others were sent out to raid neighboring plantations for more provisions. In a half-mile radius around the hill, female scouts were assigned to watch for any sign of approach by whites. Escape routes had already been precut through the trees on the back of the hill, in case the fortress should be breached. These paths were deliberately steep, easy to descend but nearly impossible to climb.[1]

Samuel Sharpe's movements during mid-January 1932 are still a matter of conjecture, though it seems likely that he stayed close to the base at Greenwich Hill. He had a spy named Hurlock—a slave whom the militia thought was "bold even to madness"—who dressed himself as a woman and brazenly went into the town of Montego Bay pretending to be a water carrier, and then switched to the identity of a cigar saleswoman when he began to feel the eyes of suspicion on him. Hurlock went from place to place, making conversation with every soldier he could find, telling colorfully fabricated stories of the violence he had seen on the north coast. In the course of these jolly exchanges, he managed to learn the sizes of the various detachments and the times at which they were going to move the following day. This intelligence went straight to Greenwich Hill.[2]

Sharpe had two subcommanders, both of whom had held elite jobs at their home plantations and evidently brought with them a substantial number of followers. Robert Gardiner, who had been the head driver at Greenwich, was his chief deputy. A clear image of him is captured by British militia officer Bernard Senior, who met him near the end of the violence and wrote, "His figure was tall and well-proportioned, his limbs muscular, and his carriage unusually upright." Others testified to his powers of oratory, which was said to nearly equal Sharpe's. George Guthrie, for example, reported staggering out of a chapel after hearing Gardiner preach. But there is some evidence that Gardiner may have doubted his own role in the leadership. Just before the rebellion broke out, he had sat listening in a church in Montego Bay as a white missionary preached on Luke 8:6—"And some fell upon a rock; and as soon as it was sprung up, it withered away, because it lacked moisture"—and the need for Christians to raise a harvest not of evil but of righteousness. After hearing this, Gardiner told a friend he would indeed sit peacefully after Christmas and not fight. But he had evidently changed his mind again.[3]

We know less about the physical appearance of the other subcommander, Thomas Dove, but he was among the most optimistic of the rebels. He was literate, and had seen stories in the London newspapers about the Anti-Slavery Society, where some of the white members would invite black members to stand next to them at public meetings. It was a show of equality that Dove found amazing and enchanting.[4]

Sharpe had no opportunity to drill his followers or to give them formal instructions as a group in which everybody would have heard the same message. He would have been personally acquainted with very few of them, as he seems to have relied on an inner ring of confidants like Thomas Dove, Robert Gardiner, and George Taylor to do most of his recruiting. Many of the newly freed slaves had been sworn in after the fires began on December 27. Indeed, all evidence suggests that Sharpe's planning and organizing was decidedly not to the purpose of slaughter. Sir Willoughby Cotton—who was in a good position to judge his enemy—said after the uprising that he did not see evidence of a strategy of conflict. He told a committee of inquiry, "The only plan I can perceive was a simultaneous rising to resist working if they were not declared free at Christmas, and the determination to burn the different properties; as to any organized plan of resistance in the field, I have never either met or heard of it."[5]

When captured rebels appeared at their brief courts-martial, their testimony, tellingly, was contradictory. They were literally begging for their lives. Some declared that they were out to burn down houses and expel the whites from the island. Others stubbornly held to the idea that the intent was to shed no blood. Many captured slaves understandably told a story of profound reluctance. James Fray was at Woodstock Estate when it was burned down. He said he approached the second in command, Robert Morris, and told him, "You are forcing us to join your people, but I do not think it is religious to do so, and besides, we have no arms."

"Come along with us," he reported Morris as replying. "If it is only a knife, it will do."[6]

If the rebels' motivations remain ambiguous, the same is not true for the white militias, whose sole raison d'être was to put down an insurrection. They had been trained for a simple thing—pacification through violence—but they had no knowledge of how to recognize, confront, and respond to a peaceful work stoppage. Sharpe's attitude toward fighting appears to have changed along with the militia's vicious response to his movement.

Yet all that we know of Sharpe's actions and any transformation from peaceful to aggressive intentions and acts come from testimony after the rebellion had started to fail, and that testimony should be read with caution. The slaves themselves were powerless to create any written record of what they witnessed, or to publicize it in any way beyond the discreet oral circles of plantation life. What can be known of Sharpe's method and motives must be seen through the lens of the Jamaican prosecutorial narrative, which sought to understand him only to the point of gathering sufficient evidence to justify his hanging.

A witness named Joseph Martin said he encountered Sharpe on December 29, 1831, leading a party of twenty men. About half of them were toting guns, he said, and "some had Macheats and some lances & swords." Sharpe himself was carrying a small machete, and seemed to be the one giving the orders. Later he started carrying a "fowling piece"—a game-hunting rifle. Robert Rose also said he saw Sharpe wielding a cutlass one day and a gun on another.[7]

Another slave reported hearing Sharpe using the explicit language of warfare. James Clarke said he was with Sharpe about a week after Christmas and heard him make a blunt statement of violence: "He was going to war and going to fight and he asked me to go with him and I said I can't go."[8]

Sharpe was reported to have said he was going to "fight white man" at a village named Struie while he was carrying a short pistol. The next day Sharpe returned and said that "they had fired at a white man there and the white man ran and they ran after him and chopped and killed him." Yet no accounts of this explosive incident—Samuel Sharpe at the scene of a homicide—appear anywhere else in the printed record, and he was not specifically charged with this crime. The name of the alleged victim was not recorded.[9]

Context is also important. Martin and Clarke were both testifying at Sharpe's trial several months after these confusing events. They may also have been under intense pressure to recall details differently from how they actually happened in order to fit a prosecution narrative. The court records do not show if they were offered immunity or light sentences in exchange for their stories. Three of the witnesses—James Clarke, Joseph Martin, and Robert Rose—were the property of an attorney named Philip Anglin Scarlett, making it highly likely they knew each other and heightening the chances they might have been able to corroborate their testimonies if they had felt any pressure to do so to save themselves punishment.

To quietly take a beating for a cause—especially one they believed to have been sanctioned by God and the king of England—appeared to have been too much to swallow in those crucial days of transformation in late December. Multiple pressures—the lack of reliable communications, the differing agendas of the various slaves involved, the unexpected chain of trash house fires, and the clumsy and eventually bloodthirsty response of the militia—all combined to throw the movement into a much more confused state of ideology and an uncertainty over who was in charge. Sharpe was said to have told an acquaintance after the fact that he had not anticipated the fires burning out of control on the night of December 27. "When this occurred," he said, "I saw the scheme was defeated. I knew that the whites would slaughter us without mercy, and our freedom would be a long while put off." William Knibb was not present to witness any of it, but he testified later that he understood Sharpe's collaborators "had no desire to burn" but instead to "confine the white persons, but not to injure them, and not to let them go again till they were promised payment for their labor." Everything changed, said Knibb, when they "broke open the stores, and got drunk, and then they fired the property."[10]

Sharpe's loss of control may also be partly attributed to an early action by the militia to interrupt the lines of communication between Greenwich Hill and Black River, to the east. Near the settlement of Stracy on the coast road, near the spot where the doomed raiding party had been captured, the rebels took aim at and shot a private of the militia. His colleagues immediately returned fire, killed at least two slaves, and then fortified their positions, cutting off the route eastward to Sharpe's messengers. Whatever instructions Sharpe might have tried to deliver about keeping a nonviolent stance were lost after that point.[11]

The militia then tried a direct attack on Greenwich Hill with a combination of bombardment with a cannon followed by an infantry attack up the hill. The St. Elizabeth and Westmoreland Regiments, with the help of two sailors, dragged a six-pound gun into place and shot it up into the slave barricades. Then two columns started the dangerous march upward.

A few rebel snipers apparently fired warning shots above the heads of the approaching soldiers. Whatever their intent, they managed to hit only one militiaman, a captain, in the collarbone. The musket ball made an odd ricochet into his shoulder blade and he collapsed on the slopes with a debilitating but nonfatal wound. This was the only reported casualty of the attack, for which the militia was in an extremely vulnerable position. Militiamen eventually reached the stone and log walls at the top of Greenwich Hill and found, to their huge surprise, that nobody was there to fight them.[12]

The lack of any significant bloodshed or numbers of dead militiamen, by bullet or any other means, stands out most from the remaining written record, all collected by whites and some of which was extracted by torture. A slave named Adam gave jailhouse testimony to Rev. John McIntyre that supports the idea of a peaceful revolution slipping into actual violence by small degrees.

"The first thing proposed was only that they should refuse to work after Christmas, but afterwards 'the word was given out' that they must burn the buildings that white people might have no place to keep guard in, otherwise they would be compelled to work," Adam told Reverend McIntyre, who assured the authorities in his summary that these were nearly the words that Adam spoke. "Lastly it was determined that all the white people should be seized in the night and placed in the stocks, and the buildings to which they were confined set fire, because if they escaped they would only go to Montego Bay to join the regiment and return to fight them."[13]

If McIntyre's summary of Adam's thoughts is to be believed, it paints a picture of a nonviolent revolution in which the revolutionaries succumbed to fear for their own lives and faced rapidly diminishing choices. Jamaican slaves would have been well schooled in the expectation that surrendering slaves would be spared retribution or death.

Rumors spread of a man-of-war battleship that had docked in Montego Bay, and it was said that it contained black troops—perhaps from Haiti—who would take the side of the slaves. Even when it was revealed that the ship was actually HMS *Sparrowhawk*, which had carried Sir Willoughby Cotton and two companies of troops from Kingston, there was still "rejoicing," for Samuel Sharpe had convinced his followers that the British were secretly on the side of the slaves and would be aiding them in their struggle for freedom. "They said, 'never mind, all the people who come from England are our friends,'" recalled Adam.[14]

Whether it came directly from Sharpe or whether it had grown organically among the temporarily free slaves in those first euphoric days of late December 1831, the belief spread that all black Jamaicans were on the verge of founding their own independent nation. "The white people made bad laws for them," summarized McIntyre of Adam's testimony. "Then when they were free, the country would belong to themselves and . . . they could make laws for themselves. Others said that when the country was their own, they could serve God better than they could now because they cannot serve two masters."

The enslaved wanted liberty in the most mundane of ways: to live out their lives in Jamaica without fear. Samuel Cunningham, a Baptist deacon who was jailed early in the rebellion and sentenced to death, put it succinctly before he died: "Liberty is sweet."[15]

When asked about the ultimate object of the rebellion, Cunningham scoffed. "Thinks there is no occasion for anyone to ask that question," wrote his interrogator. "Thinks it is sufficiently shown by their destroying their master's property and houses and taking so much care of their own. What other object should they have than taking the country for themselves?"

The revolution had begun to sputter and fail by the third week of January, and the British Regulars were reduced to conducting a mop-up operation. Approximately 145 estate houses had been totally destroyed, and many dozens more had suffered partial damage. The band of destruction spanned seventy miles.[16]

On January 20 a team of Jamaican militiamen broke through slave-held territory near Kensington, where the first signal fire had been lit; it was a major psychological victory. "They succeeded in dislodging them with the loss of one man, Mr. Charles Whelan, killed," the *Watchman and Jamaica Free Press* reported in a terse dispatch, with no mention of how many rebels might have been killed on the spot. Sharpe himself remained at large, as did Dove and Gardiner.[17]

The British Army was now making full use of its traditional alliance with the Maroons—the descendants of freed and runaway Spanish slaves who had occupied the hill country since the middle of the seventeenth century and who had made a lasting peace with the Englishmen. Cotton ordered the militia in St. Elizabeth to join forces with the Accompong Maroons, with strict instructions not to cut off the ears of dead slaves in exchange for any anticipated bounty.

Dozens of prisoners had been hauled off to Montego Bay, where an improvised jail in the courthouse had become, said an observer, "so obnoxious from the noisome stench, arising from so many *unkempt* and filthy human beings, as likely to create pestilence" that a ship in the harbor was conscripted to act as a floating lockup until enough captured slaves could be put on a trial that might last for a half hour and then executed to make room for more. Some went to their graves based only on evidence that they were members of a Baptist church, and they seemed to accept their fate just as emptily and indifferently as they had walked out to the cane fields at dawn every day during peacetime. After execution, the bodies were usually then mounted into a metal cage called a gibbet and hoisted up for public display in the center of town.[18]

As Henry Bleby recounted,

> Generally four, seldom less than three, were hung at once. The bodies remained stiffening in the breeze, till the court-martial had provided another batch of victims for the hands of Bacchus, a brutal negro, who acted as executioner. . . . Other victims would then be brought out and suspended in their place and cut down in their turn to make room for more; the whole heap of bodies remaining just as they fell until the workhouse negroes came and took them away, to cast them in a pit dug for the purpose, a little distance out of town.[19]

An exceptionally small number of accused slaves were spared the hangman. A white woman, Mary Topping, accused a female slave named Venus of speaking the same terrifying language of freedom as all the rest of the slaves when the plantations began to burn two nights after Christmas. "She said she was not sorry at all; she only regretted she would lose her room, clothes and her husband," according to Topping's testimony. Others swore they saw a torch hidden in the kitchen, along with flammable materials like rags, tar, and pitch, which seemed to indicate Venus had planned to do some burning of her own when the time came. An already condemned slave named Camilla—one of the female conspirators—had also been seen creeping around Venus's house.[20]

But several others came forward with testimony that Venus could have had no physical access to the torch hidden in the kitchen. "The prisoner was acquitted," noted the *Watchman*, with no further comment. This was one of the few instances in preemancipation Jamaica

ISLAND ON FIRE

of an enslaved person escaping death because of testimony given by other slaves.

Sir Willoughby Cotton called for a formal "Council of War" in the capital, Spanish Town, on January 21, where members of the Jamaica Assembly voted unanimously to extend the state of martial law for another month. This would cost the plantocracy a small fortune in taxes. It also meant the militia was free to do as it pleased for a few more weeks. By this point, it was battle stressed, frightened, and impatient for everything to be finished. Some units had been marched up to thirty miles a day in the Jamaican damp, on top of cliffs and through swamps, always aware of their vulnerability to sudden ambush, provisioned on constant drafts of rum and servings of wild fruit, and wearing the same filthy clothes for weeks. When they had soup, they ate it with their hands. At night they slept on the ground inside plantation outbuildings and the abandoned huts of the slaves. "The only bed was the ground, their cartridge box their pillow," wrote the soldier Theodore Foulks.[21]

In the pages of the *Watchman and Jamaica Free Press,* editor Edward Jordon decried the dozens of unauthorized killings committed by "ignorant and irresponsible" people in the militia. "Every military underling considers himself armed with power because he wears a red or blue coat, to vent his spleen, or display his illegally assumed power." As a free person who might have resembled a slave, Jordon himself was particularly vulnerable during this period. He tried to argue on pragmatic grounds that enslaved people ought not to be executed, for the rebellion would end sooner if the combatants were not convinced of their own deaths when they lay down their weapons.[22]

"If terror alone be excited in the minds of the fugitives, it is hardly possible to expect their return," Jordon wrote. "They will rather perish in the woods than run the risk of being shot after having surrendered themselves."

In one of the rare cases when a militiaman faced a court-martial for committing a war crime, Lieutenant John Gunn was accused of ordering a cold-blooded murder near the town of Falmouth. On January 12 he had marched up to the incinerated remains of Lima Estate to find all the hoes rusty and covered with dew, indicating no fieldwork had been done in some time. Gunn gathered all the slaves together, read out a death sentence for a man seemingly chosen at random—a driver named John Allen—and then directed an underling to put a pistol to Allen's head and shoot him.

Unlike all the other arbitrary murders committed during the uprising, this happened before a wide audience of witnesses, which was doubtless why it was one of the only ones to be prosecuted. The crime was also committed barely one hour after all the slaves at Lima had been granted a pardon by Sir Willoughby Cotton himself, making it likely that the general had personally lobbied for the court-martial. Gunn had been formally turned in by his own commanding officer, F. B. Gibbs, who had heard the story from the slaves who watched it happen. The murder was blatant enough for an officer to tell him, "I must take notice of this, Mr. Gibbs, if you don't."[23]

Called to testify against himself, Gunn acknowledged, "I had to perform many acts which, however repugnant to my feelings, were imperatively necessary." He said he ordered Allen's death in that same spirit because "my knowledge of the negro character in general, and particularly of the man whose death has led to this prosecution, left me no alternative." He also complained that the prosecutor was a relative of the owner of Lima Estate and was trying the case only because of the loss of "property"—that is, the life of John Allen, worth approximately 150 British pounds on the open market.[24]

One of his defenders in the militia also made a novel argument: even if Allen was innocent, his murder in front of all his friends "did more good for the restoration of order than twenty would in town."[25] The judge advocate acquitted Gunn of the crime and restored him to duty, remarking, "I have much pleasure in returning you your sword."[26]

The anecdote is telling: in the one instance where a militiaman was accused of murder, the racial prejudices on which the entire island had been built were on display. The only conceivable reason someone was motivated to seek justice was because of the cash value of the dead slave.

The full extent of the murders will likely never be known, as only a select few cases rose to public attention through the courts and the newspapers. Even those seem to have been brought to trial because of political motivations: the egregious killings that happened with the knowledge of an officer who may have been under pressure from Willoughby Cotton or another influential figure to make a public display of attempted punishment of an errant militiaman. In the end, nobody was successfully prosecuted.

One of the only other cases to reach public view surfaced weeks after the violence was over, when Private Patrick Murphy was brought to a civilian trial for killing an elderly slave named Trim. Murphy's regiment had been marching past Kensington when his party stopped for a drink of rum, and then left Murphy behind for some reason. Apparently drunk, Murphy wandered down the road to the charred remains of Williamsfield Estate and stopped at the garden gate to ask directions of Trim, a "weak, sickly man" of about sixty years of age who had been hoeing in the garden. A gunshot rang out and the overseer on the property came running over to see Trim lying on the ground with blood pouring from his chest and Murphy standing over him.

"Why did you shoot him?" the overseer asked of Murphy.

"He was saucy to me and would not show me the road," replied the private.

Murphy first tried to deny that he had shot the slave. Then he changed his story, claiming the old man had tried to attack him with a clasp knife. Two enslaved witnesses came forward to contradict this; they said that Murphy had given Trim a hard shove and poked him with a bayonet just prior to shooting him in the chest. The novelty of the trial, however, was in the fact of their testimony; less than eight years earlier under Jamaican law, no slave could bring witness against a white defendant in a court.

Murphy's defense counsel explained that the private had been out on patrol in the battlefield for twenty-six days; that he was under orders to keep his firelock loaded at all times; that he had been sick and weary; that it was common for even harmless-looking slaves to grab rifles from the hands of soldiers; that Murphy was "a steady and quiet man" who had no history of quarreling; and that the shooting could have been a tragic mistake. The jury retired for a half hour and returned with a verdict of not guilty. The foreman explained that the jury believed the killing to have been "occasioned by accident."[27]

Shortly after the hostilities ceased, the assembly passed the Bill of Indemnity, making it impossible to prosecute any more members of the militia for what they might have done during the uprising. One of the only voices against it was that of Augustus Beaumont, who had boasted earlier that he considered helping the rebels overthrow a corrupt system. But since the start of the violence he had formed the private vigilante group he called the Cornwall Rangers, and he had personally chased down and shot a slave in the back. He worried that passing such a measure might be a sign to the public that the militia thought they had "something to fear from misconduct."

Beaumont, rising indignantly and reading a statement into the record, spoke to the contrary. According to the *Royal Gazette,* "On behalf of the Corps which he had lately had the honour to command, he begged to say, they required no such indemnity—They had nothing to fear."[28]

After the rebellion was quelled, there was no shortage of horror stories that told rumors of grotesque acts committed by slaves: rapes, hatchet murders, and the improvising of jails, hastily erected in the forest, for white women. The veracity of these stories, however, is best reflected in the relatively low death toll among whites—just four-teen presumed dead in five weeks of chaos. Ten were reported to have been militiamen who died of unknown causes during the time of active deployment, and one or two were plantation employees killed in house fires, leaving only two others that were murdered outright. But few details are known. A major general named Pearce wandered away from his men in the Hanover Regiment and was hacked to death by a roving band of rebels and left to die on the road, and a man named Holmes was shot in the presence of his wife. Their names were reported before the Jamaica Assembly on April 5, 1832, with the curious statement, "Mrs. Holmes and Mrs. Pearce were the only persons whose husbands were murdered in the rebellion." Given the prevalence of bachelors in Jamaica, it may not be surprising that only two of the victims were married. But no complete list of vic-tims was made public, the circumstances of the deaths were not de-scribed in detail, and not one of the dead was specifically elevated as a martyr by the Jamaican partisan press.[29]

This noteworthy lack of documentation, even in the midst of kinetic events, suggests that even the low number of fourteen deaths may have been an exaggeration. Nearly two centuries later the con-spicuous lack of white bloodshed stands as powerful evidence of mercy among the enslaved people in a time of violence when they might have been free to do anything, as well as the persistence of the nonviolent ideology that many clung to, even as the centralized re-bellion broke into regional pockets. As Hope Masterton Waddell later reported, there were multiple instances in which enslaved people woke up their masters in the middle of the night and urged them to leave before any fires were set: "Had the masters, when they got the upper hand, had been as tender of their slaves' lives, as their slaves had been of theirs, it would have been to their lasting honor."[30]

The essentially nonlethal character of the revolt made an imme-diate impression on both sides of the Atlantic—an effect that may have been specifically intended by Sharpe and the rest of the rebels.

"Had the negroes been such savage and blood-thirsty beings as they were represented, hundreds of their white oppressors would have been sacrificed to their revenge," concluded Henry Bleby. Most of the rebel command was comprised of ardent Baptists who would not have easily countenanced acts of murder or sexual violence in their ranks. Indeed, in keeping with men and women hopeful of continuing employment, the most economically crucial property was also largely respected. The majority of the fires were confined to the trash houses—the least valuable property on the estate and the most easily replaceable.[31]

As January turned into February, what remained of the revolutionary force holed themselves up in caves, increasingly worried and uncertain. The news of Willoughby's offer of pardon for the repentant had spread widely, and it would have been impossible for any slave not connected to even the most rudimentary social networks to not have heard of it. The agonizing decision to give up would have been complicated by the knowledge of the wanton murders committed by the militias. There might have also been some doubt about the veracity of Cotton's offer, particularly for those who had not directly heard it for themselves. The pardon explicitly did not apply to those adjudged to be ringleaders, and it seems that such a definition could be applied loosely and without any evidence.

A repentant slave also had to be sure to surrender to British Regular troops, because the Jamaican militias were known to welsh on the promise of pardon and assemble a hasty firing squad. For these renegade units, said Henry Bleby, the promise of pardon "was used only as a snare to betray the unsuspecting and deluded negroes to an ignominious death."[32]

A failure to deliver an ironclad alibi of where one had been during the trouble was enough to ensure an immediate execution, even if a slave had been loyal all along. An enslaved man named Bailey had taken the enormous risk of hiding his owner's silver dinnerware and other valuable goods inside a cave so the insurgents would not loot

them. After the trouble had passed, he was busy returning the silverware to the house when a militia headed by a local butcher ("an ap-
propriate profession," Bleby noted) captured him in what looked like
a compromising position. None of his explanations were believed,
and he was quickly hanged from a branch in front of the cave. Minutes
later, other slaves informed the butcher of Bailey's innocence. The
story likely would have remained covered up had it not been revealed
in an unrelated legal proceeding several months later.[33]

Another such case happened at Great Valley Estate, where a slave
approached an officer and said he wanted to go back to work. The
officer, who appeared to be a "humane and benevolent" man, said in
a lightly mocking tone, "Oh, go along with you! I suppose you are as
bad as the rest."

The returning slave began to walk slowly out of the mill yard, but
before he got to the gate, a sergeant of the militia leveled his musket
and shot the man in the back without a word. Nobody in the militia
spoke of it afterward, but the slaves heard all about it and showed a
visitor the poor man's grave a few days later.[34]

What could be trusted in these times? Not three weeks earlier the
slaves had been told they had been made free by the king of England
and that all that stood between them and a new life was a matter of
bureaucracy. They had recently been convinced to take radical and
dangerous action based on rumors of official proclamations from the
British, and this had led to grief. They had seen a movement of nonviolent resistance based on the teachings of Jesus turned into chaos
and death.

Many had sincerely believed that British troops would have taken
their side against the hated slave-owning militia, and there were even
some spontaneous celebrations when HMS *Blanche* and HMS *Sparrowhawk* sailed into the harbor at Montego Bay carrying squadrons
of professional British troops as well as heavy artillery, a sight most
enslaved people had never seen before.

"We all believed this freedom business from what we were told and from what we heard in the newspapers—that the people in England were speaking up very bold for us," an enslaved man named Linton said from his jail cell, not without some pathos. "We all thought the King was upon our side. Gardiner constantly kept telling us that he and the other head people had been told that the King had given orders to his soldiers here not to fight against us, and that he was sending out powder and arms, and that the governor was going to go away and leave the country to us."[35]

The decision of surrender amounted to a terrible test of loyalty. To whom would they pledge their fates? To the charismatic preacher Samuel Sharpe and his promises of imminent freedom, which had led them to frantic weeks of hunger, thirst, night chills, and gunfire in the wilderness? Or to their masters back home, to whom their lives had been bound for as long as they had lived, where the work was unceasing but at least promised a bit of food, shelter, and stability?

The question also had an ominous spiritual dimension. To which God would they submit? There was the God proclaimed by the Baptists, who said they could no longer serve two masters, and that freedom was a birthright. And then there was the God of the Church of England, who commanded them to obey their masters and serve in thankfulness and humility.

A number of slaves, whether through remorse or the pragmatic demands of survival, professed renewed love for those who had been oppressing them and hatred for those who had induced them to gamble on freedom. A driver named George Gordon told the authorities he wished he could take revenge on Samuel Sharpe and Thomas Burchell for what they had done. "If I could live," he said, "I would defend my master and his property as sincerely as I have done for years, but I was led by the parsons to believe I was free."[36]

Even some of those facing certain death claimed to love those who were oppressing them. Branded as "one of the worst of the rebels" by the *Royal Gazette* and sentenced to hang, a slave named Captain Dehany was said to have begged for a biscuit so that he would not die hungry. When one was given to him, a black executioner tried to take it away, but was rebuked by a white deputy marshal. After Dehany ate the biscuit, he said "God bless white people, for them that have more sense then we negroes." He then stood up and said, "Thank you, gentlemen. I am now ready to die, which I will do like a man."[37]

The clergyman Henry Bleby, who was also present for this event, told a slightly different story about the death of "a man whose bravery and daring during the revolt had acquired for him considerable notoriety." He did not mention the pathetic request for a biscuit, and spelled the slave's name slightly differently from how the newspapers did, but did note that "Dehaney" was anxious not to let anyone conclude that he had confessed anything that would implicate the white missionaries in the revolt. "If I am guilty and deserve to die, let me die; but I won't go before God with a lie in my mouth," Bleby claimed the man was heard to say, suggesting the possibility that his final legal statement had been extracted through misleading questions or even torture.

After this statement, the man's composure was solid. As Bleby noted, "While the executioner made his revolting preparations to complete the tragedy, the cloud passed from Dehaney's brow as he calmly looked down upon the heap of dead beneath his feet; but still his eye quailed not, and his cheek remained unblanched." The man was heard to be murmuring prayers and citing the name of Jesus, even as the rope broke and his executioner had to string him up again and then roughly push him from the platform toward the dangling remains of other executed victims.

"It was sickening to behold the poor fellow's convulsive struggles, and the manner in which the suspended bodies nearest to him were elbowed and pushed about in his dying agonies," reported Bleby. This made some onlookers guffaw with laughter, which disgusted William

Knibb. He didn't go near the gallows; the flagstones underneath were slick with blood from those who had been flogged.[38]

Dehany had earlier testified that it was the intention of the slave army to burn the sugar estates from the middle of the country out toward the seashore and its towns. The white people in those areas would be lucky to escape by getting on board a ship in the harbor. But this threat had not truly existed since December 31 after the confused retreat of McLenan's army.

A basic reality awaited those who surrendered and were not shot: the dismal existence of a slave, with all of its pain, indignity, physical punishment, and humiliation. For a brief while—though they were hunted—they had had a taste of self-government and freedom. Giving up had to have been indescribably bitter.

Lord Belmore traveled on HMS *North Star* up to the worst areas of destruction at the beginning of February. He spoke to groups of assembled slaves to "inform them of the impossibility of acquiring liberation by the horrid means they have resorted to and the necessity of returning to their peaceful occupations." For nearly all of them, this was their first and last look at the highest representative of the British government on the island.[39]

As a gesture of peace, Belmore lifted martial law on February 5, 1832, and sent the British soldiers home to Kingston. Further resistance to the laws by the enslaved people would only frustrate the "humane intentions of the government to improve their condition," he said, offering no further details. After seeing the wreckage of the north shore, his communiqués to London took a less optimistic tone than his public words, and he professed dismay at the rapid pace of executions—both lynchings in the woods and those under the pretense of law. An open pit dug just outside the city of Montego Bay had been filled with corpses of those who had been hanged in the marketplace behind the courthouse. Most of them had been put there by the enormous enslaved man named Bacchus, who had been told he would be hanged himself if he didn't assist in the legalized killing. He did his job with casual efficiency, often hanging a group of enslaved people, pausing to eat his dinner while they asphyxiated, and then using his dinner knife to sever the ropes and let them drop into a pile under the gallows.[40]

When the newspapers mentioned those who were hanged, a favorite phrase was to say that the condemned person was "launched into eternity." Executions became so common in Albert Market that people stopped noticing them, and "the buying and selling, the chaffering and talking went on without interruption even as lads were led out, as they prayed, as they choked and struggled in the wind." Nevertheless, many onlookers noticed something disconcerting: the slaves often faced their sentences with a serenity that bordered on total disregard. A Royal Navy captain found that "men did not mind being shot" and did not alter their voices or faces in their last minutes. A friend of Hope Waddell reported seeing at least a dozen men "who had staked all on one great throw for freedom, lost it, and submitted to the dreadful consequences with dignity." As their wagon drew close to the gallows, they did not cry but calmly sang hymns. And when they had nooses around their necks, they behaved "with a fortitude and cool deliberation that astonished all who beheld them."[41]

At the *Watchman and Jamaica Free Press,* Jordon worried of the "dreadful ravages of this insurrection, and the evils it is likely to produce." By this he meant not the partial loss of the sugar crop or the financial burden created by the execution of hundreds of slaves or even the fiery loss of so many plantation buildings. Most free men were aware that if a deacon like Samuel Sharpe could quietly spread a gospel of liberty, such a catastrophe could easily happen again—and probably would. A certain myth of invincibility had been shattered. For more than a week around the turn of the New Year of 1832, every slave on the north shore had seen the routing of the plantocracy, the master's luxurious houses aflame, and the temporary helplessness of the militia. Only the superior firepower and discipline of the King's Regulars—and the extraordinary measures of martial law—had been sufficient to subdue them. The damage was likely permanent. The usually phlegmatic *Royal Gazette* lamented, "To renew the superstructure which has now fallen to the ground, to restore the broken confidence between master and slave, no legislative enactment can be of avail."[42]

Those enslaved people who went back to work seemed to have a changed mood about them, which disquieted the editor of the *Cornwall Courier*. Taking note of their feelings in a rare moment of empathy, he wrote, "There appears in the conduct and the character of the negroes at present a mixture of shame, disappointment and dogged sullenness. They seem to labor attentively, but not cheerfully—it is not from the heart. There is a strong measure of that depression in their countenances that seems to arise from 'hope deferred.'"[43]

The center of the disturbance—St. James Parish—was completely quiet. Almost all the rebellious slaves had calculated that their chances of living to see another day were better if they gambled on their master's restraint, though they must have known that nothing could ever be the same again. The commanders of the King's Regulars concluded that there were at most four hundred slaves still at large, and these were mostly confined to Hanover Parish on the far northwestern part of the island. It was at some point during this twilight period of the rebellion that Samuel Sharpe either gave himself up or was betrayed by one of his confidants. Bernard Senior's account is frustratingly vague, mentioning only that the top leaders of the rebellion, including Sharpe, "were captured or compelled to surrender" after avoiding several close calls.[44]

Writing twenty-four years after the fact, in flowery language and with information borrowed from local legend, the Baptist minister P. H. Cornford described Sharpe's surrender in more heroic terms: as a sacrifice to prevent blame from being heaped on the white missionaries. Having spent most of the revolt as a tempering influence, Sharpe "walk[ed] the winding ways to Montego Bay" by himself at night, where he tapped on the window of his brother William's cottage to give himself up to his former master, while ignoring pleas from his family to stay in hiding. Only in his jail cell did he find "the sweet calm of heaven, the smile of God, the dear consciousness of right." There are several problems with this lachrymose account, including the lack of evidence in British documents that Sharpe had a brother named William, but it is still more detailed than anything else that exists. By the middle of February it must have been clear to every rebel that the cause had been lost.[45]

Evidence of the failure lay all around. Where the fighting had been intense, the corpses of the fallen lay scattered in the indifferent sunshine. An outraged Henry Bleby reported one revolting scene on a mountain road which had been littered with bodies and blackened with hundreds of feeding carrion crows: "The stench was distinctly perceptible at the distance of a quarter of a mile, and when we came near the spot, was almost overpowering. There lay one body, the head of which was completely stripped of flesh by the crows; and the bare scull, still attached to the partly-clothed body seemed to grin at us as we passed over it."[46]

The expense was staggering, and some wondered if the economy could ever recover. The records of the Jamaica Assembly showed that 207 plantations had suffered either partial damage or total destruction, and the *Jamaica Courant* made sure that everyone knew the extent of the property damage by publishing a list of the torched estates on its front page. That was only the beginning. When added to the cost of raising the militia, the loss of slain and executed slaves, the lost sugar crops, and the robbed possessions, the five weeks of mutiny would cost the island 1,154,589 British pounds.[47]

The death toll among black Jamaicans was far harder to calculate because of the chaotic nature of combat, as well as the many authorized murders the militia was naturally reluctant to report. Approximately two hundred were said to have died in battle, and another 340 were recorded as having been executed for various crimes. Among those convicted were seventy-five women, suggesting that they had played a significant role in the planning and fighting. The death toll almost certainly represents an undercount of both men and women, as the militia made no record of its randomized killings.[48]

An additional 160 were sentenced to a military-style flogging with anywhere from fifty to five hundred lashes, with the helpless enslaved person pinned to the foot of the gallows—perhaps in a demonstration of the fate they had narrowly escaped and of the "mercy" they were receiving at the end of the whip. The severity of the beating was sometimes fatal in itself, as five hundred lashes with a cat-o'-nine-tails amounted to 4,500 stripes across a back that would be left resembling nothing so much as a bleeding sponge. Most of the victims were left unconscious in the marketplace; those who survived could eventually crawl and scrabble across the paving stones to a place of shelter.[49]

The spontaneous shootings and hangings slowed down in February, even as one vengeful member of the assembly wished out loud that martial law could have been extended ten days longer so that "gaols may have been swept of all their prisoners!" and as Richard Barrett awarded Sir Willoughby Cotton with a proclamation thanking him for "the humanity which has extinguished this rebellion with the smallest effusion of blood." In Montego Bay there were only fourteen executions in the first week of February, including that of a woman, Ann Bernard, who was convicted of setting fire to an unspecified part of her master's estate. The editor of the *Cornwall Chronicle* called for the execution of at least one slave chosen from every single planation—regardless of the victim's guilt or innocence—to serve as "a powerful lesson" in the value of servility. He predicted the randomized killings would have "a most salutary effect" upon the public peace.[50]

But the rapid and indiscriminate pace of the executions troubled Lord Belmore, who confessed "serious alarm" in a memorandum to London. Backing him up was the elite planter Richard Barrett, who had first been calling for rebels to be hanged during the outbreak of violence and now seemed to be softening his position in the midst of so much death. He counseled Belmore to adopt more "humane and lenient measures" at the close of martial law. Those directives were not widely followed.[51]

The drumhead courts-martial in the field had been replaced by "slave courts" which took their legitimacy from a confusing blend of military and civil statues known as party law. That meant trial by a jury, but one composed entirely of white Jamaican planters, overseers, and bookkeepers who had spent the last five weeks slogging through the forests after having seen their livelihoods destroyed. Almost nobody was acquitted in these kangaroo proceedings. Henry Bleby watched the trial of a man named Robert Carr where "two or three leading questions" were put to a man and a young boy to extract the desired answer that Carr had been seen among the rebels. This took no more than ten minutes. The judge was "an ignorant, brutal old man who had formerly been an extensive slave-dealer and importer and grown rich and callous by trading in the stolen Africans."

"Robert Carr," the judge intoned, "you have been found guilty of one of the worst crimes that can be. The sentence upon you is that you be taken tomorrow morning to Plump Pen and hanged by the neck until you are dead. You sabbie dat?" This last was Jamaican patois for "Do you understand me?"

Somebody had to whisper this sentence into a stunned Carr's ear: that he was to be hanged at his home estate in front of his friends and family between the hours of eleven and two.[52]

Another such example was made of Nicholas Doman, a driver who had reportedly shot a fellow slave who tried to stop him from burning down houses. Doman was hanged on the grounds of his own estate of Roehampton on February 14. Every slave on the property—most of whom had known him his whole life—was ordered to stop work to come watch the execution.

Doman said goodbye to all his friends, as well as his three children and wife, who were watching his last moments. "After you are dead, we will hear from you," his wife called, and he nodded assent before going to his death "with great self-possession," according to a witness. After his neck was broken on the rope, he was decapitated and his head was mounted on a lightning rod over the boiling house as an example for others.[53]

In early February an extraordinary conversation took place between one of the top leaders of the rebellion and a militia officer who had been ordered to capture him.

Captain McNeil of the Westmoreland Regiment had been camping in a secluded spot in the woods, mainly because it looked like a choice spot for the rebels to build another fortress. An enslaved woman who had been employed to do their cooking went to a nearby spring at dawn to fetch a bucket of water when a strange woman came out of the woods and identified herself as the wife of the rebel chief Robert Gardiner—second only to Samuel Sharpe in the rebel hierarchy.

She had an intriguing message from her husband:

> Tell Mr. McNeil that he need not be afraid of me, as I am so tired of my present mode of life that if he will come unarmed and unattended to the wall that skirts the deep wood by the roadside this morning at midday, about halfway between his station and this spring, and walk twenty yards straight into the wood, by a pass that is cut there for the purpose, I will be ready to deliver myself up to him, and in return, I shall only require him to make terms for my life.

McNeil was incredulous at Gardiner's claim that he would walk into the woods alone, without a gun, but he didn't want to pass up the opportunity to arrest such a high-ranking leader. So the next day he put on a sword, strapped a pistol to his waist, and went down to the appointed spot where he found a musket broken in two. This was likely Gardiner's way of signaling that he wanted peace. McNeil decided to honor the terms of the agreement and laid his own weapons on a stone wall. Then he walked back into the woods conspicuously unarmed, but nobody appeared.

A few days later, a cattleman came by the militia camp and made the same offer as the woman: Gardiner was willing to surrender if McNeil would come into the woods unarmed.

The suspicious captain told six of his men to pack two pistols each under their coats, to carry heavy sticks, and to follow him down to the path through the trees that Gardiner had described. McNeil motioned for his six henchmen to crouch at the base of the stone wall, where they wouldn't be seen. Then he walked into the woods and, true to his word this time, there stood the notorious Gardiner under a tree.

The following exchange was McNeil's recollected version of it as first published in the *Cornwall Courier* seven days later, as well as additional dialogue related by Bernard Senior. Though the occurrence of the conversation is unquestioned, the substance of the account may be doubtful, as it contains incriminating statements that Gardiner was unlikely to have made against himself while he was still technically free.

"Well, master McNeil," said Gardiner, "Now you come by yourself and without arms. I meet you according to my promise."

"Then I suppose you are the Gardiner who the rebels call their colonel?"

"I am," said Gardiner. "But I find they are a parcel of cowards and have no good spirit in them so it is no use to keep out any longer. Had they been all of my mind, and acted with me, as it was first agreed upon, there would neither have been a buckra-man living or buckra-house standing by this time in the island."

"Indeed, you talk very high," said the captain, "but you see that it was not so easily accomplished as you expected."

"No matter for that," replied the slave. "Remember you command only a small company. I command an immense army and by a single command could, at this moment, destroy you and your whole party, but I wish to shed no more blood; and having passed my word for your safety, not a hair of your head shall be injured."

"Well, Gardiner, on that point I'm satisfied but tell me the truth on another. In case of your having performed all you have told me were your intentions, what was to become of the white women?"

"Oh, Mr. McNeil, you need not ask that question for you know quite well that we should have taken them for our own wives. But that is nothing now. I'm wanting to know if you will promise myself and another our pardon if we will give ourselves up to you as officer of the party because governor's proclamation say so."

McNeil's account is to be viewed with suspicion because it would have been clear suicide for a slave to have bragged of ambitions to kill all the white men of Jamaica and have sex with their wives before surrendering and hoping to get away with his life. In his telling of the event, McNeil said he could not guarantee a pardon, only safe passage to the Earl of Belmore for a hearing.

Who was the other person who wanted to surrender, McNeil wanted to know.

"He is not far off. Dove is his name. Do you wish to see him?"

This was the third-ranking insurgent in the rebellion, and so McNeil answered, "Yes, certainly. But I tell you at once, if he is the Captain Dove named in the governor's first proclamation, he is in the same situation with respect to pardon as yourself, and I am sorry to say, I could only do for him what I am willing to do for you. At any rate, let me see him."

Gardiner looked upward toward the far reaches of the tree where Dove had been hiding the whole time. "See him there!" he pointed. "Dove, come down."

The other rebel leader jumped down from the branches with "great agility" and offered himself up for surrender.

Gardiner told his captor, "Yesterday, you made a narrow escape by coming armed, but you have acted wisely today in coming unarmed."[54]

The two slaves then linked their arms with Captain McNeil in a friendly fashion and walked together through the woods and down the hill, to the unease of the militia detachment hiding at the wall. When they reached the camp, Robert Gardiner and Thomas Dove formally surrendered, were taken to the jail at Savannah-la-Mar, thirty-two miles away, and began waiting for their hoped-for pardon from Lord Belmore.

On the road there, Gardiner talked cheerfully about the doctrine of salvation with a planter named Anthony Whitelock. He believed himself to have a kind of immunity. "When converted they believe, whatever their crimes, that they will be saved—a doctrine quite incompatible with slavery," Whitelock testified later.[55]

Before he went to his death, Robert Gardiner lamented that the non-violent principles of the rebellion had clashed with the plans for revenge held by others and that the movement was morally conflicted from the start.

He said the planning for the movement began at a secret meeting of the educated slave elite in December when Samuel Sharpe had stood up to make a speech: "The thing is now determined upon, no time is to be lost. The king of England and the Parliament have given Jamaica freedom and as it is being held back by the whites, we must take it."

Likely moved by Sharpe's powerful oratory and seeing others moved as well, Gardiner said the talk "roused" him and made him "nearly mad." He told Sharpe to stop the discussion of revolt, which made the leader angry. "What is to become of all the men I have sworn, then?" Sharpe asked. "They might as well obey me, as to die from not doing so."[56]

The slave George Guthrie took Gardiner aside and invited him and a few others to a three o'clock lunch in his quarters in Montego Bay. Wine was poured, and Guthrie made a toast which called out the hated colonel William "Little Breeches" Grignon. "In a few days may we get our rights and may 'Little Breeches' and the other gentlemen who oppose us lay under our feet."

Gardiner said he refused to drink this toast, and that others laughed at him for his reluctance. But then George Taylor insisted to the group, "Let us not spill a drop of blood. If we do, it will bring a prosecution upon our church."[57]

Testimony from Thomas Dove backs up Gardiner's insistence that he envisioned the revolt to be a peaceful one. Dove said a slave at this dinner named John Tharp had showed off a gun, which he said he got from a white man at Lethe who had also promised to show him how to make ball cartridges from lead ore.

"Tharp, if you have, you have done a very bad thing," Gardiner allegedly told him.

A few days before Christmas, Gardiner was sent over from his home at Greenwich to a neighboring estate to pick up a large quantity of rum for the slaves to drink on the holiday. He didn't hear anything more about the planned work stoppage until December 26, when a "multitude" of slaves came to see him. They had been sent over by Samuel Sharpe himself, they said, and were now under Gardiner's command. He said he slipped out the back door and tried to dodge this responsibility, but eventually gave in and led the slaves over to a planned rendezvous at the town of Hazleymph, where an even larger army under Sharpe's command came "wild, furious, blowing shells, and making a very great shouting."[58]

They all tried to burn the trash house at the plantation, but the wet sugar leaves would not catch fire. A second group marched over to Belvidere, where they successfully got the place burning. "Different regiments were then dispatched to different places, and the work began everywhere," Gardiner said. "I declare, however, that I entreated them to burn no place." He also insisted, "I particularly ordered the negroes to take no man's life."[59]

He said he advocated for a peaceful approach, even after the burning had started. The best way to do this, he said, would be to find a "respectable gentleman" traveling by on the road and ask if it was really true that King William IV had issued a freedom paper. If the report were denied, the slaves should return to the fields. If it was judged to be true, however, the slaves ought to "of course, do no work."

"We heard so much from newspapers and people talking that that we did not know what to believe or do," said Gardiner. "The negroes, however, would not take my advice, but said if they went into the road as I had told them, the white people would come and slaughter them."

After the militia surprised their brigade at Cow Park Estate, Gardiner said his men scattered into the hills and left their stash of arms behind. "From that time, we never rallied," he said, adding, "I saw therefore that it was useless to remain out any longer. I would have come in then but I was afraid to do so."[60]

The man to whom Gardiner gave this confession, Rev. Thomas Stewart, was a vicar of the established church, a defender of the existing order. How much of Gardiner's official confession may have been Stewart's ventriloquism is uncertain. It is also likely that Gardiner's denial of culpability in the military aspect of the rebellion—so at odds with his reported bravado during his surrender—was made under the duress of an impending execution. The document, for example, included praise for the "kind" treatment given to him by white people as they prepared to hang him, as well as an exclamation of regret: "Oh sir, if I had had any good friend to tell me the real truth as I now find it to be, I never would have been brought to this."

But Gardiner seemed anything but repentant to Bernard Senior. Instead he showed pride in the discipline that his untrained army had achieved in so short a time. His attitude, even in defeat, was not of a captured terrorist but of a decorated general who had put up a good fight against the army of a rival nation. As Senior noted, "He spoke even magnanimously of some encounters he had sustained with the whites, lauding, in the highest terms the valor of his own troops on those particular occasions and boasting of the havoc they had committed among the military in two or three instances." In these first engagements—particularly the winning battle at Montpelier—Gardiner's assessment was entirely correct, and Senior seems to have recognized this and given due credit to his foe.[61]

A few weeks after his capture and confession, Gardiner was brought to trial and the evidence was read against him. In an attempt to prove himself a good worker and a trustworthy man, he took off his shirt and showed the judge the unbroken skin on his back, proving that he had never been whipped by his master. But it made no difference: Lord Belmore's pardon did not materialize. For unknown reasons, Dove's own sentence was relatively lenient for the day: a life spent in a prison cell back in England.[62]

Gardiner was executed the same day as his trial. His severed head was mounted, according to Senior, "in the most conspicuous part of the rebellious district" for his onetime followers to see.[63]

Whenever Jamaica's governor thought a certain document was so important that his bosses in London should see it, he attached it to his regular dispatches sent via cargo ships, usually in special pouches kept in the captains' quarters. Lord Belmore apparently felt this way about a handwritten transcript dated April 19, 1832, and titled "The King against Samuel Sharpe," which became a permanent part of the Colonial Office records for that year.[64]

A total of eleven men testified against the prisoner Samuel Sharpe in the limestone courthouse in Montego Bay.[65] A clerk recorded their statements in a staccato patter heavy with dashes. The witness of Edward Hilton, for example, read, "Sharpe had a short gun—saw him come up—he put the others before and he was behind—he commanded them and they did as he told them—they called him schoolmaster."[66]

Five enslaved men testified that they had seen him carrying weapons at various points, and two put him directly at the scene of the murder of a white man. One of the witnesses, Edward Barrett, had himself been spotted carrying a gun during the violence, which would have meant a certain death sentence. His testimony against Sharpe may therefore have been coerced with his life hanging in the balance, and the testimony of all the others also has the flavor of coaching and collusion. Five of the witnesses belonged to a single master. Only two witnesses were called for the "evidence called in defense" and they offered nothing exculpatory—only that they had seen Samuel Sharpe at Ginger Hill Estate during the revolt, but that they saw him swear no oaths. Sharpe himself was not allowed to testify, and the entire proceedings appear to have taken less than two hours. Even so, this was the longest trial of any rebel ever recorded, and the one for which the authorities provided the most documentation.[67]

The jurors signed his death warrant that same afternoon:

> Tried and found guilty the nineteenth day of April 1832. Sentence: That the said Negro man slave named Samuel Sharpe be taken hence from the place from whence he came and from thence to the place of Execution at such time and place as shall be appointed by His Excellency the Governor and there to be hanged by the neck until dead—Valued by the jury at the sum of sixteen pounds ten shillings current money of Jamaica.

They kept Sharpe in a cell on the town square for the next month, and he had several visits with sympathetic missionaries. Perhaps still mindful of his ecclesiastic charge to stay out of politics, and probably fearing for his own safety, William Knibb kept Sharpe at arm's length during a brief jailhouse interview, asking him only to provide a statement that the white missionaries had not directly helped his revolt. Rev. Henry Bleby was more charitable, paying him multiple visits. Sharpe told him he was sorry that the sugar estates had been burned and that so many people had been killed. His only goal had been to make people free, he said, and what had been a peaceful movement had spun out of control. But he remained defiant to the end about the idealism of his cause, if not the means.[68]

"I would rather die upon yonder gallows than live in slavery!" he said. Bleby reported that Sharpe's frame expanded, his spine stiffened, and his eyes seemed to "shoot forth rays of light" when he said this. Sharpe had always been a capable speaker—it was one of the reasons he had been singled out for the ministry—and this was one of the last displays of his ability to mesmerize, even in the defense of a lost cause.[69]

In Bleby's view, Sharpe had been a leader of a nonviolent resistance that went awry because of causes outside his control. He knew "very well how matters stood both in England and the colony" and that freedom was still a matter of lengthy debate within Parliament and that it would not arrive quickly with a single proclamation from the king. His story to the rest of the slaves was an exaggeration of more complicated events. But he never sought to foment violence in the name of his cause; only to make a gaudy demonstration that might help further the crucial matter of liberty. "He did not wish to destroy the estates," Bleby later wrote, "nor did he desire that any person should be injured: his only object was to obtain freedom. But to his great disappointment he found that the spirit of revolt, once evoked, was not susceptible to control."

Such subtleties meant nothing to the white planters, some of whom compared Sharpe to the American preacher-soldier Nat Turner, whose own uprising had failed the previous summer. The *Jamaica Courant* made a local connection under the headline "The Late Insurrection in Virginia":

> From the confession of the ringleader in this insurrection, it is a remarkable coincidence that the instigator of the diabolical outrages which took place was, as was the case here, a great man among the Baptists! This wretch, who was apprehended after the whole of his gang had been secured, was executed, as we hope the leader of the present disturbances of this island will be.[70]

On the day of his hanging, May 23, 1832, Sharpe was led out to Albert Market at 12:15 P.M. A high wooden platform with dangling noose stood at the center; this was the semipermanent structure that had been erected for the dispatch of unruly enslaved people, and hundreds had died there during the rebellion. A guard of the Eighth Regiment tried to hustle him along, but Sharpe, with his hands tied in back of him, asked the guards to proceed at a slower gait so as not to humiliate him. They acquiesced, and he was permitted to walk toward his death with a "firm and even dignified step," a witness reported.

"I saw him come with his face as bright, his form as erect as if he had achieved a glorious victory," said another observer. "His calm and peaceful eye singled out his old friends and acquaintances as he passed along. To many of them, he bowed his recognition."[71]

Public executions had become a routine occurrence in Albert Market, but this one excited special interest. The correspondent from the *Watchman and Jamaica Free Press* saw "persons of all classes" crowding the walkway from the jail to the gallows for a look at Daddy Sharpe, the instigator of the uprising: "It seemed as though some important matter would be developed at the death of this aspiring man, and all were anxious to observe the last tremulous tread of the foot and the convulsive quiver of the lip." But whether through genuine peace of mind or an effort of acting, Sharpe's manner was calm.[72]

He was wearing a new suit of sparkling white clothes recently sewn for him by the family who had owned him. The women of Cooper's Hill estate been fond of him, and—to the apparent disgust of their neighbors—were among his mourners, although discreetly. They watched from the windows of a nearby townhouse, and he paused and bowed before them. The skeptical *Watchman* correspondent thought the suit lent him "that simplicity and neatness which give interest to the appearance of a corpse." Before Sharpe climbed the steps of the gallows, he was asked—as was the custom—if he wanted to make a last confession to an attending minister from the Church of England.[73]

After a glass of water mixed with a dash of alcohol was lifted to his lips, he admitted in the presence of Reverend McIntyre that he had broken laws and betrayed the king of England, as well as his owner, a lawyer also named Samuel Sharpe. "I have been disobedient to my master, who was nearer to me than I have been to him. But my mind was slippery and I was misled. I hope the younger branches of my family will make an atonement to him for my guilty conduct, and my offenses will not be visited on any of my fellow-creatures." He then looked up curiously and hesitatingly at the gallows, as if "measuring the strength of the awful structure."[74]

His captors then allowed him to pray, which he did, kneeling at the base of the wooden scaffolding he had just contemplated. His new white pants apparently slipped as he stood up and he asked the executioner to tighten the band on them lest they fall off and embarrass him when he dropped through the gallows trapdoor.

Before the anonymous executioner drew a hood over Sharpe's face, he was permitted to make a last statement, and he obliged with a few words that were as much a sermon as a dying declaration. "I have transgressed against the laws of the country and the government, and with great violation, and I am come to be a sacrifice to it, but I will soon appear before a Judge that is greater than all. I don't know that I am prepared to face my God, but I depend for salvation upon the Redeemer, who shed his blood upon Calvary for sinners." Sharpe insisted that the white Baptist ministers accused of persuading him to incite the insurrection for political reasons had done nothing wrong, and he directed a charge to them: "Let me beg to you my brethren to attend to your Christian duties, for it is the only way for you to go to salvation. I hope what I am saying does not give offense to any gentleman present. I am not speaking in boasting, but in humble boldness." As he spoke, reported the writer from the *Watchman,* his face was animated with energy and "his large expressive eyes were continually in motion."

Then a cryptic final phrase: "I now bid you all farewell. That is all I have to say." Within a few more moments, shortly after the noon hour, Sharpe's neck was snapped on the rope.

Henry Bleby said he felt like weeping that such a man with a brilliant mind "should thus be immolated at the polluted shrine of slavery." One of the brief, warm afternoon rain showers that pass over Montego Bay during the early summer months began to come down, chasing every spectator from the square.[75]

TEN

PANIC

WITH THE SLAVE REBELLION QUELLED and the northwestern shore of Jamaica in ruins, the rage of the planter class found a new target: the Protestant missionaries who had come to the island preaching a message of individual hope instead of obedience to slave masters.

Many of the dead rebels had been carrying tickets of passage to Baptist churches, and this was twisted into "evidence" that the rebellion had really been planned by white schemers who lurked in the shadows. The planters could not quite comprehend how the enslaved people, mainly illiterate and so seemingly obedient, were able to lay out a coordinated conspiracy and mount such an effective five-week attack without at least some help from white people.

"Jamaica had never before been visited by a rebellion of equal extent or organization," worried the militiaman Theodore Foulks. "The almost simultaneous movements in the disturbed districts, the uniformity of the plan, the degree of military science displayed, the possession of arms and ammunition, and the universal declaration that freedom had been granted by the King, all tend to prove, that the germ of this insurrection was not indigenous, but must have been imported from some other part of the world." Foulks was here repeating the widespread belief that the white preachers had all been behind it somehow, covering their tracks with bland-sounding appeals to philanthropy.[1]

The reactionary Anglican rector George W. Bridges thought the military response to Sharpe's rebellion was only half finished; he also wanted the violence brought home to his fellow clergymen. On January 26, 1832, he formed a reactionary group, the Colonial Church Union, to deal with the continuing threat of the white Baptist and Methodist ministers. He sent around sign-up sheets to all the militia companies and asked for a pledge of support. Those who refused to join the union should be defined, he said, as "the enemy of Jamaica." In racial ideology, rhetorical strategy, and terror tactics, this group would anticipate the Ku Klux Klan which would be formed in the aftermath of the US Civil War thirty-four years later.[2]

Posters went up around Montego Bay, proclaiming,

INHABITANTS OF JAMAICA!
Your danger is great. If you have discovered the source of your disease, lose not a moment in expelling the poison from your veins. Rally round your church and kirk, before it is too late, and defend yourselves from all who attack them: the preservation of your wives, your children, your properties, your houses—nay, of your very lives, demands it.[3]

William Bruce at the *Jamaica Courant* became the mouthpiece of the Colonial Church Union, using his newspaper to make an open call for vigilante murders of the Baptist and Methodist preachers. "I have only to say for myself," he wrote, "that if a mad dog were passing my way, I would have no hesitation in shooting him; and if I found a furious animal on two legs teaching a parcel of poor ignorant beings to cut my _____ or to fire my dwelling, my conscience would not trouble me one bit more for destroying him, than it would for the destruction of a mad dog."[4]

Bridges and Bruce made it clear that the purpose of the Colonial Church Union was to deliver some payback for what Samuel Sharpe had done—"the just recompense of rebellion"—and they directed the pent-up anger of the island against the missionaries. On February 6 a rowdy jumble of overseers, attorneys, militiamen, and shopkeepers gathered in Montego Bay and tore down the wooden Baptist chapel, board by board.[5]

The fever spread. White mobs ripped down the chapel in Stewart Town the next day. In Falmouth that night, at eight o'clock, the editor of the *Cornwall Courier*, William Dyer, was on hand to shout encouragement to the militia captains as they dismantled a Wesleyan chapel and then William Knibb's Baptist chapel with axes, ropes, and other tools brought onshore from a ship docked in the harbor; within a short time "the whole fabric was leveled to the ground," reported the *Royal Gazette*. Dyer also threatened to tar and feather any minister of the Gospel who stood in his way. A group of imprisoned slaves were ordered to throw horse dung into the baptistery.[6]

Shouted protests from the ministers and their outraged congregants did no good, as the militia—exhausted from five weeks of combat—paid them no attention. The white citizen-soldiers looked frightened and hollow-eyed. "The poor fellows cut a miserable appearance," noted an eyewitness. As pathetic as this night-time marauding might have been, it was regarded in the *Courant* as a victory for "true-hearted Jamaicans" who had distinguished themselves by "razing to the earth that pestilential hole, Knibb's preaching-shop."[7]

Missionaries knew they were targeted for their supposed role in fomenting violence among the blacks, but a few suspected more primitive motives for this explosion of pent-up anger. Wherever they made converts, they undermined the Jamaican tradition of white masters raping enslaved women. "We have already been instrumental in saving a great number of respectable women of color from that evil, and have prevented many others from entering into it," remarked one minister. Even William Burge, the attorney general for Jamaica, complained that missionaries had been "aloof" from white society and all its hedonism, and that he had never spotted a single one at a party or a dinner. Sexual possessiveness, as much as fear, may have powered the mayhem.[8]

In the days that followed the destruction of the Falmouth church, vigilante groups vandalized missionary homes, tarred and feathered several preachers, and obliterated churches in Botany Bay, Ocho Rios, Oracabessa, Savanna-la-Mar, and St. Ann's Bay. At the Baptist chapel in Salter's Hill, where William Knibb had tried in vain to convince the congregation not to rebel on the eve of the violence, a mob used gunpowder to blow off the roof. Fourteen Baptist and four Wesleyan churches were left in ruins, many of them having been burned down just as quickly as the sugar estates had been torched the previous month. Knibb later visited the remnants of the chapel at Montego Bay and saw that "the outhouse, the garden fences and gates and everything were carried away." The only signs that anything had once stood there were one small piece of wall and the top of the water well. Among those who had wrecked it was Colonel George Lawson, who had spotted the first fires of the rebellion from atop the courthouse. A joke quickly spread: the chapels hadn't been wrecked by mobs, but were "struck by lightning" or had "fallen in an earthquake."[9]

The missionaries had little doubt that the Jamaican newspapers, more than any other force, had created the frenzy against them, fueling the idea that they were secret agents in robes, the vanguard of a conspiracy hatched in radical drawing rooms back home in England. "What but religious enthusiasm, or madness, could have urged on this awful state of things?" fulminated the *Royal Gazette* on January 28, calling for the British government to cut off any further religious instruction to "such a diabolical agency as the negro slaves have proved themselves to be."[10]

The next week, a writer for the *Gazette* wandered into William Knibb's church at Salter's Hill and found a Bible on the pulpit that had been dog-eared to the eighth chapter of the book of Joshua and its vaguely belligerent verses, such as "And the ambush rose quickly out of their place, and they ran as soon as he stretched his hand—and they entered into the city, and took it, and hasted and set the city on fire" (Josh. 8:19).

This folded page of the Bible was enough to convince the anonymous correspondent that a foul conspiracy had been hatched from this house of worship. "Who then can blame the honest indignation of the people of the country against so jesuitical, so infamous an institution as the Baptists have proved themselves to be, in causing ignorant people to become murderers, incendiaries and felons of every description?" he concluded.

Few men on the island were more unalloyed in their hatred for Baptists and Methodists than William Bruce, editor of the ultraconservative *Jamaica Courant,* for which Rev. George W. Bridges wrote with a pen seemingly dipped in acid, often leaving his articles unsigned. Whether its doses of fury may have come from either Bruce or Bridges, readers of the *Courant* received their invective in fiery blasts.

"Shooting is, however, too honorable a death for men whose conduct has occasioned so much bloodshed, and the loss of so much property," someone wrote on January 6. "There are fine *hanging-woods* in St. James and Trelawny, and we do sincerely hope that the bodies of all the Methodist preachers who may be convicted of sedition may diversify the scene."[11]

The imagery of Christian preachers dangling from the gallows kept reappearing in the pages of the *Courant.* "Tar and feather them wherever you meet them," said the paper, "and drive them off the Island, excepting always, those who may merit a greater elevation—a more exalted distinction." The lynching was altogether deserved, he concluded, because the ministers had obviously been spies paid off by the Anti-Slavery Society to ensure "the destruction of the fairest portion of the British empire." It would therefore be a "grateful exhibition to the island, to see a dozen of them gibbeted."[12]

The friend and patron of the notorious Samuel Sharpe, Rev. Thomas Burchell, had been traveling back from England on the *Garland Grove* during the heat of the violence and he had been ignorant of current affairs when his ship docked in Montego Bay on January 7. A lieutenant boarded and asked the captain for a list of passengers. He found Burchell's name, and then escorted him to house arrest aboard HMS *Blanche*. "It is martial law," he explained.[13]

Burchell was ordered to sleep on a cot in the commodore's apartment and was permitted to walk only to the main mast; if he ventured farther, the guards were ordered to bayonet him. On land, meanwhile, court officials combed through his papers and letters, looking for evidence of sedition, and then found a witness, Samuel Stennet, to say he had heard Burchell encouraging the slave members of his church to fight violently for their freedom.[14]

At this moment an unlikely hero emerged: Richard Barrett, the Speaker of the Jamaica Assembly, who also served as the custos of St. James Parish. Though lying sick in bed at a friend's home in Montego Bay, he was given a large briefcase full of Burchell's letters and papers as "evidence." Too ill to sort through all of them, he asked a young man named Robert Dewar to pull all the ones that made any mention of slavery, and then reviewed the key documents himself. "Nothing on slavery," he remarked, "but what one planter might write to another." He told his associates that he was unimpressed with the legal case against Burchell and two other ministers. He furthermore complained that the affidavit against them was "taken in a hurried hand" and barely intelligible—a probable reflection of the rushed manner in which local authorities were trying to hustle the minister toward the gallows.[15]

From his sickbed Barrett sent a written order to the magistrate at Montego Bay, John Manderson, a free colored planter who had protected the clergymen from the gathering mob:

My dear Sir,

Having examined the evidence against the missionaries of the
baptist persuasion, in whose behalf you have interested
yourself very humanely, I have to inform you, that there is no
evidence in my possession that implicates Mr. Abbott and
Mr. Whitehorne; and no legal evidence implicating
Mr. Burchell. These persons must therefore be discharged
from their bail, and
I am, my dear Sir,
Your faithful and obedient servant,
Richard Barrett, *Custos.*[16]

Barrett was one of the richest men on the island, with lineage
tracing back to the seventeenth century and a family network of magistrates that ringed Jamaica. His ruling was a signal to Bridges and
the rest of the vigilantes that the sugar aristocracy favored law over
revenge, and he was likely looking across the Atlantic for how the
chaos might be perceived in Parliament. Barrett followed up this legal
order with an even more laconic message to the captain of the *Garland Grove,* the ship Burchell had taken across the Atlantic and to
which he had been transferred from the *Blanche:*

> *Montego Bay,* 10TH FEBRUARY 1832
> SIR,—You are hereby authorized to release from detention
> the person of Mr. Burchell.
> Richard Barrett, *Custos*[17]

Barrett then talked to John Roby, the local collector of customs,
who had been the one to sound the first warning of the Kensington
Estate fire on December 27. Roby was told to use private channels to
relay a message to the captain of the *Garland Grove:* that although the
preacher under his watch appeared innocent of the charge of sedition, it seemed apparent that he was an enemy of slavery to the point

where he should tell Burchell to leave the island on the first available outbound ship for his own protection, "as well as for the welfare and safety of the colony itself." The job of the missionaries was forever finished, he said, and "they never would be permitted, after what had occurred, to remain quietly in the island." Richard Barrett would later say he had only one suggestion for the missionaries: "To be off. I have no other advice to give them."[18]

Though he was liberal by the standards of the planting gentry, and had previously been a friend to the Presbyterian missionaries, Barrett's tolerance had its limits. His own view of Sharpe's revolution was that it had indeed festered in the underground of the Baptist churches before it exploded into view.

Barrett later made cryptic reference to leaders among the slaves who had disseminated "mischievous principles" to "persons of violent passions and criminal intentions" within the churches. He was here almost certainly referring to Samuel Sharpe as a guerilla military leader, a slave who had had far too much freedom to travel between plantations. He also predicted the rise of another Sharpe. "The division among the Baptists into leaders and inferior grades prepared the slaves to act under command," he said. Even so, Barrett still refused to help the vigilantes, or give any credibility to the Colonial Church Union, which he thought was an outlaw group.[19]

William Knibb had been presented with an impossible offer on New Year's Day 1832: to take up arms in the militia against his congregants. He refused, and Captain Paul Doig responded by drawing his sword and telling two attendants, "Take this man into custody—this is all he has got by preaching!" Knibb was held for three more days, then taken from Falmouth to Montego Bay at gunpoint in an open canoe. When the boat landed, visible fires were still burning across the hills. The preacher was led through the streets to the courthouse, past the bullet-riddled dead body of a rebel. A soldier beside Knibb remarked that he would soon share the same fate, and another threatened to run him through with a bayonet. Knibb was marched to the door of Sir Willoughby Cotton—who gave him a shot of brandy, but little else—and then to the house on a nearby hillside, where Richard Barrett was staying while the countryside was aflame. Barrett examined the evidence and eventually signed a writ releasing him from custody on a bail of fifty pounds.[20]

Before Knibb walked free, he asked if he could lie down on the cell floor to ease his exhaustion, and a militia soldier refused, telling him, "No, you damned villain, if you stir one step or speak one word, I will shoot you immediately; you are to be shot tomorrow morning at ten o'clock and I am very glad of it." This was a lie, but when Knibb returned to Falmouth, he found his friends had all "scattered hither and tither." A mob later showed up to his house, dressed in women's dresses and bonnets to disguise their identities. They threw rocks against his windows, breaking one of them, and yelled that they were going to tar and feather him. But perhaps fearing the power of the civil authorities, as personified by Richard Barrett, none of them had the courage to break in.[21]

Barrett himself was partially immune to popular wrath for helping save the hated missionaries, but the writer of a letter to the *Jamaica Courant* subtly insulted him as a "civilian" who shouldn't be making a military decision. "Really, Mr. Editor, the manner in which matters have been conducted here, convinces us that there is considerable unsteadiness," said the writer, who had titled his opinion "The Two Bs—Barrett and Burchell," implying more of a link than there really was. This still represented a turning point, an important symbolic break between the populist fury on the streets and the more moderate opinion of the sugar gentry, who recognized the damage an all-out pogrom against the missionaries would do to the long-term health of the island.[22]

Barrett therefore absorbed some of the popular feelings against the white missionaries from England, which were nothing short of murderous. The captain of the American ship *Robert and Rowland* said he overheard one Jamaican sugar planter say he "would not go home until he had got Mr. Burchell's heart's blood." Others felt that Burchell would probably be shot on sight if he walked the streets of Montego Bay, and a local justice of the peace decided to heighten this risk. He demanded Burchell leave the ship to appear in court to formally answer a charge that he had encouraged Sharpe's rebellion. The minister reluctantly allowed himself to be taken ashore by soldiers into the village where he had lived and worked for a decade, and was led by the arm through a dockside mob of his former neighbors— members of respectable Jamaican society who now wanted to tear out his throat.

"They began to throng around me, hissing, groaning and gnashing at me with their teeth; some with water in their mouths to spit upon me," he would later recall. "Had I never been in Montego Bay before, I must have supposed myself among cannibals, or in the midst of savage hordes of Siberia, or the uncultivated and uncivilized tribes of central Africa."[23]

"Hang him! Hang him!" they screamed, but several free colored people also clustered around the Baptist minister and dared the mobs to hurt him. Such a display of defiance would have been virtually unheard of in prerebellion Jamaica; it was a sign of how much island society had changed in only six weeks, and Burchell was convinced that this show of force saved his life. He spent the next month in a jail cell, but the court case was anticlimactic, as Stennet almost immediately confessed he had been bribed to make a false statement. Burchell was still kept in confinement for weeks following the trial, but likely only as a measure to guarantee his safety from the mobs. When he was released on March 14, he and his family were hustled to a ship in the harbor and escaped to the United States to elude further prosecution. William Knibb likewise took Barrett's advice and left Jamaica, though not in a way the planters would have liked. He sailed for London on April 26 to begin a speaking tour throughout Britain about the evils of slavery.[24]

Henry Bleby chose to stay, but thought it good for his health to stay out of sight, hiding out at a friend's house in Montego Bay for several weeks as the work of the Colonial Church Union reached its peak. When he thought it safe to go back to his rented house in Falmouth on April 5, he found a letter on his porch threatening him with tarring and feathering if he did not immediately leave town. The handwriting was deliberately childish to conceal its authorship, and it was signed with one word: "Mob."

Bleby invited a few free colored men to camp in the backyard for his protection and resisted the attempts of his intimidated landlord to evict him. As he sat down for tea one evening, he heard "the trampling of many feet" and approaching voices. He looked out the window in the moonlight and saw perhaps eighty or a hundred men in the process of smashing down his gate and advancing on the house. Once inside, a few of them said they were "constables"; others lamely muttered that they had come in for tea. Before long, they rolled a keg of warm tar into the living room, then smeared the black goo all over his clothes, denouncing him as a "damned preaching villain." A ship captain named Thomas Dobson slammed Bleby over the head with a club, threatening to touch a lighted candle to his now-flammable pants. Before this could happen, Bleby's wife knocked the candle away. A gang of free colored men then burst through the back door, brandishing logs of firewood and ready for a brawl. The white mob fled without having gotten around to the feathering.[25]

Popular anger was also growing against Lord Belmore. He had not only failed to stop the revolt with a timely debunking of the "free paper" rumor but also seemed to have dithered in the religious war. Some of his fiercest local critics then learned Belmore was on the verge of being fired by the colonial secretary, Viscount Goderich.

The two had never really gotten along. Goderich had just come down from a disastrous six months as prime minister, where he had been widely mocked for a habit of crying whenever he became agitated in debate. This earned him the nickname The Blubberer. While he was a diligent administrator, he was also prone to fuss over small details, and his dispatches had grown increasingly critical over the course of 1831. Goderich felt Belmore needed to show a stronger hand to the Jamaican planting class and their legal structures to ameliorate the condition of slaves. An irritated Belmore had to ask his secretary to make sure his own dispatches back to London were "totally devoid of sarcasm or anything which could betray personal feeling" so that he wouldn't get into even more trouble.[26]

Unhelpfully to himself, Belmore also got into a power struggle with Sir Willoughby Cotton, who enjoyed widespread popularity for his generalship during the rebellion and had made a bid to secure an appointment as lieutenant governor. Belmore refused him, and Cotton soon left the island on a trip to Honduras that he said was to help him recover from some health problems. Belmore sent an official dispatch on June 9, 1832, announcing that Cotton had sailed on HMS *Tweed* "under the advice of his medical attendants to try the effects of a Sea Voyage toward the restoration of his health, which for some time past has been much impaired." But in a separate note to the Colonial Office on the same day, prominently marked "Confidential," Belmore offered a more nuanced view of the official story: "I cannot avoid stating to your Lordship that his departure has been likewise not a little influenced by a discovery that he has not been provided with a commission as lieutenant governor." It had become obvious that Belmore's talents at colonial intrigues were weaker than those of his adversaries.[27]

Matters reached a head at the end of April, when a carefully worded dispatch from London informed Belmore that his actions were "so much at variance" with Crown policy and "highly injurious to the Slave Population" that he could no longer continue as governor. Yet he seemed to put himself on the side of the abolitionists and missionaries when he told the Jamaica Assembly in a farewell message, "The cause of your present distress results from that policy by which slavery was originally established; this fine island can never develop the abundance of its resources while slavery continues." This statement earned him the permanent distrust of the plantocracy and ended whatever remaining moral authority he enjoyed. At odds with his army, his superiors, the assembly, and most of his own citizens, Belmore was soon on his way back to England even as the terrorism of the Colonial Church Union remained unchecked.[28]

His replacement at King's House was a minor nobleman named Constantine Henry Phipps, otherwise known as the Earl of Mulgrave, a graduate of Trinity College of Cambridge University and the author of the popular romance novels *The English in Italy* and *Matilda*. Mulgrave inherited the gritty task of putting down a domestic terror organization that threatened to bring a permanent state of racial warfare to Jamaica with religion as its thin pretext. His arrival did not just signify new leadership; it was a near complete change of course.

Though Mulgrave was not a vocal abolitionist, he was a liberal on racial matters and took the unprecedented step of inviting free colored people to parties at King's House, where they danced with one another in formal waltzes. Mulgrave even allowed his wife to dance with free men of color—a gesture that horrified the island elite. Those who let their indignity be shown were coldly disinvited from future state events. Unsurprisingly, Mulgrave acted swiftly against the Colonial Church Union. One of his first moves was to make a speech at Montego Bay in front of a crowd that included twelve magistrates who had torn down the Baptist church where Samuel Sharpe had been a member. Standing just a few yards from the ruins, Mulgrave told his listeners they had to stop the "state of alarm" and "illegal threats" that had rippled through the city. His audience showed visible discomfort, but the violence dwindled to a halt.[29]

Mulgrave then lobbied his superiors in London for a royal proclamation declaring the Colonial Church Union an illegal organization.

This was granted on January 29, 1833, leaving its members on the wrong side of King William IV's pleasure and giving Mulgrave a strong hand in liquidating the power of one of Bridges's top allies, the militia colonel James Hilton, who had signed a resolution deploring Mulgrave's "hostility." The governor responded with an icy letter firing him from the St. Ann's Western Regiment on February 3, 1833. He followed it up with a circular to the custodes of all the parishes, reminding them of their loyalty to the British Empire. Eleven local officials were eventually dismissed; critics heaped scorn on the new governor, calling him a "namby-pamby novel writer." But the message was clear: violence against missionaries would be considered equal to disloyalty to the Crown.[30]

Mulgrave had survived his white domestic crisis and could now concentrate on keeping another rebellion from breaking out among the enslaved people—an outcome many feared inevitable. One correspondent to King's House had complained to Mulgrave about the impaled heads of black people that kept showing up around Jamaica. Such gruesome displays may have been intended to show "a lively sense of the dangers of rebellion," said the writer, but he feared that the real effect among the enslaved people who saw the severed heads of their friends would be "to exasperate their resentments, to harden their feelings, and thus to give any future contest which may unhappily arise a character of unbounded ferocity."[31]

Though they stood at the nexus of the island's anger, and might not have been tempted to thank Samuel Sharpe for his actions, the surrendered rebels had done their missionary allies a tremendous favor. The burnings of December 1831 had, at last, freed them to speak. The white missionaries had been under the constraint of legal silence on the injustice all around them, but the uprising wiped away the fiction of their neutrality. Henry Bleby would confess that he had been too meek, and that "our mouths had been closed about slavery up until that time." Now they could speak honestly and without fear of censorship. Knibb, in particular, was on his way to England to do just that.[32]

News of the revolt had trickled into Britain and the United States by way of the few merchant vessels that left Kingston after the declaration of martial law on December 30. Only those who had already secured their departure papers were allowed to sail, and they bore alarming reports from a burning island.

America got the news first. Captain John Percival of the *Porpoise* arrived in Pensacola, Florida, on February 8, 1832, and told an interviewer that 180 plantations had been "laid waste" and that up to thirty-six thousand slaves had rebelled against their masters—an overestimation of the actual numbers. Independent reporting from the American mainland was impossible, so these inflated numbers were accepted without question. Samuel Sharpe's identity, if not his actual name, first became known to American readers when a brief item cribbed from a Jamaican paper appeared on January 24 in the *Alexandria Gazette,* ominously reporting that "a negro preacher was at the head of the whole plot." This no doubt served to remind the paper's Virginia readers of the failed Nat Turner rebellion just five months earlier, which had also been inspired by a renegade pastor citing pointed Bible verses.[33]

The uprising received lurid treatment in the *Liberator,* a Boston newspaper dedicated to the cause of immediate emancipation and founded by William Lloyd Garrison, a reformer who wrote with a sulfurous pen, employed black reporters, and made himself the bête noir of contemptuous Southern slaveholders. The governor of Virginia, John Floyd, had complained in his diary that the *Liberator* had "the express intention of inciting the slaves and free negroes . . . to rebellion," and he blamed the paper for indirectly causing Nat Turner to go on his messianic rampage. And neither did the *Liberator* pull punches in its commentary on the similar event in Jamaica. "More blood has been shed in this single revolt, than would flow from the immediate emancipation of all the slaves in Europe and America," thundered an anonymous contributor, probably Garrison himself. "Thousands of whites and blacks already slaughtered on one island!! and yet the monster Oppression is not glutted and, nor are his apologists satisfied with the results of his bloody reign!!"[34]

The American media reaction flashed back to Jamaica as if in an echo chamber. The *Royal Gazette*—the prim journal of British loyalists—repeated the words of a US newspaper: that although most slaves had no access to education or literacy, "there were many whose intelligence ripened in a degree to enable them to comprehend their situation and the questions connected with it, and who were constantly on the alert, in observation and design, for the vindication of their supposed rights."

It was this "ripening" that the slaveholding classes of North America seemed to fear above all else: the dawning consciousness in the minds of enslaved persons that they had an inborn right to be free—and that they might take further steps to make it happen, because they already had superior numbers. All they would need in the future was a little more knowledge, a little more discipline, and some more key allies among the whites.[35]

But in the American South the response was near silence. After initial reports came in to Pensacola, Florida, and Savannah, Georgia, newspapers largely refrained from making further comment on the uprising. The *Charleston Mercury* made a passing reference to "local disturbances" in a February item about Jamaica, and then went quiet. The *Macon Telegraph* dutifully reported news from the port at New Orleans from the captain of USS *Mary Howland* who had heard from a Spanish colleague that "extensive disturbances" had taken place. Armed vessels in the port at Kingston had thought it "necessary to moor so that their guns could rake every street that laid on angle with the harbor." The item made no mention of slavery, and the paper dropped its inquiry.[36]

Britain, however, was where the political impact would run deepest, though the news took nearly two months to reach the public because of the sailing time across the Atlantic; London was therefore about a month behind Washington, DC, in learning of the largest slave uprising since the Haitian Revolution.

HMS *Mutine* was the first news-bearing ship to arrive in England, docking at the Cornish port of Falmouth on February 17, carrying Lord Belmore's first urgent dispatches to the Colonial Office and a bundle of Kingston newspapers that contained what the London *Globe* called "the most distressing and alarming accounts" of the slave insurrection. Three days later, the *Globe* devoted an entire column of the paper to the story—an enormous amount of space. That night's London *Evening Standard* went even further, filling two columns with a collection of military bulletins, Colonial Office dispatches, and clippings from Jamaican papers that went far beyond the coverage given by any American paper.[37]

As the news sank in at the beginning of spring, Elizabeth Barrett Browning made a diary entry that reflected the uncertain outlook for West Indian planting families such as her own. "It would be agreeable to know that Papa's estates are not burnt up—& still more agreeable to know where we are going!" she wrote on March 3, 1832. "Fear as well as hope deferred maketh the heart sick."[38]

William IV, the king who had been impressed with Jamaica during his Royal Navy days, was also troubled by the news. He penned a private note to Viscount Goderich at the Colonial Office registering his "conviction that slavery cannot be abolished in the West Indian colonies without entailing the loss of all those colonies."[39]

But reformers and abolitionists spotted a strategic opening. All history is made of publicity, and the press coverage of Sharpe's rebellion was helping cast a new consciousness with surprising rapidity. The *Northern Whig* of Belfast noted the violence in the Caribbean "has excited a considerable sensation in England," sending the price of sugar rocketing upward, and the *Morning Advertiser* in London compared the Jamaican uprising to the successful black revolution in Haiti thirty years earlier. "The slaves must be sooner or later set at freedom," said the paper, "whether it be or whether it be not for their benefit, and the sooner that proper steps are taken for this purpose, so much the better." *Tait's Edinburgh Magazine* praised the "indelible hankering after liberty" on the part of the rebels in Jamaica who were only challenging a system that was "essentially rotten." Any half-hearted attempt to save it would be like nailing new boards over a worm-eaten floor. More uncompromising words came from the *Nottingham Review:* "Nothing will satisfy the people short of the instant and complete extinction of negro slavery," wrote an anonymous editorialist.[40]

Within the month an alarmed Parliament met to review documents about the insurrection and the general state of slavery in the West Indies. The brewer and social reformer Thomas Fowell Buxton promised to use the opportunity to introduce a measure for total abolition of slavery, which stood a poor chance of passing but nevertheless captured the attention of parliamentary conservatives. Dudley Ryder, the representative from the former slaving town of Liverpool, concurred with a colleague "that the question was one of life and death to the colonies, and that delay must be fatal."[41]

If Samuel Sharpe had been trying to seize the attention of the mother country—just as Nat Turner had given the American South a brief window through which to reconsider slavery—he succeeded far beyond what he might have hoped. Never before had enslaved people spoken so loudly in Britain. The tangible gains of the rebellion had been slow to materialize, but they would soon coalesce into an unstoppable force.

Richard Barrett was the closest to an embodiment of Jamaica's old line as the planters could hope to find, and as attractive a model slave owner as could be put in front of the public. He had not lost any of his houses in the uprising—by all accounts, his enslaved people had courageously protected his holdings—and so he was able to defend the system in cooler language than one who had been recently ruined.

In the face of so much negative press brewing back in England, the Jamaica Assembly selected Barrett and an associate, Abraham Johnson, to travel at once to London to mount a last-ditch defense of the system that had already been in economic decline. Their plan was first to lobby individual members of Parliament and then, if they could see him, King William IV, whom they regarded as their "last hope and refuge." They set sail in early March.[42]

Barrett gave multiple speeches to conservative audiences, but one talk that he made alongside the lawyer William Burge stands out as an impassioned summary of everything he wanted to say about Jamaican slavery. It was given at London's Thatched House Tavern on St. James Street, a second-story drinking hall bedecked with candle chandeliers and famous for its literary history—Jonathan Swift had been a regular—as well as the spot for regular meetings of the Carlton Club, the Royal Yacht Squadron, and the Society of Dilettanti, among other esteemed associations that treated it as their living room. On the night of May 18, 1833, the tavern hosted "a general meeting of planters, merchants and others interested in the West India Colonies" and Barrett took the floor.[43]

He began with an appeal to British patriotism, putting slavery in the context of necessary foreign policy in the Caribbean, and then, in the same breath, seeming to put himself in agreement with those who called it a humanitarian crime. Without forced labor, without the black people "torn from Africa" by those "spoilers" in previous centuries, the nation never would have attained a firm foothold in the New World islands nor a strong check against their continental rivals. British laws and British capital had propped it up ever since the days when John Hawkins had gone hunting for humans on behalf of Elizabeth I.[44]

Then Barrett veered into self-pity, pointing out that running a slave operation was truly the only way a man could survive in Jamaica, and that the British people had effectively forced their island cousins to do it in the name of mercantile power and cheap sugar. "Thus the planter became a slave proprietor not by the choice of his will, but the force of law," he said. "It is not fair—it is not honest—it is unjust and cruel for the people of England to reproach the planter with the unavoidable condition of their own act, and to load him with obloquy at the moment they are about to make him a victim of their guilt."[45]

Now that the British citizens themselves—snug and safe on their European island—could be revealed as the true slave drivers, it needed to be said that they were subjecting their tropical countrymen to a list of horrors by threatening abolition: massacres from vengeful blacks, economic ruin, a "servile war" against their former farmworkers, who would themselves be driven back into a state of African barbarism in their liberty and forget the lessons of civilization they had learned while in bondage.

The taxpayers should expect to be funding a permanent military presence in Jamaica, Barrett warned, without mentioning the garrison of three thousand British Regulars who had been in Kingston for decades. He read aloud from a pamphlet written by a proslavery advocate from Charleston, South Carolina, who warned that the British West Indies were "about to become an archipelago of free blacks." Jamaica, in other words, would suffer the same fate that Haiti had. The "imminent and appalling" condition of black freedom and possibly even self-government would require a costly army occupation to keep the remaining white gentility safe from marauding bands of revanchist farmworkers wielding hoes and machetes. And the degraded moral state of the Jamaican planter, of which so much gossip had been made, had been exaggerated, Barrett assured his audience. Unlike the blackened demimonde of Britain's dreary industrial boomtowns, there was no murder in the tropics, no dangerous coal mining, no discrimination against Jews or free people of color.[46]

Then came a favorite argument of early nineteenth-century slave owners. Barrett averred that the health and happiness of a typical Caribbean forced laborer was far above that of a poor white who had to toil in a factory in the Midlands. He told his tavern audience that the enslaved people of Jamaica worked only ten hours a day (this was largely untrue) in the "pure and open air" of the land of sunshine, and they did not exhibit "the sickly countenances, the stunted figures, the incipient deformity and squalid appearance, the ragged and dirty persons of the laboring infants in England."[47]

He summed up with a note of defiance against the gathering forces of abolition who would impose a collective will upon their rural brethren, an argument that echoed the fire-eating secessionist rhetoric then brewing in the American South and one that also encapsulated part of the eternal tensions between metropolitan versus local governance: abolition could not succeed because the farmers would vigorously contest—even with violence—the fiat of the disconnected urban elites. "I am confident that the people of Jamaica, from the highest to the lowest, will resist it in every way," he said. "Society may be thrown into disorder; the supremacy of the laws may yield to military violence, the slaves may resume the torch and the knife; and the white inhabitants may be massacred or exiled. But not even to avoid those horrors will they surrender their rights to the arbitrary disposal of Parliament."[48]

These remarks were transcribed and later published in a pamphlet designed to help sway popular opinion in the face of the certain reckoning coming to the halls of Parliament after the recent violence. Barrett's tavern speech amounts to a collection of the classic arguments that had always been deployed in its defense: it was legal, patriotic, and prosperous; it promoted British hegemony; and slaves were actually happy.

But it was also a throwback to the mentality of a different era, and in the free-trading atmosphere of the quickly modernizing 1830s, when the entire country had been made aware of Samuel Sharpe's convincing rebellion against this supposed idyll, Barrett's points looked positively archaic.

One measure of how far the country had come was to witness a remarkable change of attitude in the city of Liverpool, which had been the logistical hub of the famous triangular trading system: manufactured goods sent to Africa, captured humans taken to the Caribbean, and sugar hauled back to England. Slavery had been a dazzling job creator, turning Liverpool into an eighteenth-century boomtown. Armies of coopers, carpenters, bank clerks, brokers, and painters who lived in the new rows of townhouses radiating out from the bustling harbor furnished everything a West Indian estate could want. Families could get rich off slavery without once having to lay eyes on an actual black person. African slave brokers, especially those living on the Bight of Biafra, had come to know Liverpool's name so well that they refused to deal with ships from any other city, and a good portion of the brokers in Jamaica were also men from Liverpool.[49]

Liverpool's town hall was adorned with stone busts of African heads and figures of elephants—well-known totems of the slaving business. Several mayors were slave dealers themselves. Local politicians had frequently reminded voters where all the money came from, and loudly resisted the cries for abolition that came from the Quakers. At election time one year, a pamphlet went out with a poem:

> If our slave trade had gone, there's an end to our lives
> Beggars all we must be, our children and wives,
> No ships from our ports, their proud sails e'er would spread
> And our streets grown with grass where the cows might be fed[50]

Other Britons who disapproved of organized abduction made dark jokes at Liverpool's expense. The artist Henry Fuseli said he could not look at its buildings without seeing "the blood of negroes oozing through the joints of the stones." This architectural metaphor became a popular national insult. When the famous actor George F. Cooke got drunk before he took a Liverpool stage, and was booed for slurring his lines, he shot back a widely quoted barb to the crowd: "I have not come here to be insulted by a set of wretches, every brick in whose infernal town is cemented with African blood."[51]

That was dramatic hyperbole, of course, but many of Liverpool's streets were, in fact, named after prominent slave traders and slavery advocates: Jonas Bond, John Earle, Richard Gildart, James Penny, Admiral George Brydges Rodney, and John Tarleton.[52] Another street with a thick cluster of slaving offices was nicknamed Negro Row. A gilded model of a slaving ship sat perched atop the spire of the Church of Our Lady and Saint Nicholas. The calling cards of elite traders came embossed with the designs of flags that flew on the masts of their Guineaman fleet. Fifteen different factories around the ports supplied ropes to the city's armada of slave ships. In the midst of the successful attempt to get the overseas trade banned in 1807, Liverpool residents sent in sixty-four petitions in support of slavery, as opposed to a paltry fourteen from the entire city of London. It was said in those days that you had a choice of being a "Liverpool Man" or a "Humanity Man." Or as a favorite saying among captains went, "Get slaves honestly. And if you can't get them honestly, get them."[53]

But as popular English sentiment began its turn against slavery, defiance of the hometown trade also arose within Liverpool itself. One lumberman, William Rathbone, had let it be known that he would not sell his wood to any builder constructing a slave ship, and he fed information to abolitionists on who owned the ships that were sailing on kidnapping missions. The banker and author William Roscoe, often scorned by London elites for his bumpkin-like accent, denounced the slave trade in scorching pamphlets and in the long two-part poem "The Wrongs of Africa," which portrayed slave rebellions in a romantic light. One passage went: "Rise, revenge, Revenge your wrongs, the expected voice exclaims / And meets a ready answer, from the tongues / Of countless numbers, from each gloomy cell / In dreadful cries return'd." Elected to Parliament, he rose to denounce the slave industry in 1807. "I have long resided in the town of Liverpool; for thirty years I have never ceased to condemn this inhuman traffic," he said, "and I consider it the greatest happiness of my existence to lift up my voice on this occasion against it, with the friends of justice and humanity." When Roscoe returned to his hometown, a group of seaman armed with bludgeons tried to block his way and a riot broke out.[54]

Also within the circle of antislavery conspirators was Edward Ruston, who had been a sailor on an African slaving mission as a young man and quickly become stricken with revulsion; he tried to sneak food and water to the captives and repeatedly chided the captain for the horror belowdecks until he was charged with mutiny. He returned to Liverpool, opened a bookstore, and wrote radical tracts celebrating the American and French Revolutions. Once he wrote a letter to George Washington to ask why he had not freed his own slaves at Mount Vernon after striking such a blow against tyranny: "In the name of justice what can induce you thus to tarnish your own well-earned celebrity and to impair the fair features of American liberty with so foul and indelible a blot?" Washington never replied.[55]

It would be from Liverpool itself that one of the greatest pieces of antislavery propaganda emerged. A parliamentary committee had sent Captain William Perry of the Royal Navy to the Liverpool docks to inspect the vessels used to transport Africans to the West Indies to ensure their dimensions were "humane." When he returned, he laid a stack of documents on the table in the middle of the House of Commons. On the top was a list of dimensions of the brig *Brookes*. A group of abolitionists from Plymouth did the math and used the description to design a replica showing rows upon rows of slaves packed like sardines across its decks in geometric precision—487 black bodies in total, in an overhead view of people as inanimate cargo.

The bald-faced diagram of the *Brookes,* said Thomas Clarkson, "seemed to make an instantaneous impression of horror upon all who saw it, and was therefore instrumental, in consequence of the wide circulation given it, in serving the cause of the injured Africans." The resulting print was soon posted in coffeehouses and printed in newspapers across the country, and Liverpool felt the sting. "Men are awakening to their situation," wrote one local doctor in a letter, "and the struggle between interest and humanity has made great havoc in the happiness of many families." In a more cold-blooded fashion, the Quaker trader Joseph Cropper made appeals to his fellow Liverpudlians in the name of open commerce and free trade, insisting that slavery was too costly to maintain and hurt the pocketbooks of ordinary citizens. "The fact and arguments which I have stated are on the same firm ground as the multiplication table or any other mathematical truth," he wrote in a letter to Zachary Macaulay.[56]

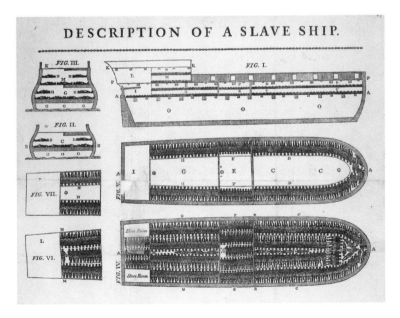

Diagram of the slave ship *Brookes. (University of York)*

Cropper's cause received a boost from the recent news from Jamaica, and it was not long after that a writer to the *Liverpool Mercury* called slavery "the most enormous evil which has ever been suffered to blast the history of man" in a letter prominently displayed by the editors. The Royal Amphitheatre in the center of town would shortly become the venue for a public debate on the wisdom of abolition—a spectacle that could not have been fathomed in the previous century. By the end of the spring of 1832, residents of Liverpool had circulated a petition to the House of Lords calling for immediate abolition.[57]

"Now is the time, therefore," said the petition emanating from what had once been Britain's greatest slave port, "for the nation to speak out loudly, boldly, universally; to call for the entire abolition of the whole system, as the only way in which the national character can be cleared from its darkest feature."[58]

But within a week, the organizers pulled back their petition. The zeal of the organizers "suddenly abated," in the words of the *Mercury*, when hundreds of people told them they would like to sign it but declined because they had no confidence that Parliament was capable of listening to the demands of the people.[59]

Samuel Sharpe's rebellion in Jamaica had coincided almost exactly with one of the most tumultuous political upheavals that Britain had seen in almost two centuries. At the center of it was Parliament, a grotesquely broken institution in which the West Indian planters held enormous influence, and through which any move to get rid of slavery would have to pass.

ELEVEN

ANOTHER ISLAND

THE GOVERNING HEART of the British Empire was inside a chamber so grimy that international visitors to London were often shocked at its appearance. Those who knocked on its front door hoping to see one of the oldest deliberative bodies in the world were shown a dowdy smoke-stained chamber joined at an awkward angle to Westminster Hall. Some expressed astonishment that the dank hall was, in fact, the storied House of Commons about which they had heard so much.

Edward IV had given the House of Commons the gift of St. Stephen's Chapel for use as a debating chamber in 1584, and it became a permanent home. This small church, which measured only thirty-three by forty-eight feet, had been fitted out with two sets of pews up on risers so that opposing factions could speak directly to each other, and it was connected to the more ostentatious House of Lords via a room decorated with medieval art. A little more than a century later, the architect Christopher Wren oversaw an extensive remodeling of St. Stephen's Chapel, to which he added galleries, closets, paneling, a new clock, and two iron pillars. But he also lowered the ceiling, making it even more claustrophobic. The renovations grew tobacco-stained and grubby over time, reinforcing the image of a dismal headquarters for such a consequential body: a sweatbox fringed with a maze of cramped hallways and tight staircases. The critic James Ralph lamented in 1736 that the structure was "so incumber'd with wretched apartments and so contemptible in the whole" as to give the British government a tarnished name. The roof leaked, and members sometimes couldn't understand one another because of bad acoustics. Air vents poked in the ceiling made it even chillier on cold days, but they provided some relief from the stench and also served another purpose: when women wanted to watch a debate, the only place where they were allowed to peer inside was through one of these holes on the roof. Only the most determined tried this.[1]

One common joke among Europeans was that the horse stables of Louis XIV's Palace at Versailles were far more elegant than the whole of Parliament. Though its defenders liked to say it was indicative of British modesty (in purposeful opposition to continental extravagance), there were also those who wished that the Catholic conspirator Guy Fawkes had succeeded in blowing Parliament up with his kegs of gunpowder in 1605. Frequent proposals for renovation were slow-walked to rejection because of the cost. This was the shabby policy-making center for the empire on which the sun never set, and where it had become increasingly clear in the spring of 1832 that the final question of slavery's continuing existence would have to be settled—somehow—as the extent of the damage and deaths in Jamaica became clear.[2]

Despite its democratic aura, the British Parliament at the time of Samuel Sharpe's rebellion was still a creaking ship of highborn privilege, with thirteenth-century sensibilities firmly rooted in its subconscious even as railroads began to creep across the land in all directions and a young generation of ambitious young factory workers and small-scale merchants were persuaded to say goodbye forever to the loamy villages where their families had farmed for centuries.[3]

The British Isles were peppered with "rotten boroughs"—fixed districts from the time of Edward I that retained the same voice in the legislature, even though the population had gone through massive change over six centuries. There were 513 seats in Parliament apportioned throughout England and Wales, and more than half the districts were populated with a total of just eleven thousand people—their lopsided authority frozen in place by the dead borders of the Middle Ages. Women had no suffrage, and barely 11 percent of men were allowed to vote: all landowners with money.

The quasi-feudal system was increasingly out of step with a rapidly changing country. Places like Birmingham and Manchester, once backwater towns, had exploded into coal-blackened cities with chuffing textile mills, new railroad projects, steam-engine houses, and hundreds of thousands of burgeoning tenements that housed wage earners who enjoyed no say in the national government, which effectively still belonged to the aristocrats and mercantilists as it had been since medieval times. And few groups had benefited more from the decrepit state of Parliament than the ring of sugar grandees known as the West Indian Interest.

The Caribbean planters had done something extremely astute in the three centuries they had spent accumulating wealth: they used some of that wealth to acquire seats in Parliament for themselves or their agents. Because there were no seats outside the British Isles, the sugar elites from Antigua, Barbados, Demerara (later a part of British Guyana) and Jamaica had dominated enough rotten boroughs by 1764 to claim a bloc of approximately fifty members of Parliament in any given year. This was enough to block "no confidence" votes against prime ministers, and it gave the planters substantial leverage and ability to trade in favors. When they could create alliances with banking and other merchant interests, they bordered on omnipotence.[4]

Breaking the West Indian stranglehold on imperial slave policy was intricately bound up with another question entirely separate from what the abolitionists were trying to achieve: How could Parliament be made less beholden to the aristocracy?

The watchword was *reform,* and it had failed several times in the past. The Act of Union in 1800 had left the House of Commons divided into two basic types of representation. There were the counties—which were Britain's historic divisions of Cornwall, Devon, Essex, Yorkshire, and the like, rooted in the geography of the Middle Ages and functioning as potent psychological touchstones—as well as parliamentary districts. And then there were the boroughs, named in a disorganized fashion through the centuries, sometimes intended to enfranchise a single village, and sometimes a giant depopulated tract of hunting ground owned by a long forgotten duke or earl. These were often up for sale.

The customary way to buy a seat in Parliament was to approach a political fixer known as a borough-jobber to find a forsaken rural area to represent. This took capital and connections. When Lord Chesterfield tried to get a seat for his son and offered 2,500 pounds to a jobber, he got a bemused response. Chesterfield wrote, "He laughed at my offer and said, That there was no such thing as a borough to be had now; for that the rich East and West Indians had secured them all."[5]

The most notorious patch of corrupt representation was from Dunwich, a former medieval port city on the North Sea that had long been abandoned and was, in fact, almost completely underwater. Even so, it sent two members to Parliament each year. Another was the postage stamp of earth on the top of a hill called Old Sarum, the seat of a vanished twelfth-century cathedral that claimed two seats, even though nobody lived there. Sham elections were typically held in a wooden shack constructed in a cornfield under a tree, and the winners were determined by fewer than a dozen nearby landowners who were taking cues from a wealthy patron. In the early nineteenth century that boss was the Earl of Caledon, who reportedly collected sixty thousand pounds for a seat. Such districts were known as "pocket boroughs" for their status of being in somebody's pocket. All a powerful man had to do was buy up at least half the dwellings in a borough and make it clear to the tenants that to vote against his interests would be inviting eviction. West Indian planters had been savvy about targeting landed noblemen who were short of funds and offering them cash for the seat or the right to appoint a stooge. Seats were not only up for sale, but it was often unclear who paid for them; this was the nineteenth-century version of "dark money" in politics.

As rapidly industrializing cities like Leeds, Manchester, Newcastle, and Sheffield mushroomed with newly dynamic economic powers but a feeble voice in national affairs, the pressures for reform grew harder to ignore. Urban citizens were also exasperated by a series of protectionist measures known as the Corn Laws, which taxed foreign grain to the benefit of gentleman farmers who could sell their food at top prices. Radical politics became fashionable in the cities, and especially among those who earned low wages. When more than sixty thousand citizens of Manchester—a city with no parliamentary representation whatsoever—gathered at St. Peter's Field on August 16, 1819, to protest their lack of representation and to hear the activist Henry Hunt give a speech, an undisciplined militia charged in to arrest Hunt and pacify the crowd; in the process eleven people were killed and at least six hundred were injured. Journalists named the incident Peterloo, after Napoleon Bonaparte's recent defeat at Waterloo, but it was not immediately clear who had been routed. A shaken Parliament responded by cracking down even harder on reformist meetings and civil liberties, yet much of the British lower and middle classes were revolted by the spectacle of drunken louts hacking women and children with sabers.[6]

Reformists got their biggest chance in 1830 upon the death of King George IV, a lover of extravagant clothes and food who had ruled for ten years. Under the constitution, the death of a sovereign also required new parliamentary elections. This gave the Whigs a prime chance to take control from the Tories, who were widely seen as allies of Old Albion and stood for a traditionally strong royal family, the spiritual hegemony of the Church of England, and aristocratic dominion throughout society. George's only child, a daughter named Charlotte, had died immediately after giving birth to a stillborn son, so the throne automatically reverted to his younger brother William Henry, who had not expected such a global responsibility to come his way.

The new King William IV was the same king that Samuel Sharpe and the Jamaican slaves had invested with near messianic qualities for his supposed desire to write them a "free paper." His racist beliefs had been considered relatively middle-of-the-road for that generation, yet history was now moving in a different direction. The economic push from the "quit sugar" movement, the constant stream of negative press about slavery, the demands of liberal reformers in the slums of Birmingham and Manchester, and the renewed vigor of the abolitionist crusaders Thomas Clarkson and William Wilberforce all helped the Whigs make advances against a flimsy Tory majority in the 1830 election, even despite the byzantine voting system.

Standing in the way was Arthur Wellesley, the Duke of Wellington, who had earned the nation's gratitude in 1815 for beating Napoleon at Waterloo but had emerged as the guardian of the old patriarchal order and the bête noire of the modernizers.[7] When he was appointed prime minister in 1828, some of his Tory colleagues were dismayed because he was an inept orator with a grating voice who enunciated words awkwardly due to several missing teeth—possibly an outcome of excessive sugar consumption. He favored blunt-force actions, both politically and personally. When the friend of one of his mistresses threatened to expose his dalliances, Wellington famously snapped, "Publish and be damned!" And he didn't care for William IV's common touch; he expressed contempt for the monarch's habit of occasionally catching hackney cabs down to Whitehall instead of fitting out the royal coach. "This," Wellington remarked acidly to a friend, "is the King of England." Later historians who examined patterns in his relationships have speculated that Wellington might have had Asperger's syndrome; he showed little affection for the soldiers who had fought alongside him at Waterloo, and had a tendency to fix a piercing stare on his visitors that left them feeling unnerved.[8]

Wellington's lack of emotional intelligence also did not serve him well politically. He seemed dangerously ignorant about the social and industrial changes sweeping his country and professed skepticism about the new technology of the railroad because he believed it was "a premium to the lower classes to go uselessly wandering around the country." He nevertheless accepted an invitation to the opening of the Liverpool and Manchester Railway in 1830, where his carriage was greeted with hisses, yelling, and a shower of rocks from the factory workers of Manchester, who were angry about Wellington's opposition to reform. The nation's constitution was as perfect as it had ever been for centuries, he told associates, and there was no sense in changing it. When he gave an uncompromising speech in opposition to any reform on November 8, 1830, he received only scorn. "Never was there an act of more egregious folly, or one so universally condemned by friends and foes," wrote a clerk of the privy council, Charles Greville, in his diary; he characterized the British government as "tottering." A mob smashed the windows at Wellington's residence at Apsley House, the ostentatious mansion he built for himself at the edge of Hyde Park and within sight of Buckingham Palace. Within a week he was relieved of his duties as prime minister and replaced with the more liberal-minded Charles Grey, by then known as Earl Grey, who was faced with a complicated mission: appeasing the conservatives with promises of stability while presenting genuine changes in front of the British public.[9]

At the same time in the spring of 1831 that Samuel Sharpe was building up a network of conspirators to audaciously protest Jamaican slavery, Earl Grey drafted proposals to expand voting rights more generally across the British Isles. But he was no zealot. He told the House of Lords that he wanted to "regulate that reform" to quell popular discontent, and he privately assured King William IV that he would try to find a peaceful settlement without going much further.

A first bill failed to garner support, but the Whigs gained even more seats and successfully pushed a bill through the House of Commons by that summer. By then, however, the people had begun to riot in major cities, spurred on by the Birmingham Political Union, a radical coalition which boasted of the loyalties of two million aggrieved Britons—far more opponents, noted its leader Thomas Attwood, than Wellington had faced at Waterloo.[10]

When the House of Lords vetoed a second attempt at reform in October 1831, it triggered an even more terrifying outbreak of violence. Mobs set fire to Nottingham Castle and rioted in Derby. In Bristol people threw rocks at constables, ransacked the mayor's house, destroyed the customs house, and freed prisoners from the jail. The rioters effectively controlled the town for three days, leaving portions of it in ruins; as many as four hundred may have died in the fighting. The Birmingham group talked of forming French revolutionary–style public militias to seize and redistribute property, and they brought in a Polish count to help them organize a resistance army. Their meetings sometimes included the singing of "La Marseillaise." London groups published a manual on street fighting titled *Defensive Instructions for the People,* which explained how to use wooden posts against mounted cavalry.[11]

Advocates for reform scrambled to fine-tune a proposal that could split the "respectable" middle-class reformers away from the revolutionary working classes. They drafted a plan to disenfranchise the worst rotten boroughs and grant representation to new industrial cities, as well as extend the vote to every male householder who could prove he paid more than ten pounds a year in rent. On May 9, 1832, a third attempt at a reform bill once again failed in the House of Lords, and a dramatic act of royal meddling almost sent Britain into full-scale revolution, a period of unprecedented anxiety that became known as the Days of May. Grey went to King William IV and suggested a bold stroke: the creation of fifty new seats in the House of Lords and the appointing of a full slate of Whigs to drown out the opposition. But William instead called on the Duke of Wellington to form a new government.[12]

This was a disastrous move. The northern cities had made it clear how they felt about the hero of Waterloo when they rained bricks and bottles down on him at the opening of the Liverpool and Manchester Railway, and the radicals of London had made a sport of breaking his windows at Apsley House. The duke was never a man of the people. A revealing view of his attitude toward the government's relation to its own people may be glimpsed in some advice that he supposedly later gave to Queen Victoria when she asked him where she should build a new palace; it should be on an island on the Thames, he said, "so that the populace cannot enact their demands by sitting down round you."[13]

Activists stepped up their call to stop paying taxes and encouraged citizens to withdraw all their money from the Bank of England under the slogan "To stop the Duke—go for gold!" In less than a week the bank lost a quarter of its assets. King William's German wife thought, fatalistically, that "an English revolution is rapidly approaching" and wondered to her friends if she might not suffer the fate of Marie Antoinette. She hoped out loud that she would show more courage to the executioner.[14]

No large-scale acts of violence broke out, as they had in the previous year, but for nearly three weeks Britain seemed on the brink of change that had not been seen since the days of Oliver Cromwell's insurgency and the beheading of King Charles I in 1649. The radical unions drew up plans to erect barricades in major cities, and the military steeled itself for conflict. Historians point to this moment as the time when the nation might have tipped the way of France and deposed its nobility with violence. The social reformer Francis Place urged caution on his more radical colleagues, but noted that they had been persuaded that "the time was coming when the whole of the working men would be ready to rise *en masse* and take the management of their own affairs."[15]

In the face of such a maelstrom, Wellington could not find enough support for a new government. In desperation, King William reappointed Grey and agreed to threaten the House of Lords with a flood of liberal-minded new members unless it acquiesced to some type of reform. Rather than cooperate, the opponents simply threw in their cards. Wellington and sixty extreme Tories staged a walkout from the House of Lords, "skulked in clubs and country houses," and did nothing to stop the bill from passing. Instead it became law by royal assent on June 7. King William's advisers encouraged him to hold a formal ceremony, but he refused, complaining of the multiple insults that had been directed against him. The final debate in the old Parliament was dismissed on a motion of Henry Hunt, whose speech at St. Peter's Field thirteen years earlier had been a harbinger of trouble. Britain had avoided its insurrection.[16]

Notably, the West Indian Interest did not vote as a unified bloc on reform, even though the passage of the Great Reform Act threatened to chip away at their power and that of slavery itself. On the crucial third reading of the bill in the House of Commons, their vote had split narrowly, with sixteen against and fourteen in favor. After a close review of their votes and speeches, B. W. Higman concluded that the West Indian Interest was no more conservative than Parliament on many social questions of the day, such as child labor, the death penalty, Catholic emancipation, or the regulation of chimney sweeps. Only 13 percent of its members' speeches had anything to do with the West Indies.[17]

Their dazzling wealth had come from sugar and slaves, but the members of the West Indian Interest also saw themselves primarily as Britons. And they had also just seen unrest in their true country— different in its methods and yet similar in its aims—that resembled the rage engulfing Jamaica. Both forces, from opposite sides of the Atlantic, now closed in against slavery.

TWELVE

FREEDOM

As WILLIAM KNIBB'S SHIP approached the old slaving port of Liverpool in June 1832, a team of bar pilots rowed out and he asked them the latest news. They told him the Reform Act had just passed, posing a serious challenge to the West Indian Interest.

"Thank God," he is reported to have said. "Now I'll have slavery down. I will never let it rest day or night until I have destroyed it root and branch."[1]

A reader can perceive a touch of Knibb's grandiosity, perhaps even megalomania, in this statement. "The impression he leaves is of a man who could not wait; life was much too urgent for the conventional niceties, which seem to matter to so many," wrote his biographer, Gordon Catherall. "He was not always polite, and his tongue on more than one occasion was caustic; but this was not unknown in the acrimonious debates of the nineteenth century."[2]

Knibb's frenetic pace doubled once he touched British soil. Before a meeting of the Baptist Missionary Society on June 19, he listened as one of his colleagues made a plea for modesty and a "temperate policy" toward slavery. Knibb was having none of it, saying he was ready to give up his salary and take his wife and children into poverty, even walk barefoot through his home country to "make known to the Christians of England what their brethren in Jamaica are suffering." He told his fellow Baptists that missionary activity could no longer continue without "the entire and immediate abolition of slavery."[3]

Baptist missionary William Knibb. His fiery speeches against slavery helped turn the tide of British public opinion. *(National Library of Jamaica)*

Though Baptists already had a national reputation for earnest and dramatic oratory and fellow parsons may have not been surprised to hear it from one of their own, Knibb nevertheless summoned deep reserves of pastoral eloquence to convince the doubters at the annual meeting of the society two days later at Spa Fields Chapel, pronouncing the names of individual slaves and investing them with an identity doubtless meant to recall the sufferings of Jesus in his final hours:

I plead on behalf of the widows and orphans of those whose innocent blood has been shed. I plead that the constancy of the negro may be rewarded. I plead on behalf of my brethren in Jamaica whose hopes are fixed on this meeting. I plead on behalf of their wives and little ones. I call upon children, by the cries of the infant slave whom I saw flogged on Macclesfield Estate, in Westmoreland. I call upon mothers, by the tender sympathies of their natures. I call upon parents, by the blood-streaming back of Catherine Williams, who, with a heroism England has seldom known, preferred a dungeon to the surrender of her honour. I call upon Christians, by the lacerated back of William Black, of King's Valley, whose back, a month after flogging, was not healed. I call upon you all, by the sympathies of Jesus. If I fail of arousing your sympathies, I will retire from this meeting, and call upon Him who has made of one blood all nations that dwell upon the face of the earth; and if I die without beholding the emancipation of my brethren and sisters in Christ, then, if prayer is permitted in heaven, I will fall at the feet of the Eternal, crying, Lord, open the eyes of Christians in England, to see the evil of slavery and banish it from the earth.[4]

The chairman of the group, John Dyer, described as a "prudent and timid man," pulled on Knibb's coat tails as a signal for him to tone down his rhetoric or be seated. But Knibb snapped back, "Whatever may be the consequences, I *will* speak."[5]

And he did, spending the summer of 1832 on a speaking tour of England, including stops in Birmingham, Manchester, Norwich, and Reading, among other places. These cities were the new industrial heartland of a rapidly changing nation and the places where the twin sentiments of reform and abolition were the strongest, as well as the likeliest source of new voters in the upcoming postreform elections. Knibb usually spoke in chapels, sometimes accompanied by his friend

Thomas Burchell, and often holding up iron slave collars for dramatic effect. In Liverpool he gave a speech on July 24 that was deemed important enough for the *Liverpool Mercury* to print a lengthy summary describing his efforts to endure the threats from "dealers in human blood." Such authentic testimony from the frontlines of Jamaica, noted the newspaper, was "kindling a fire you will not easily quench."[6]

In Exeter Hall in London two weeks later, Knibb again launched a rhetorical cannonade against slavery, calling it an irredeemable foe of Christianity and citing its multiple horrors, including the flogging of women. When he finished, he appeared exhausted, and the audience offered repeated rounds of "deafening applause." When Knibb spoke in Manchester, a member of Parliament stood up and pronounced himself convinced that slavery needed to be banned immediately. Knibb later wrote to Thomas Abbott in Jamaica to say his aim was to leave audiences in a state of "unmingled disgust" with the whites in Jamaica.[7]

Knibb's outspokenness underlines a point made by historian Mary Turner—that Samuel Sharpe and the rebellious slaves had actually done a great favor to the missionaries who had tried to dissuade them from violence. The uprising and the backlash against it stripped away all of the pretense that the missionaries were only humble observers and politically neutral about the cruelties of slavery. The rebellion had forced their honesty out into the open and let them speak with the full force of their conviction.[8]

Knibb's biggest public relations coup, however, took place not inside a chapel or a meeting hall but inside a cramped hearing room inside Westminster's Old Palace. On May 24, 1832, one day after the execution of Samuel Sharpe, a group of sympathetic members of Parliament had called for the formation of a select committee to investigate the possible effects of abolishing slavery. Cutting to the pragmatic core, the committee wanted to know if Britain would be fighting constant wars against its own enslaved citizens, or in Henry

Bleby's wording, "Will it be safe to the planters that slavery be continued?"[9]

An especially driven member of this committee was Lord Howick, the undersecretary of state for war and the colonies, who had read Belmore's correspondence from Jamaica with horror, becoming increasingly convinced that the abolitionists had been right all along. He told associates that he had thought about little else but slavery for the past two years. Moreover, Howick had family clout—he was Earl Grey's son—and he had self-assurance to the point where "he cared little for what was thought or written about him." Howick also enjoyed formidable bureaucratic assistance in the Colonial Office from playwright-turned-diplomat Henry Taylor and his colleague James Stephen, who had examined the same evidence from Sharpe's rebellion and concluded that "the evils of slavery are beyond the reach of legislation and can be remedied only by laws directly abolishing the relation of master and slave."[10]

Throughout the summer of 1832, the committee asked 8,572 questions of thirty-two witnesses, including sea captains, estate attorneys, missionaries, plantation owners, and others they could find in London who had the authority to speak firsthand to the situation in the West Indies, though—in a significant blind spot—no people who had actually been enslaved. Witnesses were all over the map, and no unified message emerged. In the words of an observer to a duplicate committee in the House of Lords, "there is not a missionary that does not speak favorably of the general quietness of the negro disposition: there is not a colonial witness who does not (when it is convenient) swear to the brutal ignorance of the slave."[11]

The select committee was nevertheless edging close to an overwhelming set of questions that had never been fully discussed in Britain, despite its three-century heritage of running slave operations. Was a black person equal in ability to the white person? Did souls of different color have equal worth? Could freed black people become good citizens? For many of the witnesses, particularly those with church affiliations, the answer to all of these was an unrestrained *yes*. Sympathetic white Jamaicans testified to enslaved people's capable intellects, sober habits, wise fiscal management, care for their own provision grounds, and love for family and friends, all of which they had personally witnessed.[12]

Then followed a pressing military question: Would they seek their freedom with violence? Few put the danger more bluntly than Jamaican lawyer William Taylor: "I believe that when the terror has worn away, they will break out again, and if they do, you will not be able to control them. They will be more successful and more methodical." Conversely, Britons who had been on hand to witness legal emancipation in Haiti and in New York state testified to the tranquility of the experience and to the immediate desire of freed slaves to become farmers and craftspeople.[13]

None seized the question with more vigor than William Knibb, who was called up to testify on July 11, 1832. Had it taken place in the modern era, Knibb's testimony would have been broadcast live and dominated the national news. He was led through a series of questions about his service as a missionary, the destruction of his chapel, the threats to run him through with a bayonet, the way he watched doomed members of his congregation go to their executions with remarkable poise and contempt for death, the blood-slick flagstones under the gallows at Montego Bay, and the bodies of those killed in the country that were subsequently eaten by vultures.[14]

Knibb spared no graphic details about Jamaica's degradations, and told stories from Samuel Sharpe's rebellion as skillfully as he would deliver a sermon. One enslaved man had told him that "if he had twenty lives he would risk them all in the cause of freedom." Another had walked right up to a militia company and said bluntly, "I will never work again as a slave; you may shoot me," which the company promptly did. Knibb repeated the story of Catherine Williams, who refused a sexual relationship with her master and then was flogged in revenge until her back was "a mass of blood." And he told the horrifying story of a Methodist schoolmaster who was made to pray with a group of suspected rebels and then murder them immediately afterward. This last anecdote so unnerved the questioner, James Graham, that he dwelt upon it for at least twenty minutes, longer than almost any other subject before the committee. Hadn't this spectacle made an emotional mark on Knibb? "None particularly," Knibb replied. "There are so many things of a painful nature always connected with martial law, particularly so in the late one."[15]

But Knibb was not as unruffled as he appeared. Not five minutes later, he erupted into one of his characteristic explosions. Graham was fixated on whether a particular minister of the established church had been present at the coerced execution, and whether he was wearing a uniform and a sword:

> Q: Did you see a clergyman of the Church of England, dressed in regimentals?
>
> A: How could I see him when I was a prisoner? During martial law, every enormity was practiced! Did you ever see a person stood over with a bayonet, and threatened to be shot if he stirred?
>
> Q: Have you ever been examined in a court of justice as a witness?
>
> A: Yes; I do not consider this as a court of justice.

A reader can almost hear the baffled pause between Knibb's angry answer and Graham's follow-up question meant to cast doubt on his mental stability.

However agitated he may have seemed, Knibb made a deep impression on his listeners. His testimony in the House of Lords so troubled the Earl of Harewood that he took Knibb into a side room and asked to know if any of the "immoralities" had been committed on his property in Jamaica. Knibb replied that he didn't think so, and the Earl gratefully shook Knibb's hand and asked that he be informed if the situation changed.[16]

The committee wrapped up its work on August 11, 1832, and turned in 538 pages of verbatim testimony of such contradictory nature that it apologized for its "abrupt and unfinished state." Yet the advocates for immediate abolition had never before presented such a detailed case directly to the British government on the fitness of enslaved people to live in freedom. The Colonial Office was then just over thirty years old and full of youthful reform-minded administrators who foresaw inevitable changes to the combination of mercantilism and slavery propping up the British West Indies. The talented writer Henry Taylor—a former resident of Barbados, a working poet, and a well-connected friend of John Stuart Mill—began working on an eighty-two-page memo arguing that another revolt was likely and the future cooperation of free colored militiamen was doubtful unless a plan for gradual freedom was adopted.[17]

The fresh activism within Parliament and the bureaucracy could not go unanswered by the West Indian Interest. They mounted posters in the towns where William Knibb spoke, accusing him of personally inciting the rebellion. They also found an orator of their own, Peter Borthwick, to make speeches defending colonial slavery with the usual arguments that chopping cane in the sunshine was healthier for workers than hard industrial labor in a Midlands textile mill and that challenging the British law on the subject was equivalent to treason. Borthwick ended his speeches with the taunting call, "Where is Mr. Knibb? Why does he not come and defend himself?"[18]

Sure enough, Knibb could not resist. On December 15, the two met in a meeting hall in Bath for a public debate, and they went at each other viciously for four and a half hours. Borthwick charged that Knibb would have been hanged for insurrection back in Jamaica if it hadn't been for the leniency of the sugar barons, and that the whole affair had been cooked up in a Baptist church by a black preacher—meaning Samuel Sharpe. Furthermore, hadn't Knibb said that a monument ought to be erected to such a "fine negro"?

Though Knibb denied ever meeting Sharpe before the revolt, he insisted that what he had actually said was that if Sharpe had been a Polish insurrectionist trying to overthrow the Russians, "many in England would have said that, instead of being considered a rebel, he deserved an imperishable monument." This may have been the first time that Sharpe's name had been spoken about in positive terms to a wide British audience, and it was a risky gesture on Knibb's part to equate Sharpe's conduct to that of a hero. Even those who were passionately in favor of abolition were not quite ready to hear of a black insurrectionist being so lauded. Knibb acknowledged as much. "Frequently during my tour," he said, "especially in Birmingham, in London, and in Manchester, I have been called to order by the audience for daring, before a British public, to call that man a rebel who only fought for his freedom." If it were treason to say so, Knibb averred, then he would gladly stand trial for it.[19]

When the chairman of the meeting asked for a show of hands from the audience as to their opinion of who had won the debate, the informal vote went overwhelmingly for Knibb, though this may have been more a result of the West Indian Interest failing to pack the audience ahead of time. Knibb's forceful stage personality also likely played a role. Some of his cocksure attitude, even grandiosity, can be glimpsed in a comment he made to a member of the Anti-Slavery Society, who was among those of his allies who had never seen Jamaica and urged him to tone down his rhetoric. "I wish you to know I am here not to risk my connection with the Society alone," fumed Knibb. "I am here to gain the emancipation of these slaves, or die."[20]

Though he appeared unhinged and manic to some of his listeners, Knibb had a keen feeling of a race against time that was not entirely in his imagination. Much would depend on the upcoming first election for parliamentary seats since the passage of the Reform Act, leaving the West India Interest hobbled. Seven of their pocket boroughs vanished overnight. Smelling an opportunity, a group of radical abolitionists broke with the mainstream Anti-Slavery Society and pressed candidates to take a public position. From the former slaving headquarters at Liverpool, James Cropper drafted a sample question: "In the event of your becoming a member of the next parliament will you vote for and seriously support the abolition of colonial slavery under such regulations as parliament may deem necessary to secure the industrious habits and orderly conduct of the negroes?" At least two hundred respondents came out as general opponents of slavery, and 104 took a public pledge to support the immediate freedom of the enslaved people. Those who refused were publically branded "irredeemable." Some on the antislavery side directed their rhetoric directly against embattled West Indian candidates, who could only give mealy mouthed defenses of the various abuses that had received press coverage like never before.[21]

Nominations opened on December 8. This was not a nationwide election held on a given day, but rather scattered contests in the newly apportioned districts that would last one month. For the first time since the twelfth century, nobody would be sent from the abandoned hilltop of Old Sarum. National sentiment had been running squarely against the Tories because they were perceived as obstructionist and hidebound. The ballots from the big industrializing cities immediately showed a strong preference for the Whigs, who were seen as independent of the deep money interests. By the time the final polls closed on January 8, it was clearly a rout. The Whigs now controlled 70 percent of Parliament, and Earl Grey would remain prime minister.

The big loser was the West Indian Interest, which lost 30 percent of its formerly safe seats; barely nineteen members now held a financial interest in Caribbean sugar. Jamaican planters had held seventeen seats in 1820, and now they were down to six.[22]

At the first session of the reformed Parliament on February 5, 1833, the Duke of Wellington surveyed the crowd and murmured, "I never saw so many shocking bad hats in my life."[23]

A large portion of the newly elected representatives from England's industrial backbone had read the news about Samuel Sharpe's revolt and taken the antislavery pledge; they were now readying themselves for a push against forced labor in the West Indies. And when King William IV sat on the throne in the House of Lords to make the monarch's traditional opening speech, he covered the Belgian Revolution, a civil war in Portugal, the termination of the charter of the East India Company, and Irish tax policy, but he said not one word about slavery. Grumbled Sir Robert Inglis, "he might at least say that it was not undeserving [of] the attention of the House."[24]

The abolitionists were at first confused, and then delighted, taking the omission as a deliberate sign that the Crown wouldn't stand in the way of abolition, as it had for decades. The fierce orator William Wilberforce had stepped down in 1825, and the abolitionists' new legislative champion was Thomas Fowell Buxton, the broad-shouldered, booming-voiced owner of a brewery who had once been cowed into submission by the West Indian Interest, complaining ten years earlier that they could "put forth a phalanx of 200 members in the House of Commons." But the earthquake of reform had shaken Parliament to the point that the old battlements were no longer standing; a frontal attack might finally be possible. The Jamaican violence had given humanitarians powerful evidence that the institution was costing Britain far more than it was giving back, and they could now make extended pragmatic arguments as well as moral ones. "If the question respecting the West Indies was not speedily settled, it would settle itself in an alarming way," warned Buxton, adding in a private letter that that the slaves "would take the work into their own hands" if the mother country did not take decisive action on their behalf. He also argued from a standpoint of realpolitik interest that hanging on to slavery could damage Britain's standing in the world if it was forced to put down another insurrection, because "a war against people struggling for their rights would be the falsest position in which it was possible for England to be placed." He cited specific testimony from the Jamaican uprising to make an overarching point: it was going to happen again.[25]

The revolt Samuel Sharpe had started on a Caribbean island was building to a culmination at Westminster—a final drive to asphyxiate slavery throughout the British Empire. But it came not through a

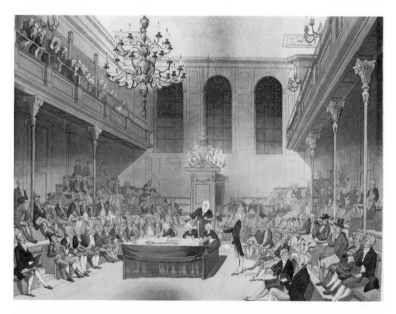

House of Commons. Some of the most consequential debates of the empire were held in a cramped and stifling room for which few members had any affection. (*British Library*)

spectacular legislative duel or an inspiring floor speech but rather through the grind of parliamentary process and the unromantic reality of dickering in the shadows.

On March 19, 1833, Buxton introduced a bill for the immediate abolition of slavery, alarming Howick and his deputies in the Colonial Office who had been concocting a secret plan to reconcile the financial burden to the planters with the humanitarian demands of the abolitionists. After counting heads and evaluating the arguments, they concluded that any successful bill would involve a straight cash payout and a gradual emancipation. Details were still sketchy. They convinced Buxton to hold off until the ministry could hold private negotiations with the West Indians.[26]

Activists ratcheted up the pressure. More than two hundred thousand copies of the tract *Three Months in Jamaica, in 1832* were printed up; it included graphic descriptions of whippings, denunciations of the "disgustingly dirty work" of slavery, and explicit comparisons of the plight of enslaved Jamaican field hands to that of British factory workers. This was a new political strategy: the struggle over slavery was being recast in class terms for the benefit of residents of a different island. At least seventy-five petitions demanding an end to slavery came in every day to both the House of Commons and the House of Lords. During one two-day period in May, both houses received upwards of five hundred lists of signatures demanding abolition. The Methodists contributed one list of nearly 224,000 signatures, not all of them legible because some of the recent converts did not know how to read or write. Buxton himself brought in a petition organized by his daughter that bore 187,000 signatures. By the end of the summer a total of 1.3 million Britons had personally weighed in—approximately 10 percent of the population. A group of them even made the most un-British of displays: a public march on the prime minister's residence on Downing Street.[27]

In a separate show of peaceful force on April 18, antislavery delegates from all over the country crowded in to tell the new secretary of state for war and the colonies, Edward Smith-Stanley, that their constituents were impatient for rapid change. The simplified idea of "freedom" had caught on with England's middle class, which found itself anxious over questions of physical and economic dominance by the aristocrats—tensions that had only been amplified by the reform crisis and a growing perception of self-dealing within the autarkic West Indian Interest. The plaintive question "Am I not a man and a brother?" found new expression; many poor Britons were more prone than ever to make the connection between their own sense of economic bondage and that of an Afro-Caribbean slave. Now they also had a semblance of mass political clout in a coalition with religious Britons outraged by the treatment of the missionaries. They had "not only caught fire themselves," wrote Zachary Macaulay, "but had succeeded in igniting the whole country."[28]

Though Stanley was a Whig, he was a conservative one, and he refused to commit to a timetable. Within a month, however, he was giving a speech to Parliament, laying out a five-point plan: children under six years of age were to be freed immediately; all others were to have a period of "apprenticeship" in which they would work for free for several years; the workday would be limited to ten hours; new magistrates would be appointed from Britain to adjudicate disputes; and the planters would split up a reparations loan of fifteen million pounds.[29]

A witness to Stanley's speech painted a vivid picture of the audience, divided between West Indian sympathizers and the energetic new coalition of Methodists, Quakers, tradesmen, and other advocates of abolition: "The moving nostrils, the parched lips, and snarling expressions of some, indicated the dread and apprehension of the moneyed man, whose cash has been as it were squeezed out of the Negro's flesh; the thought was painful, but I was amply repaid by the contrast presented by many happy countenances who seemed actually to breathe a new life."[30]

Hardcore abolitionists still balked at the cash payoff. By giving compensation for "property," was that not a tacit admission to the evil principle that had started everything—that human beings could ever be property? And if continuing slavery was to risk war, how could the government allow it to continue under a different name? They pushed back vigorously against the grace period, but British tradition was against them. "Apprenticeship" was a concept dating to Roman times in which an indentured servant, usually a teenager, could earn autonomy through a period of forced labor, usually seven years. The medieval Statute of Artificers had made this legal for centuries (until its repeal in 1814) in order to make child labor more acceptable in the textile factories. Since Caribbean slaves were typically characterized as childlike in British media depictions, the apprenticeship model seemed an attractive—even humane—concession to the planters.[31]

The Jamaican elite, meanwhile, foresaw their way of life coming to an inglorious end. Richard Barrett was watching from the crowded gallery when one of the resolutions for emancipation was read. He later said the experience was like listening to "the address of a public prosecutor against the prisoner at the bar." Many of his fellow planters predicted a bloodbath, as vengeful servants once freed might then pick up machetes and go after those who had ground them down.[32]

The example of Haiti became a favorite tool of argument for both sides. "The higher classes are in the utmost alarm at rumors of Wilberforce's intention to set the Negroes entirely free; the next step to which would be in all probability a general massacre of the whites, and a second edition of the horrors of St. Domingo," a distressed Matthew Lewis had written in 1816. Many repeated his dire prediction in the hour of slavery's demise, despite the evidence that Haiti remained a prosperous island under black rule. A Royal Navy vice admiral named Charles Fleming let it be known that "the most happy, richest, the best-fed and the most comfortable negroes that I saw in the West Indies" were in postrevolutionary Haiti and that its roads would be the envy of Europe.[33]

Still, behind the scenes, the West Indian Interest drew verbal pictures of ruin and pressured Stanley to modify the fifteen-million-pound loan into an outright grant of twenty million. At one point, Howick floated a proposal for "qualified emancipation"—that is, granting freedom to one-tenth of the enslaved people by a random lottery system and then assessing whether the transition would be peaceful enough to continue. But this idea died when tropical estate managers pointed out just how much jealousy, unhappiness, and chaos this would unleash. Stanley memorably framed the question as balancing the pecuniary interest of the West Indians with the certain knowledge "that things wrong in principle cannot be good in practice."[34]

The poet Elizabeth Barrett Browning privately rejoiced, even though it portended a financial blow to her wealthy family. "The West Indians are irreparably ruined if the Bill passes," she wrote to her friend Mrs. Martin in May 1833. "Papa says that in the case of its passing, nobody in his senses would even think of the cultivation of sugar, and that they had better hang weights to the sides of the island of Jamaica and sink it at once. Don't you think certain heads might be found heavy enough for the purpose?"[35]

The West Indian Interest faltered in the face of popular opinion, and it abdicated the fight in a similar fashion to the walkout of the House of Lords during the Reform Act debate the previous year. It also received almost no help from the Tory minority who had taken a serious blow in the recent election; only one member without a financial stake in Caribbean sugar, Sir Robert Peel, took an active role in the negotiations. But many didn't show up, and a generalized gloom and torpor prevented them from defending slavery as eagerly they had in the past. Even Wellington had to admit during an open session in the House of Lords that the Caribbean planters were "exceedingly unpopular" in the public's mind.[36]

Elizabeth Barrett Browning.

ROME, MARCH, 1859

Engraved by G. Cook from a portrait by Field Talfourd
in the National Portrait Gallery.

London Published by Smith Elder & C°. 15 Waterloo Place.

The wealth of Elizabeth Barrett Browning's family came from Jamaican sugar, but she was never comfortable with it and later became an antislavery advocate. *(British Library)*

Another traditional ally of the West Indian Interest, the non-slaveholding merchants, also proved undependable. They were more interested in the cash reparations, for many of them held notes on mortgaged estates and wanted to recoup payments. Slavery was not of short-term interest to them.[37]

By the beginning of the summer of 1833, most West Indian planters perceived that abolition was a fait accompli, that urban voters would likely hold their members accountable for whatever they did on such an emotional question, and that the House of Commons votes would be plainly against them. After the introduction of Stanley's bill on May 14, they aimed their leverage at securing the biggest possible financial package from the taxpayers. Under pressure from the Duke of Wellington, Stanley agreed to raise the price to twenty million pounds to be distributed among all the empire's slaveholders, with the apportionment calculated by slave prices and not population numbers, effectively buying the slaveholders' peace. Jamaican slave owners both on and off the island would get six million pounds—an extraordinary sum. The total payout amounted to approximately 40 percent of the British government's annual budget.[38]

The optics of this bargain revolted some abolitionists, who felt as though the enslaved people should get the money. "I am sorely disappointed in this bill," wrote the Liverpool abolitionist James Cropper in a letter to his son. "In its present shape, it is a wasteful expenditure of public money without absolutely securing anything in return." But Buxton and his allies were willing to tolerate it. For some there was a quantum of spiritual satisfaction in seeing Britain pay a tangible price for letting such an abhorrent institution continue for nearly three centuries. The collective guilt became a rough point of agreement between slaveholder and abolitionist. As Jamaican planter Alexander Barclay put it in a letter, "If the slavery of our colonies is a sin, it is the sin of the nation, and ought to be redeemed at the nation's expense." Even an ally of William Knibb, a London banker who owned three hundred slaves he had never seen, said he refused to sign any petition that didn't call for a generous payout: "I have said before that I think it is a national crime rather than an individual one and that it requires a national atonement."[39]

In the midst of this argument over money, the cautious abolitionism proponent William Wilberforce had told his friends that he felt like a clock winding down to its last hours. Though bedridden, he lived to hear of the final abolition proposal making steady progress through the House of Commons before he died on July 19, 1833. Buxton eulogized him eleven days later and mourned the fact that Wilberforce had not lived to see what was about to happen.

The bill faced its final test in the House of Lords, where old sugar money still carried some clout and where lifetime appointments could shield members from political repercussions. But in a repeat of the quiet surrender around the previous year's Reform Act, the upper house gave way without much protest, making only one minor alteration that would require an ex-slave to work overtime if they left the estate. Abolitionists even found an ally of convenience in Lord Belmore, the former governor of Jamaica, who had reclaimed his seat and said he would not stand in the way of freedom as long as it provided "justice" to property holders, though he scoffed at the idea of a successful future insurrection because "nothing is so feeble as the negroes." At the Colonial Office, Henry Taylor concluded that anything less than acceptance of the bill would have left the aristocratic class vulnerable to scorn it could no longer afford.[40]

King William IV apparently felt that same way. On August 28, the bill became law by royal assent, and with no public ceremony, as if the mutual compromises were an embarrassment to those concerned. In fact, confided Charles Greville in his diary, "all parties are dissatisfied," with the planters fearing the end of their incomes and the enslaved people not gaining true freedom. Three centuries of bondage were thus terminated with a dull bargain and a cash payout amid the grind of politics.[41]

Battered and humiliated by the insurrection and the near war of religion that followed it, the Jamaica Assembly had no choice but to endorse the will of the metropole. Its members knew that they would also be surrendering any claim on the money offered by the Crown if they refused to adopt the abolition measure. But they also made it clear to the enslaved people that they should expect few real changes in their employment condition until some unknown future date and that they would be whipped if they refused to work. On December 12, 1833, the Earl of Mulgrave gave the bill his assent. The "free paper" promised by Samuel Sharpe had finally arrived in Jamaica, making approximately 323,000 people close to freedom with a signature.

Back in 1820, Thomas Jefferson had said that a government holding on to slavery was like holding a wolf by the ears—it was impossible to keep holding on forever, but too dangerous to let go. Jamaica was about to find out what happened when the grip was softened, and then eventually released. The new governor of the colony, Howe Peter Browne, the Second Marquess of Sligo, began by issuing a printed proclamation on May 27, 1834, that he ordered posted at all sugar estates and read aloud to the slaves. It contained a dose of magnanimity embedded in a tissue of condescension:

> Our good King, who was himself in Jamaica a long time ago, still thinks and talks a great deal about this Island. He has sent me out here to take care of you and to protect your rights; but he has also ordered me to see justice done to your owners, and to punish those who do wrong. Take my advice, for I am your friend; be sober, honest, and work well when you become apprentices; for should you behave ill, and refuse to work because you are no longer slaves, you will assuredly render yourself liable to punishment. The people of England are your friends and fellow subjects—they have shown themselves by passing a bill to make you all free. Your masters are also your friends: they have their kind feeling towards you all by passing in the House of Assembly the same bill. The way to prove that you are deserving of all this goodness, is by labouring diligently during your apprentice-ship. You will, of the first of August next no longer be slaves, but from that day you will be apprenticed to your former

owners for a few years, in order to fit you for freedom. . . . I trust you will be obedient and diligent subjects to our good King, so that he may never have cause to be sorry for all the good he has done for you.

Your friend, and well-wisher,

Sligo

Governor of Jamaica[42]

The following period of transition made nobody happy and went down as a complete policy failure. The Jamaica Assembly had just told 311,070 people that they were expected to work as they had before for forty and a half uncompensated hours per week, though they could get paid for overtime work, and lashings could no longer be carried out directly by an overseer or a bookkeeper. All punishment had to be meted out by uniformed special magistrates appointed by the British government who could deputize other white people for on-the-spot brutalities. Liberty was an abstraction; the apprentices knew they were not "full free" and existed in a vague liminal state between bondage and freedom.[43]

Labor troubles started even before the ceremonial reading of the emancipation decree from the steps of King's House in Spanish Town on August 1, 1834. A group of soon-to-be apprentices at Ginger Hall Estate approached their master "in the most cool and determined manner" and told him they wouldn't work unless they were paid in cash. Only a threat of force by the magistrate—and an invocation of the name of King William IV—could convince the ex-slaves to go back into the cane fields. Nine of the ringleaders were flogged in public as a stern demonstration that white dominance was still the law. But when the day of "freedom" came on August 1, none of the dreaded explosions of violence happened. Planters doled out extra rations of beef and rum, the Baptist and Wesleyan chapels opened for a special day of worship, and "not a single man, woman, or child, was butchered to make a negro holiday," wrote a sarcastic R. R. Madden, one of the appointed magistrates, in a letter to a friend.[44]

Strikes still broke out on at least twenty-four estates in St. Ann's Parish the first week of August. A soldier reported that the ex-slaves were convinced once more that the planters were deceiving them and that the king would not have allowed them to wallow in such a state. They said were willing to work for fair pay, but swore to be decapitated or shot if they were to be treated as slaves. When they were whipped, Sligo reported later, many put on the "appearance of pleasure to their punishment, their comrades exhorting them to bear it for the sake of freedom." One elderly veteran of the cane fields, when told of the educational root of the word *apprentice,* asked the obvious question of what, exactly, he was supposed to learn at this point?[45]

A few spiteful masters squeezed what last value they could from their charges, forcing them to work during heavy rains, demanding rent for the provision grounds, quoting outrageous prices for a slave to buy his or her own freedom, eliminating the makeshift nurseries

EMANCIPATION, 1st AUGUST, 1834.

The emancipation celebration in Spanish Town, August 1, 1834. *(British Library)*

and the dedicated nursing time so as to get more labor from mothers, and putting even elderly or handicapped ex-slaves to work in the fields chopping cane. Those slaves who refused were sent to local prisons known as workhouses, where they were forced to run on treadmills and whipped so frequently that the floors became sticky with a permanent coat of blood. Stories of these cruelties spread throughout the island and caused the already beleaguered planter class to talk once more of violent secession from the Crown. "Many are there in the island who would be delighted to get up an insurrection for the pleasure of destroying the negroes and missionaries," wrote the governor to the Colonial Office. "They are, in fact, mad."[46]

The planters' dire predictions of a Haitian-style revolution turned out to be nonsense, but their forecast of an economic downturn was accurate. Sugar prices continued to fall—mainly because of new competition from Brazil, Cuba, and Mauritius—and estates continued to go into foreclosure. These trends had begun well before Sharpe's rebellion, but the specter of a paid workforce further discouraged investment from London's merchant houses and likely spooked the planters into taking land out of cultivation. Average annual production fell 21 percent during the apprenticeship period. The thirty or so special magistrates appointed by London were supposed to be insulated from "local passions" as they punished ex-slaves for alleged misbehavior, but they were held in low regard by nearly everyone they encountered. Fifteen of them died within six months of their arrival, both from the customary tropical diseases and from heavy drinking. Lurid tales of abuses in the parish prisons—including rape and torture—convinced Parliament to put them directly in the hands of the governor. At their height, the prisons held up to 3 percent of the entire black population of the island. Most agreed that the conditions for workers were, if anything, even worse than they had been under actual slavery.[47]

Realizing the near total failure of the apprenticeship experiment, the Jamaica Assembly voted to end it two years early. Had it not been for this decision, thought estate employee Benjamin McMahon, "the slaves would have been driven to repeat the attempt to break their yoke, and perhaps with far more disastrous consequences."[48]

Excitement mounted throughout the island as August 1, 1838, the day of total emancipation, drew near. The new governor, Lionel Smith, sent out a proclamation much more generous than the one issued four years earlier. "The first of August next is the happy day when you will become free—under the same laws as other freemen, whether black, white or colored," he wrote. "I, your governor, give you joy of this great blessing."[49]

Dissenting chapels were gaily lit up with candles. In Kingston, scores of young people decorated themselves with leaves and flowers; some ministers had to push their way through enormous crowds to reach their pulpits. A parade wound through the capital city at Spanish Town, with silk flags bearing slogans like "England, Land of Liberty, of Light, of Life" and the favorite motto of the abolitionists, "Am I Not a Man and a Brother?" At Salter's Hill, near where the first fires of the rebellion had erupted four years earlier, the Baptists decorated their rebuilt chapel with palm branches, fruit, and flowers. A minister held up the tools of slavery—a whip, a chain, and a shackle—and broke all of them into pieces, one by one, as the audience cheered. The remains were buried on the property, as would befit a corpse.[50]

The most dramatic ceremony, however, was left to William Knibb's congregation in Falmouth, where the members held a vigil on the night of July 31, counting down the remaining minutes of legal slavery. A few minutes before midnight, Knibb stood up at the pulpit and broke all of called for quiet, even though the church had been calm. He then pointed at a clock.

"The hour is at hand," he said quietly. "The monster is dying."

Then the congregation listened as the clock chimed the twelve bars of midnight. At the last one, Knibb shouted: "The monster is dead! The negro is free!" The church "broke out into one loud and long-continued burst of exultation and joy" that awoke Knibb's young son and rattled all the windows. "Never did I hear such a sound," Knibb later wrote.

Most stayed up all night until 5:30 the next morning when, in another symbolic funeral, they lowered a coffin filled with whips, chains, and collars into the ground. The bottom bore the name of Sir John Hawkins, who had first ventured into the African interior to capture human beings in the name of Queen Elizabeth I nearly three centuries earlier. The coffin bore a most prominent legend: "Colonial Slavery, died July 31, 1838, aged 276." Everyone present sang a hymn composed for the occasion as the sun rose:

> Now, Slavery, we lay thy vile form in the dust
> And, buried for ever, there let it remain:
> And rotted, and covered with infamy's rust
> Be every man-whip, and fetter, and chain

Several former slaves then spoke at a public meeting, promising not to forget the pain they had endured even during the period of faux freedom known as apprenticeship. "Let we remember that we been on sugar estate from sunrise a-morning till eight o'clock at night; the rain falling, the sun shining, we was in it all," said William Kerr.

Still others marveled at their newfound status as full citizens of the British Empire and not forced laborers. "I am a slave no more, and you are slaves no more—Jamaica is slave no more," said Thomas Gardner. "My dear brothers and sisters, now the black man can unite with white: no distinctions now, only of character."[51]

THIRTEEN

AFTERMATH

SAMUEL SHARPE'S UPRISING continued to reverberate beyond Jamaica, even though almost nobody spoke of him publicly and the memory of the seditious preacher was quickly effaced from the imperial memory.

An exception to this forgetting came from his minister friend Henry Bleby, who always spoke of Sharpe in generous terms and credited his efforts toward destroying slavery. "The revolt failed of accomplishing the immediate purpose of its author," wrote Bleby, "yet by it, a further wound was dealt to slavery which accelerated its destruction for it demonstrated to the imperial legislature that among the negroes themselves, the spirit of freedom had been so widely diffused as to render it most perilous to postpone the settlement of the most important question of emancipation to a later period."[1]

Emboldened by the Jamaica insurrection and Parliament's dramatic stroke, abolitionists on both sides of the Atlantic stepped up their efforts to overthrow slavery in one of its strongest redoubts: the United States. A group of influential activists founded the American Anti-Slavery Society in Philadelphia and encouraged British allies like Richard Webb Davis and George Thompson to help organize the US population against slavery. They pointed to the peaceful transition in the British Caribbean as evidence that the end of forced labor did not mean anarchy or economic ruin. The editor of the *Liberator,* William Lloyd Garrison, had been watching from the galleries of Parliament during the debates and he returned to Boston convinced that a similar political solution was possible in America.

But others drew the opposite lesson. Samuel Sharpe's rebellion—and the consequent success of British abolition—triggered a low-level panic among US slaveholders, who took note of the fact that both Sharpe and the Virginia rebel Nat Turner were Baptist preachers who had learned to read and had likely been inspired by the propaganda of white abolitionists.

In the spring of 1835 a con artist in Mississippi named Virgil Stewart wrote up a fictional account of a plot to encourage enslaved people to rebel, and anxious Southerners took the hoax seriously. On July 4, thirty people were hanged in the Tennessee cities of Memphis and Nashville and in Natchez, Mississippi, for their "complicity." On July 29 a white mob in Charleston, South Carolina, overran the post office and stole antislavery tracts. Slave owners burned Garrison in effigy, and from the White House, President Andrew Jackson said anyone passing out antislavery tracts was helping "this wicked plan of exciting the Negroes to insurrection."[2]

An important figure in Jackson's State Department wholeheartedly agreed that Jamaica's experience was a foretaste of American trouble. The US consul posted in Kingston, Robert Monroe Harrison, was a self-described "native born Virginian" and the out-of-wedlock offspring of a Tidewater aristocrat. He had nothing but contempt for those born with black skin, and tried to avoid dealing with free colored people. Harrison called enslaved Jamaicans "the most indolent and lazy people of the Earth" and dropped the epithet "wooly-headed Sambo" to refer to the editor of the *Watchman and Jamaica Free Press,* Edward Jordon.[3]

After counting ships in the Kingston docks—a favorite pastime—Harrison realized that a wave of white refugees was moving to the American South, and he predicted that if the situation continued, "the white population of the Colony will be nothing." Even more alarming to him was the prospect of Jamaican slaves being transported into the

United States, for to him it could only lead to plotting and uprising, and he sounded the alarm to Secretary of State Edward Livingston in a handwritten dispatch:

> Believing as I do that the government and citizens of the US-tates [sic]are extremely anxious to prevent the introduction of slaves into any part of our country, I do myself the honor to inform you that great numbers of *blacks* as well as persons of *color* are [unintelligible] in the habit of leaving this island thereby opening a door for the introduction of slaves who may be of the most dangerous character, most especially when the recent insurrection is taken into consideration, and the present state of the Colony.[4]

He was afraid, in essence, of a charismatic leader like Sharpe hiding among the immigrants.

Harrison developed a theory that British metropolitan liberals were plotting to export their notions of slave liberty to the United States, for they had put themselves at a commercial disadvantage by forsaking indentured labor. He warned that "emissaries will go from hence to New York and find their way to our Slaveholding States" to "poison the minds of the Negroes" and lead them toward a revolution. In fact, several in Parliament had indeed predicted that British abolition would soon be replicated worldwide.[5]

For as long as he lived in Jamaica—his posting continued until his death in 1858—Harrison never let go of the conspiracy theory that Britain's secret goal was the disruption of the plantation system in the Old South. His official dispatches warned of an alliance between freed Jamaican slaves and those of Haiti which could "throw upwards of 200,000 blacks" in an amphibious assault on Southern ports. However farfetched, these ideas were taken seriously by South Carolina senator John C. Calhoun, famous for his scabrous rhetoric against those who would deny slaveholders their rightful human property.

After the British foreign secretary, Lord Aberdeen, offered a loan in 1843 to the fledgling Republic of Texas in exchange for its settlers abolishing slavery, Calhoun felt that Harrison's conspiracy theory was coming true. He urged the immediate annexation of Texas into the United States as a slave state, citing a "great & menacing" threat from Britain to foment a race war in America, just as the Jamaica missionaries were believed to have stirred up the violence through their preaching. In this view, antislavery was not merely a pernicious social movement but also a cloak for British imperialistic designs on North America. When Calhoun became secretary of state himself in 1844, he reviewed years of Harrison's correspondence from Jamaica and found support for his belief that British abolition had been motivated not by conscience or humanitarian concerns but, somehow, by simple territorial designs on the United States. Texas was formally annexed the following year.[6]

But the paranoia from Southern interests was only matched by the dedication of those determined not to abandon the fight for total liberty. Some New England Methodist churches commemorated the August 1, 1834, British emancipation date with picnics, songs, speeches, and marches, subsequently making it into an annual celebration. "Freedom Jubilees" in forest groves soon spread across the north from Salem, Massachusetts, to Norristown, Pennsylvania, to Marlboro, Ohio.[7]

At Tranquility Grove in Hingham, Massachusetts, on the appointed date in 1842, vast crowds of people—both black and white—gathered to feast on boiled ham, cake, fruit, raisins, and lemonade under banners with mottos like "True Freedom Is to Share, All the Chains Our Brothers Bear." Medallions passed out to the crowd pictured a slave standing next to a triumphant freed man, broken shackles at his feet—an echo of the wildly successful "Am I not a man and a brother?" campaign. This new legend read "A Voice from Great Britain to America 1834."[8]

A later gathering at Tranquility Grove featured a special guest, none other than the Methodist missionary Henry Bleby, who had visited Samuel Sharpe in jail just before his execution and had since gone on to pastor a church in Barbados. Bleby wrote and spoke frequently on the cause of abolition, and directed most of his activism against slavery in the United States. At the Massachusetts picnic, he described his friend Sharpe in romantic terms, calling him the original author of British emancipation and noting that his revolt and its vengeful aftermath had become the tipping point for government action.

"By and by we began to see what it was," said Bleby. "By these means it was that the storm of indignation was raised among the British people, that led to the abolition of slavery." He was hailed with loud applause.[9]

British Caribbean freedom was celebrated with picnics and rousing speeches in the United States every August 1, even amid gathering tensions, up until the eve of the American Civil War.

Unlike the Americans, the British never had to fight an extended military conflict over the end of slavery. Samuel Sharpe's revolt was as close as it came, and this localized violence half a world away had the practical effect of forcing the question into the political arena, where it could be settled peacefully. The Jamaican revolt of 1831–1832 was, in effect, a contained version of the civil war that ended slavery in a large nation-state: bloodshed that demanded concessions.[10]

Why hadn't the Jamaican planters taken a military stand, as Southern US slaveholders did? There had been firebrands among them who had been willing to sever the ties with the Crown just as easily as their American brethren had renounced the US Constitution in order to save their property, and certainly they could have made an attempt to confiscate royal property in Kingston just as South Carolina partisans would later take over Fort Sumter.

But their cause suffered the disadvantage of geography. The Royal Navy would have easily blockaded major ports, cutting off the sugar trade with other European powers and quickly starving the planters of capital. Economic demographics were also against them. Nine out of ten Jamaicans were enslaved, compared to a slavery rate of 33 percent in the American South, where freehold farms and small artisanal businesses coexisted with large plantations. The combination of sugar and slaves had been an astonishingly successful recipe for economic growth in the Caribbean, but it came with the price of guaranteed uprisings and an undiversified economy. There was simply no real life beyond the megaplantation, where the abused majority was held uneasily at bay.

A further debilitating factor was the prevalence of absentee ownership. Sugar lords felt attached emotionally and genetically to the mother country far more than to Jamaica, and those who lived in Jamaica full-time lacked the "pride in place" felt so keenly by their slaveholding colleagues in the Southern United States. They simply weren't willing to defend their island as a distinct entity beyond its ability to generate easy wealth. Lord Mulgrave had observed, mordantly, in 1833 that most members of the Jamaica Assembly had "hardly any of them any permanent interest in the Country." The foundational contract that created Jamaican prosperity—that between attorney and absentee tycoon—was precisely the factor that made the island an unsuitable candidate for anything other than long-term dependence on the mother country.[11]

How much credit is due to Samuel Sharpe's rebellion for dealing the final death blow to British slavery? Establishing causality is a notoriously tricky business in both politics and history, and those who have studied forced servitude in the British Empire have had a lengthy argument as to what prompted the final collapse. In his landmark book *Capitalism and Slavery,* the Trinidadian scholar Eric Williams made a forceful case for economic dynamics that floated beyond the ability of planter, slave, politician, or missionary to control. The price of sugar was in free fall, West Indian plantations were going into foreclosure, once productive soil had been exhausted, and the old seafaring mercantilism was losing out to steam power and railroads. In this analysis, Samuel Sharpe's revolt and the antislavery moralism back in England were mere window dressing to inevitable change. The American historian Lowell Ragatz, in *Fall of the Planter Class,* also gives dismissive treatment to the agency of the enslaved people, preferring to focus on the Nero-like decay of elite sugar society and the breaking of the West Indian Interest in Parliament thanks to the Reform Act of 1832.

But many others have challenged the economic fatalism thesis with data that shows a robust British sugar monopoly after the Haitian Revolution, regardless of a seasonal price fluctuation. Kamau Brathwaite, Michael Craton, Richard Hart, B. W. Higman, João Pedro Marques, and Mary Turner have all, in their own ways, made a case for the liberation message spread in the tropics and the physical force of the enslaved people themselves. William L. Green, in *British Slave Emancipation,* goes further: "It was the Jamaican rebellion, not the new vigor of the anti-slavery movement, that proved a decisive factor in precipitating emancipation."[12]

The clearest picture may emerge from what was said in Parliament—in both formal debate and worried private settings—in the months following the end of the Jamaican revolt. The questions of Parliament's select committee had zeroed in on the geopolitical risk of slavery to the West Indian population, the cost of maintaining a standing army to quell further revolts, and the possibility that enslaved people, once freed, might prove an imperial asset instead of a security threat. The Colonial Office had been taken over by Whig reformers eager to make use of Sharpe's rebellion as a bureaucratic battering ram. With the West Indian Interest hobbled and contained, the opponents of slavery were more than willing to make use of recent events for their own purposes. The Jamaican violence gave them the moral and pragmatic ammunition they needed at exactly the right time, with the added force of popular sentiment. News of the uprising had spread all over Britain, and if readers weren't made nervous by more warfare in the colonies, they may have been inclined to see a touch of the heroic in the actions of people across the globe, particularly given the successful kicking against aristocratic dominance they had just witnessed at home during the Reform Act fight.

In his key role as a conduit between the Colonial Office and Parliament, the diplomat Henry Taylor was in an especially good position to assess the political effect of Sharpe's rebellion. "This terrible event," he wrote many years later, "with all its horrors and cruelties, its military slaughters and its many murders by flogging, though failing at its object as a direct means, was an indirect death-blow to slavery."

William Knibb's posthumous embrace of Samuel Sharpe is, in many ways, a distillation of this important British breakthrough. In their previous rhetoric, abolitionists had largely cast slaves as objects of pity without voices of their own or the ability to change their own fates. Speaking favorably of a domestic agent of terror was risky, and Knibb had conspicuously refused to visit Sharpe in his jail cell for longer than a few minutes. And he made almost no mention of Sharpe until he was confronted. Only then did he allow—with a touch of prescience—that if the public gave the enslaved people as much credit as it did Europeans, a statue to the doomed avatar of Jamaican freedom ought to be erected. Such a romanticized view should not diminish the essential truth of what is known about Sharpe's rebellion from all the available documentary evidence: that it was solely in the name of liberty.

This crystallized the gradual awakening that took decades to transform into a political consensus: that the soul of the black person was not out of harmony with the soul of the white, and that further resistance to this basic reality would be costly and even embarrassing. Education and religiosity had created an irreversible awareness among the enslaved people to the reality of their condition and their ability to fight back; a similar awareness accrued to the white ruling class that this transformation was both logical and human. This slow collective comprehension, affirmed by Sharpe's rebellion, was the primary deciding factor. British slavery had thrived in isolation, but it was doomed by too much intercourse with a changing world and it was likely headed for further violence and military expense, followed by ineffective measures of amelioration that would only have prolonged the anxiety and misery.

There can be little doubt that Samuel Sharpe's rebellion, with one forceful punch made in the name of liberty, hastened the cause of abolition by several years, if not decades, and provided a potent example of a successful transition to freedom that the Americans failed to heed.

Everyone involved in the events of 1831–1832 was an individual with their own fortunes at stake. Emancipation created a distinct cast of winners and losers.

The hotspur pastor George W. Bridges chose not to stay in Jamaica. His wife, Elizabeth, abruptly left him in 1834, and he moved north to Canada, where he became a passionate devotee of the new technology of photography. At the age of fifty-eight, he embarked on a seven-year trip around the Mediterranean, shooting upward of 1,700 photographs of Roman ruins in Malta, Egyptian pyramids, Algerian markets, and biblical sites in the Levant in which he visually emphasized the rubble of the Ottoman era landscape, as if calling for another crusade to liberate the region from Muslim rule. Photography was an "aristocratic art," he said, though he was only a "poor idle wanderer" running low on funds. Before he died Bridges penned a lengthy unpublished lament for his estranged wife, whose departure still grieved him. But he did manage to forget one thing: after he had left Jamaica, the energetic commentator and fiery defender of slavery never mentioned the island or its slavery in writing again.[13]

The Baptist minister Thomas Burchell, who had given Samuel Sharpe his first preaching platform, returned to Jamaica after his self-imposed exile. He bought an estate outside Montego Bay and split up the land for the use of the freed slaves in his congregation. An American visitor dropped by and found him without malice toward the planters. "He was once insulted, persecuted and imprisoned," wrote the visitor to his friend, US senator Henry Clay. "Now he is greatly at his ease, enjoying a delightful country residence." Burchell kept up his friendship with William Knibb, who had returned to Jamaica as a celebrity after his 1833 speaking tour and his memorable performance before Parliament's select committee. Many of the ex-slaves who greeted him said it seemed as if he had come back from the dead. "Him come," they said. "Him come for true. . . . Him fight de battle, him win de crown." He rebuilt his ruined church at Falmouth and found it routinely packed with worshippers. The emancipation had unleashed a wave of religious feeling on the island that ministers took to calling the Jamaican Awakening.

Knibb personally baptized up to six thousand ex-slaves, founded more than two dozen churches and schools, and translated the Bible into the patois spoken by most black residents. And when a new pastor arrived from England to take over the Montego Bay church, he introduced him to Eve, the elderly mother of Samuel Sharpe, and asked that she be looked after until the end of her days. After a baptismal service on November 9, 1845, he caught a fever and chills. Within a few days he began to vomit black ooze, a sign of the yellow fever that had claimed so many lives in Jamaica.[14]

Knibb's old friend Burchell arrived at the house quickly and sent a letter to his wife on November 14, 1845. "I write to say that brother Knibb is very, very ill with fever and has been so ever since the 12th. Drs. Carey and Anderson are both here; and I do not intend to leave him before I see a decided change." But Knibb's health spiraled downward. He told his daughters they would soon be fatherless, and asked them to keep up the schools he had founded. A stream of friends came to his bedside, and Knibb assured all of them that he trusted in Christ and was not afraid to die.

262 ISLAND ON FIRE

Knibb succumbed to his illness on the morning of November 16 in a fit of muttering, including the statement "All is well." He was buried in the yard of his church in Falmouth, and Burchell preached the funeral sermon for his old friend on the famous text from Revelation 21:4, "And God shall wipe away all tears from their eyes; and there shall be no more death, neither sorrow, nor crying, neither shall there be any more pain: for the former things are passed away."[15]

Burchell left Falmouth feeling weak and febrile himself, and it seems probable he caught yellow fever during his deathbed visit with Knibb. After vomiting blood for several days, he allowed himself to be examined by a doctor, who felt that the minister would not live twenty-four hours. "I shall soon join dear Knibb," said Burchell in his bed. "We worked together in life, and our separation will be short; I hope we will spend an eternity together in heaven."

But the diagnosis proved premature; Burchell lived through the night and soon felt well enough to administer Communion to a few congregants. Then, following his doctor's advice, he took the stagecoach to Kingston and boarded the ship *Clyde* for the four-week voyage to the more healthful climate of England. The trip was miserable; he vomited every night and found his sheets "besmeared with gore" every morning. Shipmates thought they would have to bury Burchell at sea. But he arrived in Southampton, took a train to London, and lay weakened at a friend's house until eventually dying in April.[16]

Knibb and Burchell's Methodist colleague Henry Bleby went on to a successful career as a devotional author and antislavery crusader. One of his books, *Josiah: The Maimed Fugitive,* told the story of an American runaway slave who escaped into Canada via the Underground Railroad.[17]

King William IV remained unhappy about his defeats on abolition and reform, and in 1834, he decided to get rid of his prime minister, Lord Melbourne, thus becoming the last British sovereign to dissolve a government in opposition to the will of Parliament. The decision earned him national scorn and effectively ended the last vestiges of real monarchical influence on the affairs of state. He spent his last three years veering between depression, rages, and meandering speeches. After the king's rambling performance about his hatred of France in front of a group of British soldiers at Windsor Castle, Charles Greville noted in his diary, "If he was not such an ass that nobody does anything but laugh at what he says, this would be very important." But nobody else said a word; they had come to expect such foolishness.[18]

Shortly after William died on June 20, 1837, his teenage niece Victoria was crowned queen, a title she would hold for the next sixty-three years. When she read her first speech, at the coronation, she wore black mourning clothes for William but spoke "with perfect calmness and self-possession," in the view of Greville, who vastly preferred Victoria's restrained style to that of her boisterous uncle. Her first year on the throne happened to coincide with the end of apprenticeship in Jamaica, and though she didn't have anything to do with the decision, the freed enslaved people still cheered for her, remarking that a young queen could accomplish what an old king could not.

After sailing away from Jamaica under a cloud of ignominy, Lord Belmore confronted Viscount Goderich about his dismissal, made his cautious speech in favor of abolition in the House of Lords, and then took to growing exotic plants in the greenhouses at his family estate in Castle Coole in County Fermanagh in Northern Ireland. One agave plant imported from the southwestern United States grew twenty-three feet high and showed six thousand blossoms all at once. But Belmore's high lifestyle was catching up with him; he had to sell off properties and take out loans to pay mounting debts. After a stroke, he moved to London for medical attention, and a second stroke felled him as he made his way back to Castle Coole on April 18, 1841.[19]

The hated master William "Little Breeches" Grignon suffered public scorn for his retreat at Montpelier Estate that marked the military high-water mark for the rebels. He was so embarrassed that he

actively sought a court of inquiry to clear him of all charges of cowardice or incompetence. Before this could happen, however, he was
subject to court-martial procedures in June 1832, but all charges were
dismissed after no witnesses showed up to testify. Grignon then published, at his own expense, a collection of military communiqués
and his own recollections as a seventy-seven-page booklet whose title
gives some clue as to the social pressure he felt, as well as the intense
pride of the lawyer-soldier: *Vindication of the Conduct of Colonel Grignon and of the Western Interior Regiment under His Command during
the Rebellion of 1831 & 1832*. He wrote that his booklet was intended
"to expose the many misrepresentations and calumnies with which
my character has been assailed, and, without such exposure, might
have stigmatized my reputation forever." Grignon continued to practice law in Jamaica and died in 1843, but not before receiving compensation from the British government for the fifty-four slaves he was
forced to set free.[20]

Grignon never apologized publicly for his ardent defense of
slavery, even though other Britons who had supported it began quietly edging away. Some began to adopt the sanitized term *West Indian merchant* to describe their former profession, and many left
British family histories containing this euphemism. Politicians
claimed to have stood where they did not. "I held the abolition of
slavery in the West Indies to be a religious and moral duty," insisted
Grantley Berkeley, who had not spoken a word to that effect during
parliamentary debates on the matter. In 1841, member of Parliament
Robert Peel, who had been an obstructionist in the abolition debates of the previous decade, called for Britain not to be "sullied" by
the import of sugar grown by slaves in Brazil or the United States.
He stood for many who let themselves be blown with the historical
winds.[21]

Elizabeth Barrett Browning confessed that she had been upset that
her family lost money in the emancipation, but also expressed hap-

piness at the humanitarian outcome. "Of course you know that the late bill has ruined the West Indians," she wrote to a friend. "That is settled. The consternation here is very great. Nevertheless I am glad, and always shall be, that the negroes are—virtually—free!" She lent her sympathies to American abolitionists and published a poem in a Boston magazine, *The Liberty Bell*, titled "The Runaway Slave at Pilgrim Point." Laden with sentiment and angry irony, the poem tells the story of a woman impregnated by her master who kills her baby and then herself near the spot of the nation's founding. The fourth stanza reads,

> I am black, I am black;
> And yet God made me, they say.
> But if He did so, smiling back
> He must have cast His work away
> Under the feet of His white creatures,
> With a look of scorn,—that the dusky features
> Might be trodden again to clay.[22]

The cousin she never liked, Richard Barrett, returned to Jamaica a beaten man after his eleventh-hour proslavery lobbying attempt, though he accepted the freedom of his slaves without protest and continued to allow missionaries to teach reading and writing on his properties. One day while out riding, he passed a lesson in progress to a group of children and wondered out loud, mockingly, if the preachers would "teach the goats to read." His jibe concealed the fact that the rebellion and its aftermath had been good business for him, as he purchased multiple estates in foreclosure by planters who gave up on Jamaica after the violence. But Barrett never left. He was a native son of the island, three times the Speaker of the Jamaica Assembly, respected by the rest of the elite, and, though he complained to a banker of being in debt, was still solvent at the age of fifty—by local standards, an elderly man. He held on to his seat in the assembly after being challenged for election by a free colored man who disputed Barrett's claims that he had been a secret liberal all along when it came to race relations. Barrett could only reply, weakly, that in years past the colored challenger would not have been allowed to speak up at all. To the end Barrett's loyalties lay with his true home of Jamaica and not the Britain of his ancestry. In one of his final public speeches, he complained of "usurping Parliaments" and the "straw-catching ministry" of London bureaucrats.[23]

On the morning of May 8, 1839, the year after the enslaved people were formally freed, Barrett awoke in one of his houses in the hills above Montego Bay, ate breakfast, and then went into town to conduct some business at a store belonging to a merchant named Dewar, possibly the same man who had assisted him in inspecting the papers of the missionaries during the rebellion. There he became powerfully and suddenly sick, and the symptoms did not resemble yellow fever or any other of the common tropical illness. He had to be carried up a flight of stairs to rest in the lodging of Catherine Shaw, a woman he knew. Within a few hours he died, and his friends immediately suspected he had been poisoned.[24]

Certainly there were plenty of suspects. Barrett was a glitteringly rich man, a wily politician who could be cruel and withering to his rivals. Making matters more suspicious, the coroner's jury that went to investigate found the body already gone and Catherine Shaw telling her story only in a "reluctant matter." The coroner of St. James quashed the inquest, leading the editor of the *Falmouth Post* to decry the "rascally peculations which ought to be immediately discountenanced by the public." But nobody confessed, and the truth never came out. Richard Barrett died as the probable victim of a homicide, and was buried in the backyard of his estate at Cinnamon Hill without a marker. Though he was Jamaica's most influential permanent resident, with power even exceeding that of most colonial governors, he is barely remembered today.[25]

One of the enslaved people who had belonged to his extended family, Edward Barrett, spoke for thousands of his countrymen when he gave thanks in the year of his freedom, 1838. "We have been made to stand up and see our wives flogged and we could not help them," he said. "The people of England did not see us, but God see us, and God stir up their hearts to get us freedom and now we are all free people." Life would not be easy for Edward Barrett and almost all the rest of Jamaica's 311,000 emancipated people whose individual stories were never recorded. Grueling and bitter agricultural labor was generally the only economic option, and cruelty and discrimination still defined everyday reality. But technically they were free citizens, and their descendants would know conditions that improved as the years ground on, even if their stories were never told.

There were those who didn't just get erased by the record but were erased altogether. Population statistics put the scale in perspective. An estimated 860,000 humans were unwillingly transported to Jamaica over the centuries. Through normal reproductive activity, or what the colonial officials called natural increase, there should have been at least two million black residents of the island by the time of emancipation in 1838. But instead, the register only counts 311,000. That amounts to 1.7 million people who should have existed but simply didn't. They had been killed by disease, torture, starvation, or exhaustion or had simply never been born in the first place.[26]

After Samuel Sharpe was hanged at Montego Bay, white Jamaica tried to erase his memory. Unlike other rebels, his head was not mounted on a pole: such a display might only have elevated his importance and made him even more of a martyr. Fearing an emotional and angry scene, the magistrates refused him a funeral, so a few of his friends took his body to Race Course Beach, east of Montego Bay, where they buried him in the sand. Sometime after emancipation, when all was quiet, his bones were secretly exhumed in the dark, placed in a mahogany coffin, and given an honorary resting place underneath the pulpit at First Baptist Church, where he once preached.[27]

Nobody knows where the bones are today. A letter writer in 1896 reported that "some dastardly, sacrilegious, impecunious monster" had stolen them, presumably to sell to a medical student for study or the construction of a teaching skeleton. A fire leveled the church in 1924 and destroyed Samuel Sharpe's empty coffin. Still, he would attain a sort of earthly resurrection.[28]

EPILOGUE

A GROUP OF YOUNG MEN hunched around a rod of bamboo cut from the forest. One of them produced a liquor bottle full of kerosene, and poured about half of the pinkish contents into the rod's hollow core, then twisted a rag in the top until it was secure. Somebody touched a cigarette lighter to the tip. The improvised torch came to life, a yellow crown forming.

In a bus parked nearby on the public green, a few kids of high school and middle school age sensed the appointed time was close and pulled on bright yellow T-shirts bearing the logo "Flames of Freedom." They were there for the beginning of the ceremonial run on December 27, 2017, to commemorate the 186th anniversary of the revolt that helped break the back of slavery in the British Empire, and it was starting in the town of Catadupa, on the spine of the hills above Montego Bay, where the initial violence had erupted. On the wall of the community center across from the green was a painting of a balding figure with his face caught in a cryptic Mona Lisa smile. The same face is rendered on the front of the Jamaican fifty-dollar bill: Samuel Sharpe. The revolutionary leader is today one of seven National Heroes of Jamaica, part of the reverential iconography of this sovereign Caribbean country. But this portrayal of Sharpe—rendered in 1975 on a contract from the Agency for Public Information—is only an educated guess; nobody alive knows what he really looked like. Yet every Jamaican student learns about him.

The first runner took hold of the torch and started down the pot-holed road, and when she tired, passed it on to another runner. He ran for a bit himself, then handed it off to yet another volunteer runner as a group of their friends bumped along in a pickup truck, hooting and cheering as they progressed down the one-lane road that roughly paralleled the grass-choked tracks of the Jamaica Railway Corporation, which ceased operations in 1992. Their relay was heading toward the city of Montego Bay for an afternoon event near the spot where Samuel Sharpe was executed, and then would twist back up into the hills to the tiny settlement of Kensington, where an unnamed rebel, long since dead, had set the first trash house ablaze on this same date in 1831.

As the children ran down the hill, passing the kerosene torch to each other, they were acting out a visual metaphor that recalled the exchange of clandestine plans during the ritual nighttime taking of oaths in the huts, or—in a religious interpretation—the dangerous spread of Christianity that threatened the health of the planting class.

"Sam Sharpe, Sam Sharpe," some of the runners chanted. "He's a real man," observed one of them, a pillow factory worker named Reece Levy. "He said 'no' to slavery. We'd have never got our freedom otherwise."

The relay continued down the slope of the mountains as the volunteers ran with varying degrees of athleticism, handing the torch off at approximate ten-minute intervals, past ackee and tamarind trees and cinderblock roadside shops; through open meadows and hillsides; and across cane fields long since reclaimed by the jungle. And they passed through the crossroads of Montpelier, not far from the abandoned estate where the enslaved people won their only unambiguous military victory of the uprising in the late afternoon of December 29, 1831, when at least two hundred temporarily free people armed only with rocks and a few scrounged muskets advanced in columns on the hapless Colonel William Grignon, letting out war whoops and cheers as he ordered a confused retreat.

The great house of Montpelier Estate is now a wrecked limestone skeleton covered in moss, and the plantation where sugar once grew in relentless green rows is now a jungle in the hands of the adventure tourism company Chukka, which offers daytime kayaking trips for the guests staying at the nearby all-inclusive resorts that today make up approximately a quarter of the nation's employment, supplying a constant demand for chambermaids, cooks, drivers, landscapers, caddies, waiters, clerks, and back office staff, as well as providing nearly half the gross domestic product (GDP). As for sugar, which was once everything in Jamaica, it barely registers anymore. Slightly over a hundred thousand tons are produced annually, making up less than 2 percent of the GDP.

Pleasure has taken a new form in the years since emancipation. The brand-name resorts like Couples Sans Souci, Hedonism, Hilton, Hyatt, Jewel, Sandals, and Secrets form a sealed zone unto themselves, and might as well be on a different planet with their marbled floors, Las Vegas–style buffets, crystalline beaches, poolside bars, and nightly rack rates that average eight hundred US dollars. Many of them hug the coastline of St. James Parish, near the heart of the 1831–1832 violence.

Downtown Montego Bay is considered too choked with traffic and exhaust fumes to be of much interest to tourists, but those who venture there usually find their way to the 1774 courthouse where Sharpe faced his brief kangaroo trial, the backyard market where he was hanged, and the traffic oval in front now named Sam Sharpe Square, which serves as the unofficial center of town.

A contingent of the Flames of Freedom runners arrived here in Montego Bay in the afternoon for a set of ceremonial speeches by the mayor and other officials, including a former minister of youth and culture named Syd Bartley, who had organized the event. "On a day like today," he told the crowd, "on an evening like this, the Sam Sharpe War started. And because of this, we are free today."

Though Bartley called the revolt by the name of its leader, there has never been collective agreement on what to call the events of

1831–1832. It was known at the time by British officials as the late insurrection, and by later historians as the Baptist War, the Christmas
Uprising, the Emancipation War, or the Great River Valley Slave Revolt, but the organizers of the anniversary commemoration preferred
to tag it with the name Sam Sharpe. One reason for this, perhaps, is
that it gives a familiar human face and a personality to the staggering
mass of kidnapped people who lived their lives in Jamaican slavery
and whose stories and names are forever lost.

Their stories vanished along with their names and faces. Historians
of the imperial-era British Caribbean have been frustrated by a major
and obvious gap in the record: the absence of direct slave accounts.
No completely self-created autobiography has ever emerged. Their
slavery had dealt them double mortality: mistreated and abused in
life, stripped of liberties and names, their individualities were erased
again in death. We are left only with curated fragments—brief windows through which humanities may be glimpsed through statistics.
As many scholars, including Nicole N. Aljoe, have noted, the few authentic slave narratives that emerged from the British Caribbean
were heavily influenced by the court officials, soldiers, memoirists,
abolitionists, journalists, or whoever it may have been quoting from
their stories for their own purposes. The fragments of slave life therefore have a "polyvocal" quality—the enslaved black voice mingled,
diluted, and even drowned inside the differing aims of the more
powerful teller.[1]

The effect is a kind of "ventriloquism," as scholars have termed
it, through which people in bondage are made to speak only at the
behest of a dominant power structure. Yet as Aljoe has argued, this is
not a reason to dismiss the fragments entirely, for the enslaved authors
usually had agency over their choice of particular words and could
still construct a "coherent, self-evident, self-conscious, commanding
subject," even under the heavy influence of an interlocutor—even
one who might not necessarily have wished them well. Just as the
miserly provision grounds out in the woods allowed enslaved persons

a small corner of freedom to grow their own yams and corn, raise a tiny bit of capital, feed their own family, and work for no master for one day of the week, so do the individualities of the people come through for brief moments.

We can see this in the declaration "Liberty is sweet" from an imprisoned Samuel Cunningham; from the defiant agency of the enslaved woman Phibbah, who took for herself a measure of equality in her relationship with the cruel overseer Thomas Thistlewood; in the actions of the rebel soldier Dehany, who showed mercy to a white carpenter who wandered into his camp and who himself refused to die, as he put it, "with a lie in my mouth." And so it is with Samuel Sharpe, who left no writings in his own hand and therefore kept his thinking away from the "picklock of biographers," in the memorable phrase of Stephen Vincent Benét. Sharpe's true motivations are only captured in refracted glimpses, mainly from the testimony of those about to hang and from the jailhouse recollections of Henry Bleby, who reported his best-quoted words: "I would rather die on yonder gallows than live in slavery."

The descendants of enslaved people took on an even more lopsided majority on the island after emancipation, and several hundred of them made another attempt to overthrow the government in 1865 during a labor protest that turned into a riot in the town of Morant Bay. They went on to control most of Saint Thomas in the Vale Parish before British troops moved in and quashed it with the same vigor as they had the 1831 revolt. The Jamaica Assembly lost faith in its own ability to govern itself and put itself directly under authority of Great Britain as a Crown colony. Self-rule gradually returned, and the descendants of enslaved people gained more and more control through parliamentary elections and reforms, even as the ultimate authority still resided with a British governor-general who answered to the Colonial Office in London.

Jamaica's true political detachment from Britain arrived during the winding up of the empire after World War II, and it was granted full territorial sovereignty in 1962. Along with independence came an urgent need to create a sense of nationhood. A parliamentary committee designed a flag featuring a gold saltire vaguely reminiscent of the backbone of the Union Jack, with green and black sections in its quadrants.[2] The color green was said to represent the verdant beauty of the island, and black the hardships that the people endured in colonial times. (The symbolism of the latter was changed in 1996, and the official statement now reads: "The sun shineth, the land is green and the people are strong and creative.") Parliament also held a public competition to select a national anthem, and the winning entry, composed by Rev. Hugh Sherlock, was titled "Jamaica, Land We Love."[3]

Two dominant political factions had already emerged to control the newly empowered Parliament: the free-market Jamaican Labor Party (JLP), headed by the first prime minister, Alexander Bustamante, and the more social democratic People's National Party (PNP), which formed warm relations with Fidel Castro's Cuba in the 1970s even as it captured a majority of seats in the national parliament. This overture, as well as the accompanying economic reforms from the PNP, provoked alarm within the US Central Intelligence Agency, which provided secret training to the JLP to help rig elections, destabilize the government, and forestall a possible communist "domino effect" in the Caribbean.

Against this fraught backdrop in 1975 the government ordered an expansion of its portfolio of the Order of National Heroes—a coveted official status for historical figures. At the time, this pantheon included only five people: the separatist advocate Marcus Garvey, the Morant Bay martyrs Paul Bogle and George William Gordon, PNP founder Norman Manley, and Bustamante himself. A small committee of party loyalists was told to locate inspiring revolutionary figures from the preemancipation era, and they focused on Samuel Sharpe, who had been neglected—almost forgotten.[4]

The committee invited the poet and historian Kamau Brath-waite, then teaching at the University of the West Indies in the Kingston suburb of Mona, to prepare the first modern apologia of Samuel Sharpe, a short book titled *Wars of Respect* that frames him as an uncompromising social revolutionary, a proto-Marxist fighting a system of capitalist oppression who "had made the discovery—long before his time—of the impact of industrial strike action upon the industrial system." Brathwaite de-emphasized the religious side of Sharpe's mission and cast him as a hero of the colonial black underground which had attained consciousness of its role as an exploited underclass.

"Marxism was the language of the day," recalled Arnold Bertram, a PNP official who served on the committee. "The wider context was resistance to plantation slavery."[5]

Though the 1970s rediscovery of Samuel Sharpe came at the time of Jamaica's relations with Castro and the US attempts to tamper with national elections, there were also other powerful cultural forces at work, including the persuasive call of reggae singer Bob Marley (raised in the Kingston ghetto of Trench Town) to "stand up for your rights" and the influence of black empowerment thinking from American cities like Chicago, New York, and Oakland. A new sense of Afro-Caribbean pride encouraged a recasting of the island's history away from a British version founded exclusively on racial categorizations, forced labor, and systematic oppression toward one more focused on self-reliance, pride in achievement, individual agency, and optimism. And one consequential story fit perfectly with that emphasis.

The government declared Samuel Sharpe a National Hero on October 1, 1975, an honor that unleashed a number of others. Sharpe's story was inserted into the public school curriculum all over the island. His face went on the paper currency. "Right Excellent" was to be appended before his name in all official correspondence. The Agency for Public Information hired the portrait artist to guess at his

SAM SHARPE

No portrait of Samuel Sharpe was painted in his lifetime. This approximation, commissioned by the Jamaican government in 1975, graces the fifty-dollar note. *(National Library of Jamaica)*

appearance. A statue went up near the spot where he was executed in the former Charles Square in Montego Bay, now renamed Sam Sharpe Square. Prime Minister Michael Manley was on hand for the announcement in the new hero's hometown, at which "there was a crowd of blank faces," said Bertram, who was also in attendance.[6]

Few people outside the universities even knew Sharpe's name at that point. Yet the elevation of one who had convincingly stood up to the bloodthirsty militia—a figure whose actions had likely hastened the inevitability of emancipation, an appealing one-man mixture of the pious and the outlaw, a man of humble circumstances who stood morally tall even as his gave his life for his beliefs—all this was seen as a personification of Jamaica's difficult journey toward understanding, and even celebrating, the painful elements of its past. At a ceremony at National Stadium, Manley called Sharpe's canonization "the final act of justification of this nation's sense of its own history and, by extension, of the sense of our destiny."[7]

But even as Sharpe became a national symbol, he still contained an irresolvable paradox in his person. Was he a man of war, who wanted to burn down the great houses and seize the island for black self-rule, as had been done in Haiti? Or was he a man of peace, who insisted on Gandhian nonviolence and only wanted enslaved people to be paid for their work?

Because Sharpe was never allowed to speak for himself, and his ideas were filtered through the menacing legal proceedings that followed the insurrection, the documentary record, frustratingly, contains evidence to support both polarities. Rev. Henry Bleby claimed that Sharpe told him in jailhouse conversations that he only wanted freedom without violence, and Robert Rose, among many others, said he heard Sharpe order the enslaved people to simply sit down and "not trouble anybody." No witness reported him killing anyone, and when he showed up at Ginger Hill Estate, he didn't hurt any of the occupants.

Rev. Devon Dick of the Boulevard Baptist Church in Kingston, who wrote his doctoral dissertation on the Native Baptist influence in nineteenth-century Jamaica, considers the pacifist argument persuasive. "He was not about destroying property and destroying lives," Dick explained. "He was a preacher who wanted better working conditions. A leader can't control everybody."[8]

Dick also pointed to the oft-stated reverence for the king of England professed by many enslaved people—hardly the attitude of those who wanted to overthrow a monarchical establishment. An earlier proponent of the pacifist theory, Rev. C. S. Reid, concluded that Sharpe was "against fighting for fighting's sake" and must have "groaned with despair" when he saw the fires at Kensington and realized the plan had gone awry.[9]

And yet, Sharpe was seen at Ginger Hill as the clear leader of a warlike group armed with cutlasses. Multiple witnesses said he was seen carrying a "fowling piece," a weapon resembling a shotgun; others saw a machete in his hands. At least one man said Sharpe was present at an ambush that resulted in a homicide. Most problematically, the sit-down strike never fully materialized because the house torching and the hostage taking began almost immediately.

Those who advocate for the revolutionary interpretation of the evidence include Verene Shepherd, a professor of social history at the University of the West Indies and a scholar of the enslaved resistance, who views the systematic chain of fires on the night of December 27 as irrefutable evidence of a widespread signal to take up arms—a "flaming telegraph," in the words of Brathwaite. "Let no one tell you that Sam Sharpe and the rest of the martyrs were foolish enough to think the British wouldn't come after them with their allies," Shepherd told a crowd at the anniversary celebration. "So even if they had a plan to resist with nonviolence, they also had a Plan B."[10]

Arnold Bertram, who was instrumental in the National Hero movement, agreed: "Tactically, he was not a pacifist. He was a man for freedom, and he would have done whatever it took. Like what Malcolm X said, 'By any means necessary.' I have always understood Sharpe that way."[11]

An irony of Jamaican historiography is that this view parallels the dominant opinion of the nineteenth-century British slaveholders: that Sharpe was a violent radical. He was certainly treated as such by the authorities and went to a criminal's death. But the reinterpretations of him by the Baptist missionaries, which began in the decades after his execution, still carry a powerful charge. Rev. P. H. Cornford set the trend in 1855 with a florid secondhand account of his role as a holy man who tried to restrain the vengeful impulses of his followers, and his decision to surrender as a march to his own Calvary.[12]

Indeed, there are those who look at Sharpe and cannot help but see thematic notes that recall the life of Jesus: born into low circumstances, a gap in the documentary record that excludes childhood, a life of manual labor followed by a brief public ministry near the age of thirty, the gathering of like-minded friends, the sending out of intermediaries, the mingled rhetoric of peace and violence, an induction ceremony, an expected revolution against an empire, a startling reinterpretation of religious texts, a quiet surrender to the civil authorities, the acceptance of death with great composure, a public execution, the lack of any surviving words of his own writing, and—most critically—an extended posthumous dispute about what he truly meant and what he truly wanted.[13]

Noncanonical history also plays a role in Samuel Sharpe's legacy, just as the Gnostic Gospels offer an expanded view of Christ's early life. A body of oral history surrounding the rebellion still circulates in Jamaica—unconfirmed by anything in the contemporary printed literature, which had been controlled entirely by the British, but still noteworthy, not falsifiable, and not contradicted by any documentary evidence.[14]

A teenage Samuel Sharpe was said, for example, to have been sold to a Miss Williams, who ran a Montego Bay hotel named The Stag, but to have been sent back to his master after he destroyed one of Williams's musical instruments in a fit of early piety. He had been taught to ride a horse by a man named Bigga, who was the driver at Cooper's Hill Estate. His field lieutenants, Thomas Dove and Robert Gardiner, had been among his friends on the same plantation where he grew up, which is why they followed him so eagerly. He may have received some early theological instruction from the preacher and part-time barber Moses Baker—who himself had been influenced by teachings in nonviolence from a Quaker named Isaac Lascelles Winn—which is why Sharpe had been so insistent that the rebellion be peaceful. The enslaved people on Richard Barrett's plantation, contrary to the popular reports that portrayed him as a kind master, actually staged a mini-revolution on his estate some time before the revolt by starting a fire in the boiling house; the incident had been hushed up by an embarrassed Barrett and kept out of the newspapers. Sharpe told several of his followers the revolt would be foretold by a bright star fixed to the corner of a crescent moon. Two white sailors from the Royal Navy, disgusted by the slaughter, deserted their ships around New Year's Day and joined the rebels in their fight in the countryside of St. James Parish. None of this can be found in traditional scholarship, but it is still held as true.[15]

Jamaican oral history also possesses a critical detail about the fires on December 27, 1831: the identity of the first arsonist. One account points to John Dunbar, a man who served as a kind of physician among the enslaved people at Tulloch Estate near Kensington, who got drunk and overzealous that night when he should have been following Sharpe's orders to stay peaceful. Another version says it was an unnamed female slave who touched a lighted torch to the cane leaves with a defiant statement: "I know I shall die for it, but my children shall be free." Though there is no contemporary documentation for either account, the latter version is recounted on a historical marker in the mountain crossroads of Kensington. About a mile down the hill from this marker, the Jamaican government has built a small amphitheater—painted in the national colors of green, gold, and black—several yards away from the undisputed spot where the first blaze of the insurrection had been set.[16]

The torch relay ended at this amphitheater on the night of the 186th anniversary, and a caterer handed out Styrofoam boxes of fish and jerk chicken to about three hundred people who showed up for a night of music and speeches from elected officials. Many of the speeches were laced with prayers, just as the bands slipped gospel songs like "Lord I Lift Your Name on High" into their playlists alongside reggae tunes and ballads. Today's Jamaica is one of the most Christianized nations in the hemisphere—the missionaries had won that particular battle—and religious discourse slips effortlessly into the official language of the state.

Off to one side, a group of young adults gathered around a wooden board stacked with paper money to play the dice game Crown and Anchor. Pint bottles of Wray & Nephew rum were cracked open; patches of air became scented with the inevitable smoke of ganja. Somebody had placed the bamboo rod upright next to the stage, and the torch made flickering shadows against iron shackles and cuffs brought over from a nearby museum. The lights of Montego Bay glittered in the distance, framed by the nearby ridgelines, and it was easy to imagine how a fire set here would have been visible for miles in every direction. Then Verene Shepherd took the stage.

"I feel like I'm on holy ground here, do you?" she called to the crowd through her microphone. "Special spot, special spot," somebody called back. They were not wrong: what happened here in a mountainous region of a Caribbean island had gathered enough momentum to shift the course of world history.

Shepherd told the crowd the story of the anonymous woman who was said to have started the first trash house fire on the night of December 27, 1831. "Yes, it led to her death," she said, "but it gave birth to abolition within the British Empire. I'm going to rename her tonight. Guess what I'm going to name her? 'Fire.' Tonight we christen 'Fire.' This time we want to have the flames of passion in our hearts. As I look across the hills, I can almost see the fires lit in 1831. I believe the hills were joyful that night as they witnessed our ancestors stand against oppression and torture."[17]

Her voice rose. "Ancestors, we see you! We hear you every time we sing or dance. Everything we do, the roots are in what our ancestors did to survive."

282 ISLAND ON FIRE

As midnight passed, and the night's culmination approached, Syd Bartley called up a nineteen-year-old student named Sashagay Silk, who was dressed in coarse cloth—what a slave of the early nineteenth century would have worn. He passed her the microphone, and she spoke the appointed line: "I know I shall die for it, but my children shall be free."[18]

She leaped from the stage, grabbed the burning torch, and ran up the hillside toward the ruins of Kensington Estate, where the broken stone still lay in the field, coated with night dews. A small crowd of bystanders followed her, stumbling over the stone, as she reached a large makeshift hut of bamboo poles, grass, and palm leaves specially constructed for the occasion—a model of a plantation trash house— in full view of the amphitheater below.

The woman touched her burning torch to the grass stacked up inside, and it caught fire and spread to the bamboo and palm leaves, even as Bartley called to the audience.

"Burn it down!" he yelled into the microphone. "Burn it down!"

The house of leaves burst into full orange-yellow combustion, as the crowd stood up with the reflections shining on their faces and called back as a chorus; the gathered voices grew louder as the flames danced upward and filled the valley with light and shadows.

"Burn it down!" he said.

"Burn it down!" they said.

"BURN IT DOWN!"

NOTES

BIBLIOGRAPHY

ACKNOWLEDGMENTS

INDEX

NOTES

Abbreviations

AOS   *Papers in Explanation of the Measures Adopted by His Majesty's Government, for Giving Effect to the Act for the Abolition of Slavery throughout the British Colonies, Part I, Jamaica 1833–1835,* April 16, 1835

Bulletins   *Bulletins of State Intelligence &c,* 1832, compiled from the *London Gazette*

CO   Original correspondence between the Colonial Office and the governor of Jamaica (UK National Archives)

PD   *Parliamentary Debates,* third series,, vol. 17, April 2, 1833–May 20, 1833 (British Parliamentary Documents)

PP   *Parliamentary Papers* (British Parliamentary Documents)

SC   *Report from the Select Committee on the Extinction of Slavery throughout the British Dominions,* August 11, 1832 (British Parliamentary Documents)

SI   *Jamaica: Slave Insurrection. Return to an Address to His Majesty,* June 22, 1832 (British Parliamentary Documents)

SPP   *Slaves: Papers Presented to Parliament By His Majesty's Command* [. . .], vols. 2, 16, 1830–1831 (British Parliamentary Documents)

USC   Despatches from U.S. Consuls in Kingston, Jamaica, 1796–1906, Record Group 59, T31 (US National Archives)

Votes   *Votes of the Honourable House of Assembly of Jamaica*, February 28–April 28, 1832 (Jamaica Archives)

WIC   *West India Colonies* (British Parliamentary Documents)

Introduction

1. *WIC*, No. 7, p. 22.
2. George Lawson to Lord Belmore, December 28, 1831, CO 137 / 181.
3. John Roby to Lord Belmore, December 27, 1831, CO 137 / 181.
4. Lawson to Belmore, December 28, 1831.
5. *Cornwall Courier*, December 30, 1831; reprinted in the *Connecticut Courant*, January 24, 1832.
6. Senior, *Jamaica as It Was*, p. 179; Waddell, *Twenty-Nine Years in the West Indies*, p. 57.
7. Lawson to Belmore, December 28, 1831.
8. Richard Barrett to Lord Belmore, December 31, 1831, CO 137 / 131.
9. Barrett to Belmore, December 31, 1831.
10. *SPP*, vol. 2, pp. 9–13; Hall, *In Miserable Slavery*, p. 74.
11. Transatlantic Slave Trade Database, Emory University, http:/ /www .slavevoyages.org/ database.
12. Legacies of British Slave-Ownership, University College London, http:/ /www.ucl.ac.uk/lbs.

1. A Suburb of Hell

1. Burnard, "Prodigious Riches," pp. 505–523.
2. Leslie, *A New and Exact History*, p. 364; McNeill, *Mosquito Empires*, pp. 97–98.
3. *Interesting Tracts*, p. 29.
4. McNeill, *Mosquito Empires*, p. 99.
5. Bonnick, *Rooms without Doors*, p. 204. See also Barrett, *The Barretts of Jamaica*, pp. 5–13. Pimento is another name for allspice.
6. Dunn, *Sugar and Slaves*, p. 178.
7. Howard, *Kingston*, p. 38.
8. Ward, *A Trip to Jamaica*, p. 14; Lewis, *Journal*, p. 160.
9. Dunn, *Sugar and Slaves*, p. 187; Lewis, *Journal*, p. 162.

10. Burnard, *Master, Tyranny and Desire*, p. 85; Robertson, "Ambivalent Cosmopolitanism," pp. 608, 619; Levy, "Through European Eyes," p. 41; Brown, *The Reaper's Garden*, p. 1.

11. Ward, *A Trip to Jamaica*, p. 16; Dunn, *Sugar and Slaves*, p. 39; Jones, *Diary*, p. 14.

12. Foulks, *Eighteen Months in Jamaica*, p. 67; William Fisher, letter, WYK1263/1/17, West Yorkshire Archive, Leeds, UK. Fisher survived his stay in Jamaica. See also McNeill, *Mosquito Empires*, p. 102.

13. Nugent, *Journal*, p. 18.

14. Brown, *The Reaper's Garden*, p. 16; Burnard, "Prodigious Riches," p. 520; Ragatz, *The Fall of the Planter Class*, p. 54; Dallas, *The History of the Maroons*, pp. 359, 370; Roughley, *Jamaica Planter's Guide*, p. 4. For an analysis of just how thoroughly the attorney system shaped the economy, see especially Higman, *Plantation Jamaica*, pp. 88–91.

15. Long, *The History of Jamaica*, vol. 2, p. 433; Green, *British Slave Emancipation*, p. 5; Cundall, *The Press and Printers of Jamaica*, p. 4. For a description of an atypically elegant mansion near the capital, see Petley, *White Fury*, pp. 64–66.

16. Leslie, *A New and Exact History*, p. 36; Levy, "Through European Eyes," p. 33.

17. Hewlett, *Elizabeth Barrett Browning*, pp. 119–121; Elizabeth Barrett Browning to Hugh Stuart Boyd, May 19, 1831, in Browning, *Elizabeth Barrett to Mr. Boyd*, p. 137.

18. Dunn, *Sugar and Slaves*, p. 335; Brathwaite, *The Development of Creole Society*, p. 65.

19. Greene, *Evaluating Empire*, p. 74; Green, *British Slave Emancipation*, p. 5; Long, *The History of Jamaica*, vol. 2, p. 279; Nugent, *Journal*, 132.

20. Stewart, *An Account of Jamaica*, p. 123. See also Holt, *The Problem of Freedom*, p. 87.

21. Lewis, *Journal*, p. 149; Madden, *A Twelvemonth Residency*, p. 149; *SC*, p. 10. For a discussion of how Jamaica's "frontier" characteristics overshadowed its cosmopolitan elements, see Brathwaite, *The Development of Creole Society*, p. 267.

22. Nugent, *Journal*, p. xxxi; Long, *The History of Jamaica*, vol. 2, p. 19. The conception of eighteenth-century Jamaica as a more cosmopolitan place than some of its critics have alleged has recently been argued by some scholars (including Robertson in "Ambivalent Cosmopolitanism"), but

contemporary accounts are numerous and persuasive on its cultural distance from the metropole.

23. Leslie, *A New and Exact History*, p. 353.

24. Patterson, *The Sociology of Slavery*, p. 48; Brathwaite, *The Development of Creole Society*, p. 28.

25. Bryan Edwards, quoted in Hart, *Slaves Who Abolished Slavery*, p. 89.

26. Madden, *A Twelvemonth Residence*, p. 151.

27. Foulks, *Eighteen Months in Jamaica*, p. 42; Levy, "Through European Eyes," p. 38; Nugent, *Journal*, p. 57, 81.

28. Burnard, *Mastery, Tyranny, and Desire*, p. 3.

29. Burnard, *Mastery, Tyranny and Desire*, p. 156.

30. Burnard, *Mastery, Tyranny and Desire*, p. 156; Macaulay, *Life and Letters*, p. 7; Moreton, *West India Customs*, p. 78.

31. *Falmouth Post*, October 14, 1835, quoted in Holt, *The Problem of Freedom*, p. 92.

32. Fisher, letter; *SC*, p. 6.

33. *SC*, p. 63, 507; Patterson, *The Sociology of Slavery*, p. 42; Legion, *A Second Letter*, p. 59. Some bookkeepers and attorneys confessed they had not seen a single white woman in years, and would not have the slightest idea how to talk to one if they had the opportunity. See Waddell, *Twenty-Nine Years in the West Indies*, p. 21. The trysts sometimes turned into lasting relationships. One of the most prominent planters in Jamaican society, Simon Taylor, was an unmarried man who was known to have "families" of colored children on each of his many plantations, and he had a relationship with a woman named Grace Donne that lasted thirty years. Even the hot-tempered Thomas Thistlewood developed a lasting bond with an enslaved woman named Phibbah. "At night Phibbah slept in the hammock in the hall; would not come to bed," he wrote. About a month later, he noted in a hurt tone that "Phibbah did not speak to me all day." When he accepted a job on another plantation, they were both distraught: "Phibbah grieves very much, and last night I could not sleep, but vastly uneasy, &c." She bore him a son, John, and the three presented themselves to their neighbors as a family. Thistlewood eventually called Phibbah his "wife" and wrote her into his will, setting her free upon his death. See Hall, *In Miserable Slavery*, p. 67; also Paugh, *The Politics of Reproduction*, p.79: "In relationships characterized by such uneven power dynamics, consent is extremely difficult to define."

34. Patterson, *The Sociology of Slavery*, pp. 159–160.

2. Deacon Sharpe

1. Knibb, *Memoir*, p. 46.
2. Catherall, *William Knibb*, pp. 16, 20, 94.
3. Brathwaite, *The Development of Creole Society*, p. 259; *SC*, p. 388; Baptist Missionary Society, *Letter of Instructions*, p. 13, quoted in Brathwaite, *The Development of Creole Society*, p. 258.
4. Turner, *Slaves and Missionaries*, p. 57; Catherall, *William Knibb*, p. 49.
5. "A Return of Slaves," June 28, 1817, National Archives, London, T 71 / 203, cited in Kreitzer, "Kissing the Book," p. 11. Some accounts of Sharpe's boyhood give his birthplace as Croydon Estate, near the town of Catadupa, but that information is drawn from a January 3, 1832, reward poster offering three hundred Jamaican dollars for his capture. On it he is named as "General Ruler, Samuel Sharpe or Tharp, also Daddie Ruler Sharpe, or Tharp, director of the whole, and styled also Preacher to the Rebels, belonging to Croydon Estate, St. James." Kreitzer and other scholars believe that, in the heat of the rebellion, Sharpe had been confused with another enslaved man named Tharp and that the Croydon reference should therefore be treated as a mistake. There are no nineteenth-century slave owner's returns that place a young Samuel Sharpe at Croydon; he is listed only at Cooper's Hill.
6. "A Return of Slaves," June 28, 1832, National Archives, London, T 71 / 223, reproduced in Kreitzer, "Kissing the Book," p. 22; *Jamaica Almanack*, pp. 92, 128.
7. Bleby, *Death Struggles of Slavery*, p. 128; Bleby, *Speech*, p. 5. Sharpe's relatively privileged status as a youth mirrored that of attempted revolutionary leaders within slave societies in the United States—notably, that of Nat Turner and Denmark Vesey. Vesey's seafaring master, Captain Joseph Vesey, treated him more like a personal assistant than a laborer, for example. See Lofton, *Denmark Vesey's Revolt*, p. 15.
8. Reid, *Samuel Sharpe*, p. 57. Baker was an African American native of New York City who evacuated with British soldiers to Jamaica after the Revolutionary War. He set up successful churches in St. James and Westmoreland Parishes that were later absorbed into the work of white missionaries. See Baptist Missionaries, *A Narrative of Recent Events*, p. 1; Brathwaite, *The Development of Creole Society*, p. 163.
9. Bleby, *Death Struggles of Slavery*, p. 127.
10. Bleby, *Death Struggles of Slavery*, p. 127.

11. Clarke, *Memorials of Baptist Missionaries*, p. 101. See also Cornford, *Missionary Reminiscences*, p. 28. This was another point of commonality between Sharpe and the South Carolina rebel leader Denmark Vesey: they both shared the gift of literacy and would later use selected passages from the Bible to inspire their followers. A class of unemployed white men in Jamaica were known as "walking buckras" who would circulate among the estates and read newspapers to the enslaved people out loud in exchange for a few coins or a drink of rum. Though estate managers considered them a nuisance, one of them might have been Sharpe's conduit for the latest British papers. See *SC*, p. 96.

12. The United States enacted the Act Prohibiting the Importation of Slaves the same month.

13. Corfield, "Elizabeth Heyrick," p. 42. See also Hochschild, *Bury the Chains*, p. 325.

14. Boswell, *The Life of Samuel Johnson*, p. 146.

15. Coleridge, "On the Slave Trade," p. 138.

16. Abbott, *Sugar*, p. 185; Heyrick, *Immediate, Not Gradual*, pp. 31, 34.

17. Plasa, *Slaves to Sweetness*, p. 41.

18. Anthropos, *The Rights of Man*, p. 36.

19. Hochschild, *Bury the Chains*, p. 193; *Leicester Journal*, July 31, 1829; Reddie, *Abolition!* p. 214; *SC*, p. 45.

20. Heyrick, *Immediate, Not Gradual*, p. 33, emphasis in the original.

21. Wiltshire antislavery association, quoted in Corfield, "Elizabeth Heyrick," p. 46.

22. The *Leicester Chronicle* praised her a year later on May 5, 1832, as having articulated the antislavery cause "more strongly, more clearly, and more righteously" than any other abolitionist.

23. Corfield, "Elizabeth Heyrick," p. 61.

3. King Sugar

1. Hentzner, *Travels in England*, p. 59.

2. Hargreaves, "Queen Elizabeth and Her Teeth," pp. 286–288.

3. Hentzner, *Travels in England*, p. 100; Yudkin, *Pure, White and Deadly*, p. 12.

4. Abbott, *Sugar*, p. 48; Mintz, *Sweetness and Power*, p. 135.

5. Abbott, *Sugar*, p. 15.

6. Mintz, *Sweetness and Power*, p. 14.

7. Glasse, *The Art of Cooking*, pp. iii, 317.

8. Abbott, *Sugar*, p. 68.

9. Abbott, *Sugar*, pp. 61–69.

10. Mintz, *Sweetness and Power*, p. 73; Brendon, *The Decline and Fall*, p. 16.

11. Witherspoon, *The Works of John Witherspoon*, p. 315; Riland, *Memoirs of a West India Planter*, p. 8.

12. Williams, *Capitalism and Slavery*, p. 94.

13. Nelson, *Architecture and Empire in Jamaica*, p. 260.

14. McClelland, "Redefining the West India Interest," p. 143.

15. Wentworth, *The West India Sketchbook*, p. 70.

16. Chen, *The Taste of Sweet*, pp. 22–27.

17. Lustig, "Fructose," pp. 1307–1321. Taking the link further, Lustig has documented remarkable consistencies in the metabolism of sugar and that of alcohol.

18. Willis, *The Remaining Medical Works*, n.p.

19. Nugent, *Journal*, p. 95.

20. Elizabeth Barrett Browning to Mary Russell Mitford, January 12, 1842, in Browning, *Letters of Elizabeth Barrett Browning to Mary Russell Mitford*, vol. 1, p. 331.

21. Marks, *The Family of the Barrett*, p. 423; Barrett, *Richard Barrett's Journal*, p. xii; Richard Barrett to Elizabeth Barrett Williams, August 2, 1825, SD.538, MS 681/1/3, College Library, Eton College, Windsor, UK.

22. Marks, *The Family of the Barrett*, p. 342.

23. Godwin, *Lectures*, p. 16.

24. Marks, *The Family of the Barrett*, p. 341; Second Marquess of Sligo to Lord Glenelg, June 18, 1836, quoted in Burn, *Emancipation*, p. 154n.

25. *Jamaica Almanack*, p. 118; see also Robertson, "Ambivalent Cosmopolitanism," p. 160.

26. Legacies of British Slave-Ownership, University College London, http://www.ucl.ac.uk/lbs/search; Patterson, *The Sociology of Slavery*, p. 9; McMahon, *Jamaica Plantership*, pp. 143–144.

27. *SC*, p. 319; Roughley, *Jamaica Planter's Guide*, p. 116.

28. Senior, *Jamaica as It Was*, p. 59; Petley, *White Fury*, p. 8; Brathwaite, *The Development of Creole Society*, p. 232.

29. Hart, *Slaves Who Abolished Slavery*, p. 16; Burn, *Emancipation*, pp. 42–44. The driver sometimes delegated the task of whipping to an associate known

as the jumper, or Johnny Jumper; Brathwaite, *The Development of Creole Society*, p. 155.

30. Roughley, *Jamaica Planter's Guide*, pp. 191–192.

31. Beckles and Shepherd, *Liberties Lost*, p. 130. Even though the industrialized system depended on efficiency, enslaved people found many ways to resist their oppression. One common method of self-defense was the construction of what Jamaican sociologist Orlando Patterson has identified as a "Quashee" personality—the deliberate display of incompetence or stupidity. Having been stripped of family, religion, art, meaningful work, physical comfort, and all dignity, slaves developed private rebellions of the heart and elaborate methods to conceal the true self. They would work only when forced, and never with enthusiasm. This not only permitted the enslaved person a tiny measure of revenge and sly satire, but it also allowed the white masters to feel as though their disdain and coercive behavior was justified. The violent contempt of the whites and the quiet daily revolt of the blacks had become mutually reinforcing—a signature feature of Jamaican society. See Patterson, *The Sociology of Slavery*, p. 177.

32. Ragatz, *The Fall of the Planter Class*, p. 16.

33. Kaplan, *The Black Presence*, pp. 76–77; Scott, *The Common Wind*, p. 58; Brathwaite, *The Development of Creole Society*, p. 253.

34. SC, p. 56; Vasconcellos, *Slavery, Childhood, and Abolition*, p. 74; Waddell, *Twenty-Nine Years in the West Indies*, p. 23.

35. SC, p. 266.

36. Brathwaite, *The Development of Creole Society*, p. 218.

37. SC, p. 68; Cooper, *Facts*, p. 11; Lewis, *Journal*, p. 185.

38. Waddell, *Twenty-Nine Years in the West Indies*, pp. 37–38.

4. The Door of No Return

1. Pregnancy was dangerous in Jamaica. At one plantation, Worthy Park, only six children were born in an average year to seventy-seven women in their prime childbearing years. Some slave women responded by aborting their own children, sometimes under pressure from their overseer or their own fellow enslaved people. In at least one case, a Jamaican woman killed her own children rather than subject them to the pain of slavery—an event reminiscent of the case of Margaret Garner, an American slave who escaped

into Ohio with her three children in 1856, and then, when cornered in a house, killed her two-year-old daughter with a knife and attempted to take the lives of her two other children because, she later explained, she could not bear to see her offspring sent back in bondage. The Garner case horrified American newspaper readers, became the subject of an opera and later inspired Toni Morrison in the 1987 novel *Beloved*. Considerably less attention was devoted to the case of Sabina Park, who lived near the Half Way Tree village outside Kingston. She murdered her three-month-old child, telling a witness she "had worked for buckra already and she would not be plagued to raise the child . . . to work for white people." Such outright infanticide was rare, but such attitudes were common among slave mothers who were known to express sorrow for having had children in the first place. See Patterson, *The Sociology of Slavery*, pp. 106–111; and Paugh, *The Politics of Reproduction*, pp. 93–94. For a discussion of changes in the "buy versus breed" attitude between 1780 and 1807, see Turner, *Contested Bodies*, pp. 46–52. "Buy rather than breed" was no longer possible on a wide scale after the end of the slave trade in 1807. See also Mullin, *Africa in America*, p. 20; and Petley, *White Fury*, p. 49.

2. Perbi, *Indigenous Slavery in Ghana*, pp. 111–120.

3. Hakluyt, *The Principal Navigations*, p. 94.

4. Williams, *Capitalism and Slavery*, p. 187. Williams further argues in this still-debated 1944 book that revenues from the slave trade financed the Industrial Revolution in Britain, and that Britain was finally persuaded to abandon the practice not because of a moral awakening but because it had become economically unsustainable. Williams's thesis received a sharp challenge from Seymour Drescher in his 1977 *Econocide: British Slavery in the Era of Abolition*, which contended that the plantation economy was as strong as it had ever been. For an extended discussion, see Davis, *Inhuman Bondage*, pp. 231–249.

5. Matthews, *A Voyage*, p. 158.

6. Davies, *The Royal African Company*, p. 44. It had been preceded by an outfit named the Company of Royal Adventurers Trading into Africa, which had, in the judgment of Davies, more the flavor of "an aristocratic treasure hunt than of an organized business," p. 41. For a discussion of how Africans never thought of themselves as tribal, see Wright, *African Americans in the Colonial Era*, p. 18. See also Beckles and Shepherd, *Liberties Lost*, p. 86.

7. Pettigrew, *Freedom's Debt*, p. 11; Brendon, *The Decline and Fall*, p. 19; Nguah and Kugbey, *Shackles in Darkness*, pp. 22–23. Some claimed these payments were made to create warfare between rival nations so that refugees from the combat zones could then be captured, dragged to the coast, and shipped off to North America. The degree to which European traders started these wars for their own benefit, or merely positioned themselves to receive the human spoils, remains murky. The repentant slaver John Newton claimed the African wars would immediately end "if the Europeans would cease to tempt them by offering goods for slaves." But many Africans—arranged into nation-states generally much smaller than European countries—disagreed with this outside analysis, pointing out they engaged in sporadic territorial conflict long before the first European traders appeared. "We Dahomeans are surrounded by enemies who make incursions, we must defend ourselves," a king named Kpengla is reported to have told a British visitor in 1785. "Your countrymen, therefore, who allege that we go to war for the purpose of supplying your ships with slaves, are grossly mistaken." The accuracy of the quote—given to a British official who was reading the king newspaper accounts of abolitionist debates—remains disputed, but John Thornton has argued that the spirit remains consistent with the geopolitical picture and the tide of popular sentiment along the Slave Coast. Thornton also points out that African legal systems did not generally recognize the private ownership of land, but placed high capital premiums on human beings to cultivate land not already under tillage. See Thornton, *Warfare*, p. 135; and Thornton, *Africa*, pp. 87–97.

8. Park, *Travels*, p. 225.

9. Adams, *Remarks*, p. 130.

10. Hart, *Slaves Who Abolished Slavery*, p. 33; Matthews, *A Voyage*, p. 152; Brown, *The Reaper's Garden*, p. 39; A. and I. Churchill, *Collection of Voyages and Travels* (London, 1744–1746), quoted in Hart, *Slaves Who Abolished Slavery*, p. 44.

11. Lawrence, *Fortified Trade-Posts*, p. 165; Monrad, *Two Views from Christiansborg Castle*, p. 258; Beckles and Shepherd, *Liberties Lost*, p. 84.

12. Matthews, *A Voyage*, p. 152; Falconbridge, *An Account of the Slave Trade*, p. 18.

13. A Genuine "Dickey Sam," *Liverpool and Slavery*, p. 4.

14. A Genuine "Dickey Sam," *Liverpool and Slavery*, p. 4; Beckles and Shepherd, *Liberties Lost*, p. 83; Brendon, *The Decline and Fall*, p. 23; Linebaugh and Rediker, *The Many-Headed Hydra*, p. 151.

15. "An Abolitionist," *The Negro's Memorial*, p. 124. Nguah and Kugbey, *Shackles in Darkness*, p. 37. Taylor, *If We Must Die*, p. 392. "The holds of slave ships," wrote Taylor, "were perhaps the sites where African-American resistance first developed into a coherent and somewhat unified movement. . . . It was aboard slave ships that men and women of different backgrounds first forged, by means of necessity, valuable bonds of solidarity that were to remain strong and fundamentally important for many enslaved Africans and their descendants." Taylor, *If We Must Die*, p. 81.

16. Ottobah Cugoano, in Carretta, *Unchained Voices*, p. 149. Cugoano was born in present-day Ghana in approximately 1757, was sold into slavery, and transported to the Caribbean. Later emancipated by his master in Britain, he became an abolitionist and wrote a short book entitled *Thoughts and Sentiments on the Evil and Wicked Traffic of the Slavery and Commerce of the Human Species*, which contains one of the only known firsthand accounts of a transatlantic voyage from the perspective of an enslaved person. See also Bosman, *Guinea*, p. 282; and Beckles and Shepherd, *Liberties Lost*, pp. 89–90.

17. Thome and Kimball, *Emancipation in the West Indies*, p. 343; Foulks, *Eighteen Months in Jamaica*, p. 24.

18. Madden, *A Twelvemonth Residence*, p. 78; Williams, "Early Kingston," p. 5; Nelson, *Architecture and Empire*, pp. 91–92; Stewart, *An Account of Jamaica*, p. 34.

19. Equiano, *The Interesting Narrative*, p. 58. The University of Maryland historian Vincent Carretta has found reason to question Equiano's account based on a baptismal record from St. Margaret's Church in 1759 that recorded his birthplace as "Carolina" and a Navy muster roll from 1773 that said he was native to South Carolina. As an ardent abolitionist, he had a strong motivation to make the truth of the Middle Passage known to a wide readership, and it had been theorized that Equiano heard details of what the voyage was like from his fellow slaves—perhaps even his father—and expropriated them years later. Whether he was an actual eyewitness or a secondhand reporter, the details line up with all other testimony about the experience.

20. O'Malley, *Final Passages*, p. 39.

21. Brown, *The Reaper's Garden*, p. 188; Bickell, *The West Indies*, p. 36. The comparison of human chattel to livestock was a common one throughout the Atlantic world, and dated to mentions of slavery in ancient Greek writings. It extended to the domestication of both livestock and kidnapped Africans through the process of extended juvenilization called neoteny. Jacoby,

"Slaves by Nature?," pp. 90–91. See also Patterson, *The Sociology of Slavery*, p. 177.

22. Turner, *Contested Bodies*, p. 46. There was an irony in this common view of the buyers. "Rejected in theory, on the grounds of their physical frailty, women ended up, nevertheless, as the chief manual laborers on the plantation," wrote Caribbean historian Lucille Mair. See Mair, *Women in Jamaica*, p. 75.

23. John Newton, quoted in O'Malley, *Final Passages*, p. 39.

24. Clement Noble, quoted in O'Malley, *Final Passages*, p. 43; Long, *History of Jamaica*, vol. 2, pp. 332, 485.

25. Mustakeem, *Slavery at Sea*, p. 163; Beckles and Shepherd, *Liberties Lost*, p. 118.

26. *The Humming Bird*, p. 81.

27. Brendon, *The Decline and Fall*, p. 23; Mullin, *Africa in America*, p. 86; Brathwaite, *The Development of Creole Society*, pp. 321–328.

28. Burnard, *Mastery, Tyranny and Desire*, p. 17. The modern consensus on dirt eating is that it was indeed an attempt to gain calories, however unpleasant. See Kiple, *The Caribbean Slaves*, p. 101; testimony of William Fitzmaurice, Select Committee on Slave Trade, 1790–1791, quoted in Patterson, *The Sociology of Slavery*, p. 264.

29. One of Fox's close friends, William Penn, went on to found the province of Pennsylvania on a royal charter from King Charles II, who gave him the land as a repayment to a debt owed to Penn's father, Sir William Penn, who had helped capture Jamaica for the British in 1655.

30. *Defoe's Review*, January 10, 1712.

31. Mullin, *Africa in America*, pp. 28, 251; Brathwaite, *The Development of Creole Society*, p. 164; Stewart, *An Account of Jamaica*, p. 251; Williams, *Capitalism and Slavery*, p. 37.

32. Abbott, *Sugar*, p. 110; *SC*, p. 93. See also Legion, *Second Letter*, p. 38.

33. *SC*, p. 488.

34. *SC*, pp. 289, 485; Burnard, *Mastery, Tyranny and Desire*, p. 153; Long, *The History of Jamaica*, vol. 2, pp. 410–411.

35. Mullin, *Africa in America*, p. 155.

36. Foulks, *Eighteen Months in Jamaica*, pp. 47–48, emphasis in the original.

37. *SC*, p. 19; Beckles and Shepherd, *Liberties Lost*, pp. 155–56. The shortage of food for Jamaican slaves triggered one of the more bizarre incidents in British naval history. Scientists at the Royal Society of Arts in London had

the idea that breadfruit native to Tahiti might also be successfully grown in Jamaica and offered a premium for a captain to take a load of trees from \ the South Pacific\ to the Caribbean to try the experiment. Captain William Bligh of HMS *Bounty* made the attempt, but on his way to Jamaica on April 28, 1789, nineteen members of his crew, including his master's mate, Fletcher Christian, mutinied against him and set him and his loyalists adrift in launches. With the loss of only one man, Bligh successfully made it to the Dutch settlement at Timor forty-seven days later, having traveled in an open boat more than four thousand miles. Christian and the rest of the mutineers were not so lucky; they picked up eleven women and six men in Tahiti and sailed the *Bounty* to a spectacularly isolated rock named Pitcairn Island, where they fought among themselves about food and sex to the point that only one mutineer was left alive. Bligh made a successful second voyage from 1791 to 1793 that brought breadfruit to Jamaica. But the entire *Bounty* adventure had been for nothing. Breadfruit got planted and it grew, but the "ardor subsided as the novelty wore off," said an observer of the experiment. See Dallas, *The History of the Maroons*, p. 353.

38. Stewart, *A View of Jamaica*, pp. 270–271.

39. Hall, *In Miserable Slavery*, p. 177.

40. Stewart, *An Account of Jamaica*, pp. 270–271. The enslaved people drew some identification from a traditional West African mythical figure Anansi, who was a spider-shaped man, fragile and small, but blessed with a superior cunning that allowed him to outwit his many enemies: a charming rogue similar to the Br'er Rabbit of the American South. Through the stories they told about Anansi, the enslaved people could see and interpret their own methods of subverting the daily humiliations of forced labor. Anansi could summon his wits to do what seemed impossible, like gather all the world's stories into a kettle or catch a leopard in a hole in the ground. To the Jamaican slaves, it could seem at nightfall like merely surviving to work another day was also an impossible task.

41. Patterson, *The Sociology of Slavery*, p. 245; Okagbue, *African Theatres*, p. 20; Ottenburg, "Humorous Masks," p. 337. Patterson has theorized the gathering represented a syncretic blend of various West African harvest rituals that the enslaved people recalled from their former lives—especially the yam festivals of the Ibo people from what is now western Nigeria.

42. Beckles and Shepherd, *Liberties Lost*, p. 146.

298 NOTES TO PAGES 72–80

43. Trelawny, *An Essay concerning Slavery*, p. 5.

44. Gaunt, *Where the Twain Meet*, p. 156.

45. McKee, "From Violence to Alliance," p. 29; Thompson, *Fight to Freedom*, p. 293.

46. Craton, *Testing the Chains*, pp. 125–139. See also Hart, *Slaves Who Abolished Slavery*, pp. 130–150; and Linebaugh and Rediker, *The Many-Headed Hydra*, p. 221.

47. Linebaugh and Rediker, *The Many-Headed Hydra*, p. 221.

48. Brown, *The Reaper's Garden*, p. 148.

49. Hart, *Slaves Who Abolished Slavery*, pp. 151–155.

50. Gardner, *A History of Jamaica*, p. 141.

51. James, *The Black Jacobins*, p. 88; Geggus, *Slavery, War and Revolution*, p. 12.

52. Girard, *Toussaint Louverture*, pp. 174–175.

53. Dallas, *The History of the Maroons*, p. 455; Brathwaite, *The Development of Creole Society*, p. 247. Many of the Haitian slaves had previously lived in Jamaica. See Scott, *The Common Wind*, pp. 52, 69; and Geggus, *Slavery, War and Revolution*, p. 89. Lord Effingham to Henry Dundas, September 7, 1791, quoted in Scott, *The Common Wind*, p. 142.

54. Gardner, *A History of Jamaica*, p. 239; Ferrer, *Freedom's Mirror*, p. 152; Loker, "An Eighteenth-Century Plan," p. 134.

55. Thomas Jefferson to James Monroe, July 14, 1793, in Jefferson, *Papers*, vol. 26, p. 503. See also Scott, *The Common Wind*, pp. 143, 153; and Adams, *Works*, p. 437.

56. The Negro Code, or Code Noir, was a set of laws drawn up in 1685 under the reign of Louis XIV intending to bring order and law into the practice of slavery in the French colonial sphere. Among other mandates, it required Roman Catholic baptisms, prohibited unauthorized gatherings, and forbade the torture of disobedient enslaved people, though beatings were permitted.

57. Burnard, *Mastery, Tyranny and Desire*, p. 137.

58. James, *The Black Jacobins*, p. 23.

5. The Plot

1. *SC*, p. 103; Waddell, *Twenty-Nine Years in the West Indies*, p. 34; Brathwaite, *The Development of Creole Society*, p. 20.

2. *SC*, p. 129.

3. *SC*, pp. 242, 162. For his own part, William Knibb admitted preaching only parts of the New Testament that would have been palatable to slaveholders, specifically avoiding even key passages beloved to Baptists like "the truth shall make you free" (John 8:32) for fear that it might be misunderstood. "I thought it my duty so to do," he said. See Hinton, p. 177. Some of the missionaries rationalized their compromised position by thinking of the similar shackles put on Saint Paul, who preached early Christianity to enslaved listeners under the baleful watch of the Roman Empire.

4. Scott, *The Common Wind*, p. 77. A governor of British Guiana observed the year before that "nothing can be more keenly observant than the slaves are of all that affects their interest." Ibid.

5. *PP*, vol. 47, pp. 214–215, 212.

6. Higman, "The West Indian 'Interest,'" p. 4; Burn, *Emancipation*, pp. 23–25. In the midst of this economic depression, Richard Barrett wrote home to his aunt to explain why he would not be sending a remittance home to England to keep his uncle from being bothered by creditors. "But the poverty of the Island is dreadful. Bad as sugar sells rum sells even worse—& scarce any estate can pay the Island contingencies." He still felt compelled to reassure her that a revolt of the slaves was nowhere in sight, rumors to the contrary. "As to the quiet of the Island—take my word for it, that there is no danger," he wrote. "The negroes were never better disposed & all that you hear to the contrary comes from ignorant townpeople, & as cowardly as they are ignorant." See Richard Barrett to Mary Barrett Lockhead, January 18, 1825, SD.502.1, MS 681/1/3, College Library, Eton College, Windsor, UK.

7. Burnard, *Mastery, Tyranny and Desire*, p. 149.

8. Multiple rebellions across the Atlantic world—including the one in 1816 in Barbados and in 1823 in Demerara—featured drivers as top conspirators, probably owing in large part to the reservoir of trust they had built up among the field hands.

9. "Postscript to the Royal Gazette," *Royal Gazette* (Kingston, Jamaica), March 1832.

10. John Whittaker, quoted in Scott, *The Common Wind*, p. 10.

11. Bleby, *Death Struggles of Slavery*, p. 111. It is worth noting that the dependence on slaves who had a degree of economic autonomy as early co-conspirators was a common feature of revolts on both sides the Atlantic, dating to Wat Tyler's 1381 serf revolt in Britain and extending into the uprisings led by Gabriel, Nat Turner, and Denmark Vesey in the United States. See Egerton, "Slaves to the Marketplace," p. 632.

12. Bleby, *Death Struggles of Slavery*, p. 112.

13. "The King against Samuel Sharpe," CO 137 / 181.

14. *PP*, vol. 47, pp. 217–218.

15. Bleby, *Death Struggles of Slavery*, p. 112.

16. Foulks, *Eighteen Months in Jamaica*, p. 84.

17. Bleby, *Death Struggles of Slavery*, p. 129.

18. Aljoe, *Creole Testimonies*, p. 15.

19. *SI*, p. 21.

20. *SC*, p. 257.

21. Geggus, *Slavery, War and Revolution*, pp. 3, 8.

22. Da Costa, *Crowns of Glory*, pp. 177–184; Davis, *Inhuman Bondage*, pp. 216–218; Craton, *Testing the Chains*, 278–280. A white Protestant minister named John Smith, a spiritual mentor to Jack Gladstone, was convicted of inciting the slaves to rebel, and was sentenced to death, but died in his prison cell before the sentence could be carried out.

23. Bleby, *Death Struggles of Slavery*, p. 128.

24. Marson, *Belmore*, p. 147. The Temple of Dendur is now on permanent display in the Metropolitan Museum of Art in New York City—still including its aristocratic graffito.

25. Bleby, *Death Struggles of Slavery*, p. 238; Marson, *Belmore*, pp. 176, 179.

26. *PP*, pp. 7–17.

27. *SC*, p. 206; Bleby, *Death Struggles of Slavery*, pp. 141–143.

28. *SC*, pp. 121, 122, 130; Barrett, *Journal*, p. 102.

29. *SC*, p. 121.

30. Hart, *Slaves Who Abolished Slavery*, p. 246.

31. Porter, *Overture to Victoria*, p. 79.

32. Knight, *William IV*, p. 4.

33. Greville, *Diaries*, p. 122.

34. Greville, *Diaries*, p. 370. One of the stories William liked to tell his visitors involved his service near the end of his father's war to keep the American colonies. He went to New York City on a mission in 1782 to bolster the resolve of the loyalists and wandered around the city unescorted. "The town is built in the Dutch way, with trees before the houses," he wrote in a letter. "The streets are in general narrow and very ill-paved." Some Continental Army spies evidently spotted him on these walks, and the news was relayed to George Washington, who immediately concocted a plan to kidnap William as a bargaining chip. A colonel devised a plan to raid the house of Admiral Robert Digby, where the prince was staying, and abduct them both

via a whaleboat launched from the New Jersey shore. Washington gave his approval to "make the attempt in any manner, and at such a time, as your judgment may direct," cautioning only against "offering insult or indignity to the persons of the Prince or Admiral." The Americans scuttled the amphibious operation after news of it was leaked to the British, who then doubled the security around the house on Hanover Square. See Ziegler, *King William IV*, p. 38; and McBurney, *Abductions*, p. 171.

35. Ziegler, *King William IV*, p. 69.

36. Ziegler, *King William IV*, p. 98; Foulks, *Eighteen Months in Jamaica*, p. 110.

37. Macauley, *Life and Letters*, p. 221.

38. Barrett, *Journal*, p. 31.

39. *PD*, March 23, 1832; Bleby, *Death Struggles of Slavery*, p. 132.

40. Bleby, *Death Struggles of Slavery*, p. 133, emphasis in the original.

41. Bridges, *A Voice from Jamaica*, pp. 8, 400.

42. Bleby, *Death Struggles of Slavery*, p. 82; Bridges, *The Annals of Jamaica*, p. 400.

43. Bleby, *Death Struggles of Slavery*, p. 84; Macaulay, *Anti-Slavery Monthly Reporter*, vol. 3, p. 374; Lord Belmore to Viscount Goderich, November 30, 1831, CO 137 / 182; Dunkley, *The Life of Rev. George Wilson Bridges*, p. 87.

44. *Jamaica Courant*, August 15, 1831, emphasis in the original. Dorcas is the name of a rich widow in Acts 9:39.

45. *Jamaica Courant*, August 11, 1831.

6. Swear to Me

1. This language echoes the angry words of the *New York Weekly Journal* of June 23, 1741, which denounced "the business" of a supposed plot by enslaved blacks and poor whites to burn whole neighborhoods in New York City in a fifth-column attempt to help the Catholic powers of France and Spain. See Linebaugh and Rediker, *The Many-Headed Hydra*, p. 204.

2. *SI*, p. 29.

3. Legion, *A Second Letter*, p. 112.

4. "The King against Samuel Sharpe," CO 137 / 185.

5. *PP*, vol. 47, p. 215.

6. Hart, *Slaves Who Abolished Slavery*, p. 257.

7. Mullin, *Africa in America*, p. 67.

8. An act of the Jamaica Assembly outlawing the religion made it punishable by death for any enslaved person to possess any of the reagents of

an obeah spell, including "Blood, Feathers, Parrots Beaks, Dog Teeth, Alligators Teeth, broken Bottles, Grave Dirt, Rum, Egg-shells." *Acts of the Assembly*, 1769, vol. 1, p. 55, quoted in Brathwaite, *The Development of Creole Society*, p. 162.

9. Brown, *The Reaper's Garden*, p. 5.

10. Hart, *Slaves Who Abolished Slavery*, p. 295.

11. Allmendinger, *Nat Turner and the Rising in Southampton County*, p. 14; Foner, *Nat Turner*, p. 43.

12. Foner, *Nat Turner*, p. 3; Allmendinger, *Nat Turner and the Rising in Southampton County*, p. 198. For an analysis of the probable death toll among enslaved people not participating in the rebellion, which is far lower than previous historians had concluded, see Breen, *Deluged in Blood*, pp. 99–105. Allmendinger largely concurs; see *Nat Turner and the Rising in Southampton County*, pp. 203–207.

13. Turner, *Confessions*, p. 26.

14. Foner, *Nat Turner*, p. 8. See also Allmendinger, *Nat Turner and the Rising in Southampton County*, pp. 210–211.

15. *Morning Post* (London), September 26, 1831.

16. *Liverpool Albion*, reprinted in the *Lancaster Gazette* (Lancaster, UK), October 1, 1831; *Morning Advertiser* (London), December 23, 1831.

17. *Royal Gazette* (Kingston, Jamaica), October 1, 1831; *Watchman and Jamaica Free Press* (Kingston, Jamaica), October 7 and October 15, 1831.

18. *Watchman and Jamaica Free Press* (Kingston, Jamaica), October 15, 1831.

19. Reid, *Samuel Sharpe*, p. 66; Turner, *Slaves and Missionaries*, p. 156; Higman, *Plantation Jamaica*, p. 51.

20. *Bulletins*, p. 47.

21. Senior, *Jamaica as It Was*, p. 173.

22. *PP*, vol. 47, p. 214.

23. *SC*, p. 257.

24. Waddell, *Twenty-Nine Years in the West Indies*, p. 51.

25. George Lawson to William Grignon, December 27, 1832, quoted in Grignon, *Vindication*, p. 25.

26. William Knibb to Bruce Dyer, February 14, 1832, quoted in Knibb, *Memoir*, pp. 117–118.

27. Cox, *Baptist Missionary Society*, p. 83; *SC*, p. 260; Turner, "The Jamaica Slave Rebellion," p. 116.

28. Knibb, *Memoir*, p. 199.

29. Clarke, *Memorials*, p. 103.

7. The Fires

1. Mathieson, *British Slavery and Its Abolition*, p. 212.

2. Senior, *Jamaica as It Was*, p. 179.

3. Craton, *Testing the Chains*, p. 303.

4. Waddell, *Twenty-Nine Years in the West Indies*, p. 55.

5. Bleby, *Death Struggles of Slavery*, p. 8.

6. *PP*, vol. 47, pp. 199–200. See also *SI*, p. 18.

7. This is a reference to a rumor that an unnamed white missionary had told the enslaved people that a star appearing at the corner of a half-moon would be a mystical sign to rise up in revolt. Astronomical data for December 27, 1831, shows a waning moon in its last quarter, but the legend about the star was not repeated in court testimony or memoir by any enslaved person or missionary. See Commissioners, of Longitude *The Nautical Almanac*, p. 133. It seems possible that the author of the account—militiaman Bernard Senior—may have conflated a vivid detail from the Nat Turner rebellion that had been a source of news and discussion in Jamaica. Turner had reportedly seen the sun turn a bluish-green color on August 13, 1831, and took it as a cue from heaven to begin his rebellion.

8. Senior, *Jamaica as It Was*, pp. 224–226.

9. *Watchman and Jamaica Free Press*, January 4, 1832.

10. *Watchman and Jamaica Free Press*, January 4, 1832; Mathieson, *British Slavery and Its Abolition*, p. 212.

11. Dunn, *Sugar and Slaves*, p. 262.

12. Waddell, *Twenty-Nine Years in the West Indies*, p. 56.

13. Craton, *Testing the Chains*, p. 304.

14. Waddell, *Twenty-Nine Years in the West Indies*, p. 57.

15. Craton, *Testing the Chains*, p. 305.

16. "Postscript to the Royal Gazette," *Royal Gazette* (Kingston, Jamaica), January 1832.

17. "Supplement to the Royal Gazette," *Royal Gazette* (Kingston, Jamaica), February 1832. It is impossible to say how many times this dynamic was repeated at various estates throughout the rebellion, but militiaman Bernard Senior also mentions enslaved people acting to save their master's property and even fighting against the rebels. Many enslaved people claimed to have liked their masters even as much as they hated their enslavement, and as Genovese has noted of plantation owners in the American South, some of them—like Richard Barrett in Jamaica—thought of themselves as moder-

ating reformers working within a brutal system to bring better conditions to their labor force. See Genovese, *Roll, Jordan, Roll*, 123–149.

18. Senior, *Jamaica as It Was*, p. 180. An alternative—and more probable—explanation is that the rebellious slaves never expected to leave their lives of agricultural labor, only to be paid a wage for it. This is consistent with Samuel Sharpe's own words. Destroying the blacksmith's shops would have only made an economic recovery more difficult.

19. Senior, *Jamaica as It Was*, p. 181; Foulks, *Eighteen Months in Jamaica*, p. 75.

20. Deposition of William Annand, January 2, 1832, CO 137 / 181; see also Hart, *Slaves Who Abolished Slavery*, p. 256.

21. Craton, *Testing the Chains*, p. 308.

22. Higman, *Plantation Jamaica*, p. 121; *Watchman and Jamaica Free Press* (Kingston, Jamaica), January 4, 1832.

23. Ragatz, *The Fall of the Planter Class*, p. 32; Buckley, "The Frontier," pp. 154, 159.

24. McMahon, *Jamaica Plantership*, p. 93.

25. Foulks, *Eighteen Months in Jamaica*, p. 62.

26. Foulks, *Eighteen Months in Jamaica*, p. 57.

27. Foulks, *Eighteen Months in Jamaica*, p. 62.

28. Waddell, *Twenty-Nine Years in the West Indies*, p. 58.

29. *SC*, p. 276.

30. Foulks, *Eighteen Months in Jamaica*, p. 76.

31. "Supplement to the Royal Gazette," *Royal Gazette* (Kingston, Jamaica), February 1832; Craton, *Testing the Chains*, p. 307.

32. *St. Jago de la Vega Gazette* (St. Jago de la Vega [Spanish Town], Jamaica), January 7, 1832.

33. *SC*, p. 275.

34. *Watchman and Jamaica Free Press* (Kingston, Jamaica), January 4, 1832.

35. Rouse, *Rugby School*, p. 185.

36. Gronow, *Reminiscences*, p. 12.

37. *Watchman and Jamaica Free Press* (Kingston, Jamaica), January 4, 1832.

38. McMahon, *Jamaica Plantership*, p. 97.

39. Richard Barrett to Lord Belmore, January 1, 1832, CO 137 / 181.

40. Grignon, *Vindication*, p. 72; William Grignon to Robert Watt, Esq., December 29, 1832, quoted in Grignon, *Vindication*, p. 33.

41. *Watchman and Jamaica Free Press* (Kingston, Jamaica), January 4, 1832; *Watchman and Jamaica Free Press* (Kingston, Jamaica), January 21, 1832; Legion, *A Second Letter*, p. 152.

42. Foulks, *Eighteen Months in Jamaica*, p. 84.

43. Grignon, *Vindication*, p. 72. See also Craton, *Testing the Chains*, p. 307.

44. Bleby, *Death Struggles of Slavery*, pp. 13, 15.

45. Foulks, *Eighteen Months in Jamaica*, p. 76.

46. *Watchman and Jamaica Free Press* (Kingston, Jamaica), January 4, 1832.

47. Willoughby Cotton to Lord Belmore, January 2, 1832, *Bulletins*, p. 85.

48. *Watchman and Jamaica Free Press* (Kingston, Jamaica), January 4, 1832.

49. *Watchman and Jamaica Free Press* (Kingston, Jamaica), January 4, 1832.

50. *SI*, p. 18.

8. One Common Ruin

1. Bleby, *Death Struggles of Slavery*, p. 22; McKee, "From Violence to Alliance," p. 28; Campbell, *The Maroons of Jamaica*, p. 245.

2. Hart, *Slaves Who Abolished Slavery*, p. 270.

3. French-speaking Maroons played a far less sympathetic role toward European slaveholders in the Haitian Revolution, offering asylum and armed support to the rebel slaves. See Fouchard, *The Haitian Maroons*, pp. 292–300.

4. *Watchman and Jamaica Free Press* (Kingston, Jamaica), January 11, 1832.

5. Senior, *Jamaica as It Was*, p. 233.

6. Foulks, *Eighteen Months in Jamaica*, p. 81.

7. Foulks, *Eighteen Months in Jamaica*, p. 77.

8. Senior, *Jamaica as It Was*, pp. 212, 234; Foulks, *Eighteen Months in Jamaica*, p. 81.

9. *PP*, vol. 47, pp. 221; see also Craton, *Testing the Chains*, 310.

10. Marks, *The Family of the Barrett*, p. 399.

11. Bleby, *Death Struggles of Slavery*, p. 32.

12. *Watchman and Jamaica Free Press* (Kingston, Jamaica), February 4, 1832; *Cornwall Courier* (Cornwall, Jamaica), January 11, 1832.

13. Senior, *Jamaica as It Was*, p. 190.

14. Bleby, *Death Struggles of Slavery*, p. 38; McMahon, *Jamaica Plantership*, p. 96.

15. Bleby, *Death Struggles of Slavery*, pp. 43, 62; McMahon, *Jamaica Plantership*, p. 91.

16. *Watchman and Jamaica Free Press* (Kingston, Jamaica), January 11, 1832.

17. *Watchman and Jamaica Free Press* (Kingston, Jamaica), January 21, 1832; *Watchman and Jamaica Free Press* (Kingston, Jamaica), January 4, 1832.

18. "Postscript to the Royal Gazette," *Royal Gazette* (Kingston, Jamaica), January 1832.

19. Bleby, *Death Struggles of Slavery*, p. 23, emphasis in the original.

20. *Cornwall Chronicle*, Quoted in *Watchman and Jamaica Free Press* (Kingston, Jamaica), February 4, 1832.

21. "Postscript to the Royal Gazette," *Royal Gazette* (Kingston, Jamaica), January 1832.

22. *Watchman and Jamaica Free Press* (Kingston, Jamaica), February 18, 1832; "Postscript to the Royal Gazette," *Royal Gazette* (Kingston, Jamaica), February 1832.

23. Bleby, *Death Struggles of Slavery*, p. 32; The *Cornwall Chronicle* (Cornwall, Jamaica), February 11, 1832, puts this phrase in the mouth of George Brown, also killed that day. It seems likely that Bleby may have confused the speaker of the quote.

24. *Cornwall Chronicle* (Cornwall, Jamaica), February 11, 1832; reprinted in the *Watchman and Jamaica Free Press* (Kingston, Jamaica), February 1832.

25. "*Supplement to* the Royal Gazette," *Royal Gazette* (Kingston, Jamaica), February 11, 1832.

26. Egerton, "A Peculiar Mark of Infamy," p. 153. US authorities also ordered this done after rebellions in Louisiana and Virginia. For a discussion of how the Bakongo people, in particular, viewed Africa as the place of life and the Americas as the land of the dead, see Adderley, *"New Negroes from Africa,"* p. 220.

27. *Watchman and Jamaica Free Press* (Kingston, Jamaica), January 11, 1832.

28. *Watchman and Jamaica Free Press* (Kingston, Jamaica), January 7, 1832.

29. *Watchman and Jamaica Free Press* (Kingston, Jamaica), January 4, 1832.

30. *Watchman and Jamaica Free Press* (Kingston, Jamaica), January 11, 1832.

31. *Watchman and Jamaica Free Press* (Kingston, Jamaica), January 11, 1832.

32. *Watchman and Jamaica Free Press* (Kingston, Jamaica), January 11, 1832.

33. *Watchman and Jamaica Free Press* (Kingston, Jamaica), January 21, 1832.

34. Craton, *Testing the Chains*, p. 310; "Postscript to the Royal Gazette," *Royal Gazette* (Kingston, Jamaica), January 1832.

35. *Watchman and Jamaica Free Press* (Kingston, Jamaica), January 14, 1832.

36. *Royal Gazette*, (Kingston, Jamaica), February 11, 1832.

37. *Watchman and Jamaica Free Press* (Kingston, Jamaica), January 21, 1832.

38. Foulks, *Eighteen Months in Jamaica*, p. 81.

39. Bleby, *Death Struggles of Slavery*, p. 20.

40. "Postscript to the Royal Gazette," *Royal Gazette* (Kingston, Jamaica), January 1832.

41. *Watchman and Jamaica Free Press* (Kingston, Jamaica), January 14, 1832.

42. *Watchman and Jamaica Free Press* (Kingston, Jamaica), February 4, 1832.

43. *Watchman and Jamaica Free Press* (Kingston, Jamaica), January 14, 1832.

44. *Watchman and Jamaica Free Press* (Kingston, Jamaica), January 11, 1832.

45. *Watchman and Jamaica Free Press* (Kingston, Jamaica), January 14, 1832.

46. *Watchman and Jamaica Free Press* (Kingston, Jamaica), January 11, 1832.

47. Douglas, *The Golden Age of the Newspaper*, pp. 13–14; Roberts, "Edward Jordon," pp. 7, 9.

48. Huntzicker, *The Popular Press*, p. 165.

49. *SC*, p. 137.

50. Bleby, *Death Struggles of Slavery*, p. 24.

51. *Watchman and Jamaica Free Press* (Kingston, Jamaica), January 14, 1832.

52. *Watchman and Jamaica Free Press* (Kingston, Jamaica), January 21, 1832.

9. Launched into Eternity

1. Brathwaite, "The Slave Rebellion," p. 12.

2. Senior, *Jamaica as It Was*, p. 182.

3. Senior, *Jamaica as It Was*, pp. 184, 211, 260; *Votes*, 1B/5/1A/37; Baptist Missionaries, *A Narrative of Recent Events*, p. 26. From a jail cell Gardiner would tell the preacher of that sermon of his regrets: "Your word melt we, we no hold up our head."

4. *SC*, p. 257.

5. Hart, *Slaves Who Abolished Slavery*, p. 258.

6. *SI*, p. 72.

7. "The King against Samuel Sharpe," CO 137 / 185.

8. "The King against Samuel Sharpe," CO 137 / 185.

9. "The King against Samuel Sharpe," CO 137 / 185.

10. Bleby, *Speech*, p. 11. This paraphrased secondhand recollection was made twenty-six years after the fact. See also *SC*, p. 231; and Legion, *Second Letter*, p. 152.

11. Senior, *Jamaica as It Was*, p. 203.

12. Senior, *Jamaica as It Was*, p. 205.

13. *SI*, p. 21.

14. *SI*, p. 21.

15. *Votes*, 1B/5/1A/37. See also *SI*, p. 76.

16. Senior, *Jamaica as It Was*, pp. 279–285; *Jamaica Courant* (Kingston, Jamaica), February 24, 1832.

17. *Watchman and Jamaica Free Press* (Kingston, Jamaica), January 25, 1832.

18. *Watchman and Jamaica Free Press* (Kingston, Jamaica), January 21, 1832; Craton, *Testing the Chains*, p. 316.

19. Bleby, *Death Struggles of Slavery*, p. 27.

20. *Watchman and Jamaica Free Press* (Kingston, Jamaica), January 21, 1832.

21. *Watchman and Jamaica Free Press* (Kingston, Jamaica), January 28, 1832; Foulks, *Eighteen Months in Jamaica*, p. 63.

22. *Watchman and Jamaica Free Press* (Kingston, Jamaica), January 25, 1832.

23. Bleby, *Death Struggles of Slavery*, p. 53.

24. "Supplement to the Royal Gazette," *Royal Gazette* (Kingston, Jamaica), January 1832.

25. Bleby, *Death Struggles of Slavery*, p. 57.

26. *Watchman and Jamaica Free Press* (Kingston, Jamaica), January 28, 1832.

27. *Watchman and Jamaica Free Press* (Kingston, Jamaica), March 24, 1832.

28. "Postscript to the Royal Gazette," *Royal Gazette* (Kingston, Jamaica), March 1832.

29. For the brief accounts of Holmes and Pearce, see Bleby, *Death Struggles of Slavery*, pp. 39–43. Bleby's memoir, written twenty-six years after the revolt, does not contain an accounting of white casualties. The *Jamaica Almanack* of 1828 lists Alexander Holmes as a proprietor with one slave in Trelawny, but does not list Pearce at all, suggesting that—if he existed—he may have been a recent arrival in a time of population decline. For a catalog of ludicrously improbable stories of sexual assault that appear in no other newspaper or court accounts, see Senior, *Jamaica as It Was*, pp. 214–221. The other graphic account from a militiaman, Foulks, conceals his lack of documentation with a disingenuous claim of prudence: "Other anecdotes, the fruits of this terrible insurrection, might be still produced; but some of them are of a character, so abhorrent from all delicacy of feeling, as to render them unit for the public eye or public ear"; see Foulks, *Eighteen Months in Jamaica*, p. 98. The lack of documentation in the reactionary *Jamaica Courant* is also a curiosity, as the newspaper published a comprehensive list of properties destroyed by flames, but no names of victims.

30. The fear that rebellious slaves wanted to rape white women was a common mistaken belief in other Atlantic uprisings as well; see Jordan, *White over Black*, pp. 152–154. As Davis, *Inhuman Bondage*, p. 22, notes, "In the nineteenth century, British slaves thus showed considerable wisdom and self-discipline when they focused their violence on property and took what must have been extraordinary measures to avoid the killing of whites." The historical consensus that fourteen whites died appears to have been reached some time after the events, for the death toll does not appear in surviving contemporary press accounts. See Mathieson, *British Slavery and Its Abolition*, p. 214; and Waddell, *Twenty-Nine Years in the West Indies*, p. 66.

31. Bleby, *Death Struggles of Slavery*, p. 44. An argument could also be made that the trash houses were set fire because of the incendiary and visible quality of the resulting blazes, but the number of blacksmith shops and sugar works that were spared destruction should also be taken into consideration.

32. Bleby, *Death Struggles of Slavery*, p. 16.

33. Bleby, *Death Struggles of Slavery*, p. 46.

34. Bleby, *Death Struggles of Slavery*, p. 50.

35. *Votes*, 1B/5/1A/37; *SI*, p. 29.

36. *Kingston Chronicle* (Kingston, Jamaica), January 31, 1832, quoted in *Watchman and Jamaica Free Press* (Kingston, Jamaica), February 4, 1832.

37. *Watchman and Jamaica Free Press* (Kingston, Jamaica), February 11, 1832. See also "Supplement to the Royal Gazette," *Royal Gazette* (Kingston, Jamaica), February 1832.

38. Bleby, *Death Struggles of Slavery*, p. 34; *SC*, p. 246.

39. Craton, *Testing the Chains*, p. 312; *Watchman and Jamaica Free Press* (Kingston, Jamaica), February 1, 1832.

40. Craton, *Testing the Chains*, p. 312; Bleby, *Speech*, p. 7; Marks, *The Family of the Barrett*, p. 400; *SC*, p. 281.

41. *Royal Gazette* (Kingston, Jamaica), February 25, 1832; *Cornwall Chronicle* (Cornwall, Jamaica), quoted in *Watchman and Jamaica Free Press* (Kingston, Jamaica), February 11, 1832; *SC*, p. 292; Waddell, *Twenty-Nine Years in the West Indies*, p. 66.

42. *Watchman and Jamaica Free Press* (Kingston, Jamaica), February 11, 1832; *Royal Gazette* (Kingston, Jamaica), February 25, 1832.

43. *Cornwall Chronicle* (Cornwall, Jamaica), February 25, 1832, quoted in *Jamaica Courant* (Kingston, Jamaica), March 3, 1832.

44. Senior, *Jamaica as It Was*, p. 266.

45. Cornford, *Missionary Reminiscences*, p. 25.

46. Bleby, *Death Struggles of Slavery*, p. 21.

47. Craton, *Testing the Chains*, p. 312. This would be equivalent to about $170 million US dollars in today's money when adjusted for inflation.

48. Beckles and Shepherd, *Liberties Lost*, p. 201.

49. Craton, *Testing the Chains*, p. 314.

50. *Cornwall Chronicle* (Cornwall, Jamaica), quoted in *Royal Gazette* (Kingston, Jamaica), February 4, 1832; *Watchman and Jamaica Free Press* (Kingston, Jamaica), February 11, 1832.

51. Lord Belmore to Viscount Goderich, April 9, 1832, CO 137 / 182.

52. Bleby, *Death Struggles of Slavery*, pp. 36–39.

53. *Cornwall Chronicle* (Cornwall, Jamaica), reprinted in *The Watchman*, February 25, 1832.

54. This exchange has been assembled from slightly differing accounts published in the *Cornwall Chronicle* and reprinted in *The Watchman* of February 25, 1832, as well as a longer narrative given by Bernard Senior in *Jamaica as It Was*, pp. 254–261.

55. *Votes*, 1B/5/1A/37.

56. Sharpe was speaking to Anglican rector Thomas Stewart on February 11, 1831, in the jail at Savannah-la-Mar. See *Votes*, 1B/5/1A/37.

57. *Votes*, 1B/5/1A/37.

58. *SI*, Confession No. 8, p. 36.

59. *Votes*, 1B/5/1A/37; *SI*, Confession no. 8, p. 36.

60. "Supplement to the Royal Gazette," *Royal Gazette* (Kingston, Jamaica), March 1832.

61. Senior, *Jamaica as It Was*, p. 260.

62. Senior, *Jamaica as It Was*, p. 260.

63. Senior, *Jamaica as It Was*, p. 266.

64. "The King against Samuel Sharpe," CO 137 / 181. See also Kreitzer, "Kissing the Book."

65. This was the same building from whose roof the militia had spotted the first fire at Kensington Estate.

66. "The King against Samuel Sharpe," CO 137 / 181. See also Kreitzer, "Kissing the Book."

67. Kreitzer, "Kissing the Book," pp. 5–6.

68. Cornford, *Missionary Reminiscences*, p. 34.

69. Bleby, *Death Struggles of Slavery*, p. 116.

70. *Jamaica Courant* (Kingston, Jamaica), February 14, 1832.

71. Reid, *Samuel Sharpe*, 92. See also Cornford, *Missionary Reminiscences*, p. 35.

72. *Watchman and Jamaica Free Press* (Kingston, Jamaica), June 2, 1832.

73. *Watchman and Jamaica Free Press* (Kingston, Jamaica), June 2, 1832.

74. *Watchman and Jamaica Free Press* (Kingston, Jamaica), June 2, 1832.

75. Bleby, *Death Struggles of Slavery*, p. 118; see also Cornford, *Missionary Reminiscences*, p. 36.

10. Panic

1. Foulks, *Eighteen Months in Jamaica*, p. 102.

2. Another parallel was the South Carolina Association, a group of vigilantes composed mainly of wealthy citizens of Charleston, which formed immediately after Denmark Vesey's rebellion of 1822. The city also asked the state government to fund an arsenal to guard against further rebellion and intimidate the black majority; it eventually became the Citadel, the state's military academy. See Lofton, *Denmark Vesey's Revolt*, p. 199; and Robertson, *Denmark Vesey*, p. 115.

3. Cox, *Baptist Missionary Society*, p. 131.

4. Gaunt, *Where the Twain Meet*, p. 252. The omitted word may have been "throat" or a reference to male sexual organs.

5. Burchell, *Memoir*, p. 226.

6. Cox, *Baptist Missionary Society*, p. 145. See also Clarke, *Memorials*, p. 107.

7. Bleby, *Death Struggles of Slavery*, p. 167.

8. Legion, *Second Letter*, p. 50.

9. *SC*, pp. 254, 236; Cox, *Baptist Missionary Society*, p. 108; Bleby, *Death Struggles of Slavery*, p. 168.

10. *Royal Gazette* (Kingston, Jamaica), January 28, 1832.

11. *Jamaica Courant* (Kingston, Jamaica), January 14, 1832, quoted in Bleby, *Death Struggles of Slavery*, p. 155, emphasis in the original.

12. *Jamaica Courant* (Kingston, Jamaica), January 11, 1832; Bleby, *Death Struggles of Slavery*, p. 155.

13. Burchell, *Memoir*, p. 185.

14. Cox, *Baptist Missionary Society*, p. 92.

15. *Jamaica Courant* (Kingston, Jamaica), February 17, 1832; Clarke, *Memorials*, p. 146.

16. Barrett, *The Barretts of Jamaica.* p. 86. See also Cox, *Baptist Missionary Society*, p. 217.

17. Cox, *Baptist Missionary Society*, p. 213.

18. *Votes*, 1B/5/1A/37, appendix 18, page 310; Baptist Missionaries, *A Narrative of Recent Events*, p. 56.

19. *Votes*, 1B/5/1A/37, appendix 18, p. 311.

20. Baptist Missionaries, *A Narrative of Recent Events*, p. 33; *SC*, p. 233; Cox, *Baptist Missionary Society*, p. 90.

21. Baptist Missionaries, *A Narrative of Recent Events*, p. 35; *SC*, pp. 237–238.

22. *Jamaica Courant* (Kingston, Jamaica), February 17, 1832.

23. Cox, *Baptist Missionary Society*, pp. 103–104.

24. Baptist Missionaries, *A Narrative of Recent Events*, p. 46; Catherall, "Thomas Burchell," p. 354.

25. Bleby, *Death Struggles of Slavery*, pp. 216–229. See also *Watchman and Jamaica Free Press* (Kingston, Jamaica), April 4, 1832.

26. This bad relationship was indicative of a broader power struggle—between reformers in the Colonial Office and the guardians of the status quo in the West Indian colonies—regarding the improvement of slave conditions. "We tried everything," wrote Goderich's deputy Henry Taylor. "The controversy went on year after year; the Assemblies raged abroad; the saints wailed and howled at home; the Crown maintained an outward aspect of moderation." See Taylor, *Autobiography*, vol. 1, p. 122.

27. Lord Belmore to Viscount Goderich, June 9, 1832, CO 137 / 185.

28. *Parliamentary Review and Family Magazine* (London), 1833, vol. 2, p. 507. See also Mathieson, *British Slavery and Its Abolition*, p. 218; and Marson, *Belmore*, p. 184.

29. Bleby, *Speech*, p. 31; Gaunt, *Where the Twain Meet*, p. 256.

30. Cox, *Baptist Missionary Society*, p. 205.

31. Anonymous to the Earl of Mulgrave, July 5, 1832, CO 137 / 182.

32. Bleby, *Speech*, p. 14.

33. *Alexandria Gazette* (Alexandria, VA), January 24, 1832.

34. *Liberator* (Boston), March 3, 1832.

35. *Royal Gazette* (Kingston, Jamaica), February 25, 1832.

36. *Macon Telegraph* (Macon, GA), February 4, 1832; Rugemer, *The Problem of Emancipation*, pp. 109, 116. It is not surprising that the *Charleston Mercury* should have said little; this was the same newspaper that had essentially refused to cover the 1822 Denmark Vesey uprising in its own city. See Lofton, *Denmark Vesey's Revolt*, p. 162.

37. *Globe* (London), February 20, 1832; *Evening Standard* (London), February 20, 1832.

38. Browning, *Diary*, p. 221. She was riffing on Proverbs 7:12: "Hope deferred maketh the heart sick / but when the desire cometh, it is a tree of life."

39. William IV, quoted in Burn, *Emancipation and Apprenticeship*, p. 104.

40. *Northern Whig* (Belfast), February 21, 1832; *Morning Advertiser* (London), February 11, 1832; *Northampton Mercury* (Northampton, UK), April 7, 1832; *Tait's Edinburgh Magazine* (Edinburgh, UK), February 1832. *Nottingham Review and General Advertiser for the Midland Counties* (Nottingham, UK), February 24, 1832.

41. *Atlas* (London), March 18, 1832.

42. Barrett and Burge, *Speeches*, p. 1.

43. Barrett and Burge, *Speeches*, p. i.

44. Barrett and Burge, *Speeches*, p. 4.

45. Barrett and Burge, *Speeches*, p. 4.

46. Barrett and Burge, *Speeches*, p. 7.

47. Barrett and Burge, *Speeches*, p. 61.

48. Barrett and Burge, *Speeches*, p. 62.

49. A Genuine "Dickey Sam," *Liverpool and Slavery*, p. 112; Williams, *Capitalism and Slavery*, p. 59; Richardson, Schwarz, and Tibbles, *Liverpool and Transatlantic Slavery*, p. 27.

50. Anonymous poem, quoted in Trepp, "The Liverpool Movement," p. 266.

51. Trepp, "The Liverpool Movement," p. 265; Brendon, *The Decline and Fall*, p. 17.

52. The street named after James Penny—Penny Lane—was later made famous in a song by the Beatles.

53. Sanderson, "The Liverpool Abolitionists," p. 197.

54. Williams, *Capitalism and Slavery*, p. 59. See also Trepp, "The Liverpool Movement," pp. 273, 284.

55. Howman, "Abolitionism in Liverpool," p. 287.

56. Clarkson, *The History*, p. 112; A Genuine "Dickey Sam," *Liverpool and Slavery*, p. 89; Charlton, "James Cropper," p. 59.

57. *Liverpool Mercury*, May 4, 1832.

58. *Liverpool Mercury*, May 11, 1832.

59. *Liverpool Mercury*, May 18, 1832.

11. Another Island

1. Ralph, *A Critical Review*, p. 57.

2. Farrell, "The Old Palace." See also Shenton, *The Day Parliament Burned Down*, p. 29.

3. Many Britons were in agreement with onetime parliamentary reporter Charles Dickens's assessment that the body "does so little and talks so much" and that the most consequential thing that happened inside it was the guardsman clearing it of members each evening and locking its doors. Inefficiency and halting movement had been bred into it, ever since its origins as an awkward compromise between the thirteenth-century ring of barons that had forced Henry III to live up to the power-sharing ideas outlined in the Magna Carta. They called this advisory council Parliament, from the Norman French word *parler*, "to talk." King Edward I soon instituted the tradition of summoning two knights from each shire and two citizens from each town for consultation, as well as to extract money and troops for his foreign military adventures. Parliament usually met in different parts of England as the king traveled through his lands, but also near London's gigantic Westminster Hall, a ceremonial barn for coronations and high-profile criminal trials that had been erected atop a Roman-era garbage midden next to the River Thames. The citizen representatives sat apart from the shire knights and eventually claimed for themselves the right to approve new taxes and to elect their own members. This division was the origin of the bicameral Parliament: the increasingly dynamic House of Commons, where ideas originated, and the more sclerotic House of Lords, where ideas were altered or quashed.

4. Abbott, *Sugar*, p. 170.

5. Ragatz, *The Fall of the Planter Class*, p. 52.

6. Some angry locals who had witnessed the carnage founded the *Manchester Guardian*—later simply the *Guardian*—as a media tool to keep alive the hopes of reform.

7. One gruesome aftereffect of the decisive Battle of Waterloo, which killed up to forty-eight thousand soldiers, was the quick arrival of scavengers from London who set upon the corpses' teeth with pliers for later sale to denture makers. Overconsumption of sugar had created an oral hygiene crisis among Britons of all social classes, and the false teeth manufactured by dentists often contained real ones purloined from condemned criminals, bodies dug up from graveyards, and slain soldiers. A complete set of upper

teeth could fetch the equivalent of year's wages for a working person. The underground trade resulted in a slang term for dentures: "Waterloo teeth."

8. Grehan, *Voices*, p. 312; Davidson, *Downing Street Blues*, p. 53.

9. Greville, *Diaries*, p. 61.

10. Cannon, *Parliamentary Reform*, p. 203; Butler, *The Passing of the Great Reform Bill*, p. 313.

11. Harrison, *Crowds and History*, pp. 289–301; Royle, *Revolutionary Britannia?*, p. 78.

12. Hilton, *A Mad, Bad, and Dangerous People?*, p. 423.

13. Fraser, *Words on Wellington*, p. 163.

14. Creevey, *Papers*, p. 300.

15. Royle, *Revolutionary Britannia?*, p. 75. Place later acknowledged that he wanted the elites to be frightened, so he had to create visible fright on his own face.

16. Pearce, *Reform!*, p. 300; Butler, *The Passing of the Great Reform Bill*, p. 415.

17. Higman, "West Indian 'Interest,'" pp. 17–18.

12. Freedom

1. *Primitive Methodist Magazine* (Stoke-on-Trent, UK), vol. 66, 1885, p. 268. See also Catherall, *William Knibb*, p. 60.

2. Catherall, *William Knibb*, p. 140.

3. Knibb, *Memoir*, p. 143; Cox, *Baptist Missionary Society*, p. 193.

4. Knibb, *Memoir*, pp. 147–148.

5. *Primitive Methodist Magazine* (Stoke-on-Trent, UK), vol. 66, 1885, p. 268. See also Underhill, *Life of James Mursell Phillippo*, pp. 102–103.

6. Knibb, *Memoir*, p. 151; Catherall, *William Knibb*, p. 54.

7. Knibb, *Memoir*, pp. 156, 177.

8. Turner, *Slaves and Missionaries*, p. 173.

9. Bleby, *Speech*, p. 12.

10. Quoted in Griffith-Hughes, "A Mighty Experiment," p. 51; Taylor, *Autobiography*, p. 131. The growing abolitionist sentiment within the Colonial Office can be perceived in a dispatch sent by Taylor's superior, Viscount Goderich, to Lord Belmore on March 1, 1832, just as Samuel Sharpe's revolt had been quelled. "So long as the islands were peopled by the importation of native Africans, who lived and died in heathenism, the relation of master and slave might be expected to be permanent," he wrote. "But now that an

indigenous race of men has grown up, speaking our own language and instructed in our religion, all the more harsh rights of the owner, and the blind submission of the slave, will inevitably at some period, more or less remote, come to an end." Goderich to Belmore, March 1, 1832, quoted in Holt, *The Problem of Freedom*, p. 19.

11. *SC*, p. 538.

12. *SC*, p. 3.

13. *SC*, pp. 23, 210, 215.

14. *SC*, pp. 234–273.

15. *SC*, p. 247.

16. Knibb, *Memoir*, p. 173.

17. *SC*, p. 3; Holt, *The Problem of Freedom*, p. 20; Brathwaite, *The Development of Creole Society*, p. 245. As Taylor later acknowledged, his plan founded on the Spanish *coartado* system to have enslaved people gradually buy their way out of freedom was never put into action. Howick thought so little of this self-manumission idea that he promised to leave his office, and vote against it in Parliament if it was ever introduced. Taylor, *Autobiography*, p. 128.

18. Knibb, *Memoir*, p. 176.

19. Knibb, *Memoir*, pp. 159–165. See also Catherall, *William Knibb*, p. 67.

20. Catherall, *William Knibb*, p. 59.

21. Charlton, "James Cropper," p. 71; Anstey, "Religion and British Emancipation," p. 50.

22. Higman, "The West Indian 'Interest,'" p. 4.

23. Fraser, *Words on Wellington*, p. 12.

24. *PD*, February 6, 1834.

25. Buxton, *Memoirs*, p. 301; Higman, "The West Indian 'Interest,'" p. 2; Thomas Fowell Buxton to Mr. East, October 15, 1832, quoted in Craton, "What and Who to Whom and What," p. 277; *PD*, May 24, 1832.

26. *SC*, p. 114; see also p. 208.

27. Gross, "Negro Slavery," p. 71; Whitely, *Three Months in Jamaica*, pp. 3, 22; Drescher, *Capitalism and Antislavery*, p. 147.

28. Zachary Macaulay to Henry Brougham, May 13, 1833, quoted in Anstey, "Religion and British Emancipation," p. 50.

29. Holt, *The Problem of Freedom*, p. 30. In Henry Taylor's view, the speech had been written more by his Colonial Office colleague James Stephen than it was by Stanley. See Taylor, *Autobiography*, vol. 1, p. 133.

30. Drescher, *Capitalism and Antislavery*, p. 150.

31. Griffith-Hughes, "A Mighty Experiment," p. 3.

32. Barrett and Burge, *Speeches*, p. 2.

33. Gaunt, *Where the Twain Meet*, p. 259; *SC*, p. 199.

34. *PD*, May 14, 1833.

35. Elizabeth Barrett Browning to Mrs. Martin, May 27, 1833, in Browning, *Letters*, p. 21.

36. Gross, "Negro Slavery," p. 79; *PD*, May 2, 1833.

37. Higman, "'The West Indian 'Interest,'" p. 12.

38. Marques, *Who Abolished Slavery?*, p. 37.

39. Charlton, "James Cropper," p. 75; Barclay, *Effects of the Late Colonial Policy*, p. 5; *SC*, p. 295.

40. Marson, *Belmore*, p. 188; *PD*, August 12, 1834.

41. Greville, *Diaries*, p. 119.

42. *AOS*, Enclosure no. 12, p. 41.

43. Wilmot, "Not 'Full Free,'" p. 5.

44. Madden, *A Twelvemonth Residence*, p. 6.

45. Second Marquess of Sligo to Cecil Spring-Rice, quoted in Wilmot, "Not 'Full Free,'" p. 5; Burn, *Emancipation and Apprenticeship*, p. 172 (quoting a freed slave from Tobago who spoke about what was also on the minds of many in Jamaica). See also Holt, *The Problem of Freedom*, p. 56.

46. Lionel Smith to Lord Glenelg, May 17, 1838, quoted in Taylor, *Autobiography*, p. 244. In the words of Swithin Wilmot, the awkward compromise "made a mockery of the labor system which claimed to be preparing slaves for freedom"; Wilmot, "Not 'Full Free,'" p. 9. One of the few published works in the voice of a slave emerged from the British Caribbean in this twilight period of slavery; *A Narrative of Events Since the First of August, 1834* related the first-person experiences of James Williams, a laborer on an estate belonging to the Senior family in St. Ann's Parish. Williams told a story, rendered in a Creole dialect, of frequent whippings and the "dungeon," or prison, to which he was sentenced to ten days for failing to turn sheep out to pasture on time. This room, he said, was "cold and damp and quite dark—a little bit of a cell, hardly enough for me to lie full length; them give me a pint of water and two little cocoa or plantain a day;—hardly able to stand up when we come out, we was so weak; massa and misses said we no punished half enough." Williams, *Narrative*, p. 7. Diana Paton has suggested that this editorial decision to render Williams' speech in patois "would have drawn on romantic assumptions that elevated the supposedly simple and natural on the grounds that those who were closer to the 'primitive' had greater access to the truth." Williams, *Narrative*, p. xxxiv. See also Temperly, *British Antislavery*, p. 31.

47. Griffith-Hughes, "A Mighty Experiment," pp. 57, 75; Holt, *The Problem of Freedom*, p. 58; Paton, *No Bond but the Law*, pp. 43–44, 97.

48. McMahon, *Jamaica Plantership*, p. 109.

49. Cox, *Baptist Missionary Society*, p. 245.

50. Cox, *Baptist Missionary Society*, p. 245.

51. Kerr-Ritchie, *Rites of August First*, p. 33. See also Cox, *Baptist Missionary Society*, pp. 253–258.

13. Aftermath

1. Henry Bleby, *Death Struggles of Slavery*, p. 1.

2. Rugemer, *The Problem of Emancipation*, p. 141.

3. USC, July 9, 1832; Mitton, "The Free World Confronted," pp. 141–143. Harrison had been away from the island when the rebellion broke out, recuperating from a head injury in Pensacola, Florida. Though he also hinted at how his "patriotism and zealous feelings" had been perceived "perhaps a little too warm for the region" and had provoked opposition among some of his British contacts in the region. He filed a report on April 10, 1832, that put an optimistic face on the matter: "It was generally understood on our arrival that the insurrection had been completely put down which no doubt is the case, so far as regards the safety of the Colony as everything is too well organized to apprehend any serious danger the occasional alarms may happen and injury to private persons." But a later dispatch written on April 14, after he had a private meeting with Lord Belmore, took a graver tone. His supervisor in Washington, DC, summarized the report with the following notation: "Hostile feelings of the colonists against the mother country—property destroyed during the late insurrection estimated at two or three million sterling. Emigration to the U.S.—great distress in the island (common to all the W.I. colonies) from the policy of the British government— asks for an office with a salary attached." Harrison spent more time in self-pity over his empty pockets than he did taking notice of any of the conditions on the sugar estates. "My consulate is not likely to be a lucrative one," he complained at one point. "My situation in a pecuniary point of view is anything but comfortable." USC, December 23, 1831, and September 7, 1831.

4. USC, May 16, 1832.

5. Rugemer, *The Problem of Emancipation*, p. 173. The American writers James A. Thome and Joseph A. Kimball paid a call on Harrison six years after the rebellion and adjudged him a "true hearted Virginian, both in his gen-

erosity and his prejudices in favor of slavery. . . . He talked of abolition just as a Virginian of an aristocratic family might be expected to talk." Their impression must have been solidified when Harrison went on to say that Jamaican free blacks were "the most degraded and ignorant of all the negroes he had seen." The visitors noted, however, that the aging Harrison had never once traveled more than six miles outside the safe zone of Kingston, making his expertise on the state of Jamaican affairs somewhat dubious. Thome and Kimball, *Emancipation in the West Indies,* p. 347.

6. Rugemer, *The Problem of Emancipation,* p. 141; Davis, *Inhuman Bondage,* p. 239.

7. Kerr-Ritchie, *Rites of August First,* p. 62.

8. Kerr-Ritchie, *Rites of August First,* p. 63.

9. Bleby, *Speech,* p. 4.

10. Earlier rebellions in 1816 in Barbados and 1823 in Demerara also made political impressions in London and aided the argument for emancipation, though not with the same force or ultimate effectiveness as the Sharpe uprising.

11. Higman, *Plantation Jamaica,* pp. 291–293; Lord Mulgrave to Viscount Goderich, March 2, 1833, quoted in Holt, *The Problem of Freedom,* p. 81.

12. Green, *British Slave Emancipation,* p. 112. See also Matthews, *Caribbean Slave Revolts,* pp. 1–27; and Marques, *Who Abolished Slavery?,* pp. 36–37.

13. Lord, "'Faithful Delineations,'" p. 116; Dunkley, *The Life of Rev. George Wilson Bridges,* p. 104.

14. Knibb, *Memoir,* p. 194; Gurney, *Familiar Letters,* p. 139; Reid, *Samuel Sharpe,* p. 56.

15. Burchell, *Memoir,* p. 383.

16. Knibb, *Memoir,* pp. 389, 526.

17. Long, *Doctoring Freedom,* p. 40.

18. Greville, *Diaries,* p. 122.

19. Marson, *Belmore,* p. 191.

20. Grignon, *Vindication,* p. 75; Legacies of British Slave-Ownership, University College London, http://www.ucl.ac.uk/lbs.

21. McClelland, "Redefining the West Indian Interest," p. 149.

22. Marks, *The Family of the Barrett,* p. 423.

23. Richard Barrett to John F. Badley, April 5, 1838, SD.891, MS 681/1/3, College Library, Eton College, Windsor, UK; *Falmouth Post* (Falmouth, Jamaica), October 7, 1835, quoted in Holt, *The Problem of Freedom,* p. 100; Robertson, *Gone Is the Ancient Glory,* p. 160.

24. Marks, *The Family of the Barrett*, p. 468.

25. Barrett, *The Barretts of Jamaica*, pp. 107–108.

26. Transatlantic Slave Trade Database, Emory University, https://www.slavevoyages.org/voyage/database.

27. Reid, *Samuel Sharpe*, p. 94.

28. *Jamaica Advocate* (Kingston, Jamaica), August 29, 1896, quoted in Reid, *Samuel Sharpe*, p. 57.

Epilogue

1. Aljoe, *Creole Testimonies*, p. 15.

2. A curiosity of the Jamaican flag is that it is the only one among contemporary nations that does not include at least one of the colors red, white, or blue.

3. Jamaican National Symbols, National Library of Jamaica, http://nlj.gov.jm/jamaican-national-symbols/.

4. Among the first widely disseminated studies of the rebellion was Turner, "The Jamaica Slave Rebellion," in 1968.

5. Arnold Bertram, interview with the author, Kingston, Jamaica, December 29, 2017.

6. Bertram interview; *The Gleaner* (Kingston, Jamaica), October 21, 1975.

7. *The Gleaner* (Kingston, Jamaica), October 21, 1975.

8. Rev. Devon Dick, interview with the author, Kingston, Jamaica, December 29, 2017.

9. Dick interview; Reid, *Samuel Sharpe*, p. 65.

10. Brathwaite, "The Slave Rebellion," p. 15; Verene Shepherd, interview with the author, Kingston, Jamaica, December 29, 2017. See also Beckles, "Caribbean Anti-Slavery," p. 369.

11. Bertram interview.

12. Cornford, *Missionary Reminiscences*, p. 35.

13. Arnold Bertram does not go quite this far, but he has compared Sharpe's life to that of St. Paul. See Bertram, "Remembering Sam Sharpe."

14. The documented history and the oral tradition are in occasional conflict over small issues. Larry Kreitzer of Regent's Park College, University of Oxford, came to the United Theological College of the West Indies in October 2012 to present his findings, from the UK National Archives, that Sharpe had been born in 1805 rather than the traditionally presumed date of 1801, making him younger at the time of the rebellion than thirty-one,

and that his birth name was Archer. Kreitzer said this talk was not well received by the audience, as the information contradicted what had been understood about Sharpe, and that oral sources were deemed to be, in some important ways, more trustworthy than British documents. Larry Kreitzer, interview with the author, Oxford, UK, November 21, 2017.

15. Shalman Scott, interview with the author, Montego Bay, Jamaica, December 26, 2017. See also Scott, "Sam Sharpe's Journey." Scott has said that some of his information came from Tony Hart, whose family had purchased the grounds of what had been Cooper's Hill Estate, where Sharpe grew up. See also Allen, "The Hart Family"; Payne, "Baptist Work"; and Brathwaite, "The Slave Rebellion."

16. Cornford, *Missionary Reminiscences*, p. 32. This is the first appearance of the quote, published twenty-four years after the event in an untrustworthy sentimental account by a white missionary. See also Scott, "That Kensington Fire."

17. Shepherd credits Olivia Grange, minister of culture, gender, entertainment, and sport for the "fire" sobriquet. Email to author, January 7, 2020.

18. The first known mention of these words is in Clarke, *Memorials,* p. 103, which was written more than three decades after the rebellion.

BIBLIOGRAPHY

Archival Sources

British Parliamentary Documents

Bulletins of State Intelligence &c, 1832, compiled from *The London Gazette*. Westminster, UK: R. G. Clarke. (*Bulletins*)

Jamaica: Slave Insurrection. Return to an Address to His Majesty, June 22, 1832. [London]: Printed for the House of Commons, June 28, 1832. (*SI*)

Papers in Explanation of the Measures Adopted by His Majesty's Government, for Giving Effect to the Act for the Abolition of Slavery throughout the British Colonies, Part I, Jamaica 1833–1835. [London]: Printed for the House of Commons, April 16, 1835. (*AOS*)

Parliamentary Debates, third series, vol. 17, April 2, 1833–May 20, 1833. London: T. C. Hansard, 1833. (*PD*)

Parliamentary Papers, vol. 47, 1831–1832. London: House of Commons. (*PP*)

Report from the Select Committee on the Extinction of Slavery throughout the British Dominions, August 11, 1832. London: J. Haddon, 1833. (*SC*)

Slaves: Papers Presented to Parliament by His Majesty's Command [. . .], vols. 2, 16, 1830–1831. London: R. G. Clarke, 1827. (*SPP*)

West India Colonies: Slave Insurrection. Return to Addresses to His Majesty, dated 9 & 15 March 1832. [London]: Printed for the House of Commons, March 16, 1832. (*WIC*)

Despatches from U.S. Consuls in Kingston, Jamaica, 1796–1906, National Archives, College Park, Maryland, USA, Record Group 59, T31. (USC)

Moulton-Barrett archive, College Library, Eton College, Windsor, United Kingdom. (MS 681/1/3)

Records of the Colonial Office: Jamaica, original correspondence, Secretary of State, National Archives, United Kingdom. (CO 137 / 181–185)

Votes of the Honourable House of Assembly of Jamaica, February 28–April 28, 1832. Jamaica Archives, Spanish Town, Jamaica. (*Votes,* 1B/5/1A/37)

William Fisher correspondence, West Yorkshire Archive, Leeds, United Kingdom. (WYK1263/1/17)

Newspapers and Periodicals

Alexandria Gazette (Alexandria, VA)
Anti-Slavery Reporter (London)
Atlas (London)
Charleston Courier (Charleston, SC)
Charleston Mercury (Charleston, SC)
Cornwall Chronicle (Cornwall, Jamaica)
Cornwall Courier (Cornwall, Jamaica)
Defoe's Review (London)
Evening Standard (London)
Gleaner, The (Kingston, Jamaica)
Globe (London)
Jamaica Courant (Kingston, Jamaica)
Lancaster Gazette (Lancaster, UK)
Liberator (Boston)
Liverpool Mercury
Macon Telegraph (Macon, GA)
Morning Advertiser (London)
Morning Chronicle (London)
Morning Post (London)
Niles Weekly Register (Baltimore)
Northampton Mercury (Northampton, UK)
Northern Whig (Belfast)
Nottingham Review and General Advertiser for the Midland Counties (Nottingham, UK)
Parliamentary Review and Family Magazine (London)
Primitive Methodist Magazine (Stoke-on-Trent, UK)
Public Ledger and Daily Advertiser (London)

Royal Gazette (Kingston, Jamaica)

St. Jago de la Vega Gazette (St. Jago de la Vega [Spanish Town], Jamaica)

Watchman and Jamaica Free Press (Kingston, Jamaica)

Wesleyan-Methodist Magazine (London)

Books and Articles

Abbott, Elizabeth. *Sugar: A Bittersweet History*. Toronto: Penguin Canada, 2008.

"An Abolitionist." *The Negro's Memorial, or Abolitionist Catechism*. London: Hatchard, 1825.

Adams, Captain John. *Remarks on the Country Extending from Cape Palmas to the River Congo*. London: G. and W. B. Whitaker, 1823.

Adams, John. *The Works of John Adams*. Vol. 8, *Letters and State Papers, 1782–1799*. Boston: Little, Brown and Company, 1853.

Adderley, Rosanne Marion. *"New Negroes from Africa": Slave Trade Abolition and Free African Settlement in the Nineteenth Century Caribbean*. Bloomington: Indiana University Press, 2006.

Aljoe, Nicole N. *Creole Testimonies: Slave Narratives from the British West Indies, 1709–1838*. New York: Palgrave Macmillan, 2012.

Allen, Desmond. "The Hart Family: Sam Sharpe Would Make His Peace with Tony Hart Today." *Jamaica Observer* (Kingston, Jamaica), February 26, 2006.

Allmendinger, David F., Jr. *Nat Turner and the Rising in Southampton County*. Baltimore: Johns Hopkins University Press, 2014.

Anstey, Roger. "Religion and British Emancipation." In *The Abolition of the Atlantic Slave Trade: Origins and Effects in Europe, Africa and the Americas*, edited by David Eltis and James Walvin. Madison: University of Wisconsin Press, 1981.

Anthropos. *The Rights of Man, (not Paine's,) But the Rights of Man, in the West Indies*. London: Knight and Lacey, 1824.

Avena, Nicole M., Pedro Rada, and Bartley G. Hoebel. "Evidence for Sugar Addiction: Behavioral and Neurochemical Effects of Intermittent, Excessive Sugar Intake." *Neuroscience and Biobehavior Reviews* 32 (2008), pp. 20–39.

Baptist Missionaries. *A Narrative of Recent Events Connected with the Baptist Mission in This Island*. Kingston, Jamaica: Edward Jordon and Robert Osborn, 1833.

Barclay, Alexander. *Effects of the Late Colonial Policy of Great Britain* [. . .]. London: Smith, Elder, 1830.

Barrett, R. A. *The Barretts of Jamaica.* Winfield, KS: Wedgestone, 2000.

Barrett, Richard. *Richard Barrett's Journal.* Winfield, KS: Wedgestone, 1983.

Barrett, Richard, and William Burge. *The Speeches of Mr. Barrett and Mr. Burge at a General Meeting of Planters, Merchants and Others Interested in the West-India Colonies Assembled in the Thatched-House Tavern on the Eighteenth of May, 1833.* London: A. J. Valpy, 1833.

Beckles, Hilary. "Caribbean Anti-Slavery: The Self-Liberation Ethos of Enslaved Blacks." In *Caribbean Slave Society and Economy: A Student Reader,* edited by Hilary Beckles and Verene Shepherd. New York: New Press, 1991.

Beckles, Hilary, and Verene Shepherd. *Liberties Lost: Caribbean Indigenous Societies and Slave Systems.* Cambridge: Cambridge University Press, 2004.

Bertram, Arnold. "Remembering Sam Sharpe and the Emancipation Rebellion, 1831–32." *The Gleaner* (Kingston, Jamaica), December 16, 2016.

Bickell, Richard. *The West Indies as They Are* [. . .]. London: J. Hatchard and Son, 1824.

Blackburn, Robin. *The Making of New World Slavery: From the Baroque to the Modern, 1492–1800.* London: Verso, 1997.

Blackett, R. J. M., *Making Freedom: The Underground Railroad and the Politics of Slavery.* Chapel Hill: University of North Carolina Press, 2013.

Bleby, Henry. *Death Struggles of Slavery.* London: Hamilton, Adams, 1853.

———. *Speech of Rev. Henry Bleby, Missionary from Barbadoes, on the Results of Emancipation on the W.I. Colonies.* Boston: R. F. Wallcut, 1858.

Bonnick, Ron. *Rooms without Doors: A Historical Glimpse into the Family of Elizabeth Barrett Browning.* Bloomington, IN: Xlibris, 2016.

Bosman, Willem. *A New and Accurate Description of the Coast of Guinea, Divided into the Gold, the Slave, and the Ivory Coasts.* London: Ballantyne, 2007.

Boswell, James. *The Life of Samuel Johnson, LL.D.* London: J. M. Dent, 1906.

Brathwaite, Kamau. *The Development of Creole Society in Jamaica, 1770–1820.* Oxford: Clarendon Press, 1971.

———. "The Slave Rebellion in the Great River Valley of St. James, 1831–32." *Jamaican Historical Review* 13, no. 1 (1982), pp. 11–30.

————. *Wars of Respect: Nanny and Sam Sharpe*. Kingston: Jamaica Information Agency, 1977.

Breen, Patrick H. *The Land Shall Be Deluged in Blood: A New History of the Nat Turner Revolt*. New York: Oxford University Press, 2015.

Brendon, Piers. *The Decline and Fall of the British Empire, 1781–1997*. New York: Alfred A. Knopf, 2008.

Bridges, George Wilson. *The Annals of Jamaica*. 2 vols. London: John Murray, 1828.

————. *A Voice from Jamaica in Reply to William Wilberforce, Esq., M.P.* London: Longman, Hurst, Rees, Orme, Brown, and Green, 1823.

Brown, Vincent. *The Reaper's Garden: Death and Power in the World of Atlantic Slavery*. Cambridge, MA: Harvard University Press, 2008.

Browning, Elizabeth Barrett. *Diary by E.B.B.: The Unpublished Diary of Elizabeth Barrett Browning, 1831–1832*. Edited by Philip Kelley and Ronald Hudson. Athens: Ohio University Press, 1969.

————. *Elizabeth Barrett to Mr. Boyd: Unpublished Letters of Elizabeth Barrett Browning to Hugh Stuart Boyd*. Edited by Barbara P. McCarthy. New Haven, CT: Yale University Press, 1955.

————. *Letters of Elizabeth Barrett Browning*. London: Macmillan, 1899.

————. *The Letters of Elizabeth Barrett Browning to Mary Russell Mitford, 1836–1854*. 3 vols. Edited by Meredith B. Raymond and Mary Rose Sullivan. Winfield, KS: Wedgestone, 1983.

Buckley, Roger N. "The Frontier in the Jamaican Caricatures of Abraham James." *Yale University Library Gazette* 58, nos. 3–4 (1984), pp. 152–162.

Burchell, Thomas. *Memoir of Thomas Burchell: Twenty-Two Years a Missionary in Jamaica*. Edited by William Fitzer Burchell. London: B. L. Green, 1849.

Burn, W. L. *Emancipation and Apprenticeship in the British West Indies*. London: Jonathan Cape, 1937.

Burnard, Trevor. *Mastery, Tyranny and Desire: Thomas Thistlewood and His Slaves in the Anglo-Jamaican World*. Chapel Hill: University of North Carolina Press, 2004.

————. "'Prodigious Riches': The Wealth of Jamaica before the American Revolution." *Economic History Review* 54, no. 3 (2001), pp. 506–524.

Butler, J. R. M. *The Passing of the Great Reform Bill*. London: Longmans, Green, 1914.

Buxton, Thomas Fowell. *Memoirs of Sir Thomas Fowell Buxton*. London: John Murray, 1848.

Campbell, Mavis C. *The Maroons of Jamaica, 1655–1796: A History of Resistance, Collaboration and Betrayal.* Trenton, NJ: Africa World Press, 1990.

Cannon, John. *Parliamentary Reform, 1640–1832.* Cambridge: Cambridge University Press, 1973.

Carretta, Vincent, ed. *Unchained Voices: An Anthology of Black Authors in the English-Speaking World of the Eighteenth Century.* Lexington: University Press of Kentucky, 2003.

Catherall, Gordon A. "Thomas Burchell, Gentle Rebel." *Baptist Quarterly* 21, no. 8 (1965), pp. 349–363.

———. *William Knibb: Freedom Fighter.* Liverpool: Janay, 1972.

Charlton, K. "James Cropper and Liverpool's Contribution to the Anti-Slavery Movement." *Transactions of the Historic Society of Lancashire and Cheshire* 123 (1972), pp. 57–80.

Chen, Joanne. *The Taste of Sweet: Our Complicated Love Affair with Our Favorite Treats.* New York: Crown, 2008.

Clarke, James A. *The Lineaments of Wrath: Race, Violent Crime and American Culture.* New Brunswick, NJ: Transaction, 1998.

Clarke, John. *Memorials of Baptist Missionaries in Jamaica [. . .].* London: Yates and Alexander, 1869.

Clarkson, Thomas. *The History of the Rise, Progress and Accomplishment of the Abolition of the African Slave Trade, by the British Parliament.* New York: John S. Taylor, 1836.

Coleridge, Samuel Taylor. "On the Slave Trade." In *The Watchman: The Collected Works of Samuel Taylor Coleridge,* edited by Lewis Patton. New York: Routledge and Kegan Paul, 1970.

Commissioners of Longitude. *The Nautical Almanac and Astronomical Emphemeris for the Year 1831.* London: T. Bensley, 1828.

Cooke, Sir Robert. *The Palace of Westminster: Houses of Parliament.* New York: Burton Skira, 1987.

Cooper, Thomas. *Facts Illustrative of the Condition of the Negro Slaves in Jamaica.* London: J. Hatchard and Son, 1824.

Corfield, Kenneth. "Elizabeth Heyrick: Radical Quaker." In *Religion in the Lives of English Women, 1760–1930,* edited by Gail Malmgreen. Bloomington: Indiana University Press, 1986.

Cornford, Phillip Henry. *Missionary Reminiscences; or, Jamaica Retraced.* Leeds, UK: J. Heaton and Son, 1856.

Cox, Francis, A. *History of the Baptist Missionary Society, from 1792 to 1842* [. . .]. 2 vols. London: T. Ward, 1842.

Craton, Michael. "Slave Culture, Resistance and the Achievement of Emancipation in the British West Indies, 1783–1838." In *Slavery and British Society 1776–1846,* edited by James Walvin. London: Macmillan, 1982.

———. *Testing the Chains: Resistance to Slavery in the British West Indies.* Ithaca, NY: Cornell University Press, 1982.

———. "What and Who to Whom and What: The Significance of Slave Resistance." In *British Capitalism and Caribbean Slavery: The Legacy of Eric Williams,* edited by Barbara Lewis Solow. Cambridge: Cambridge University Press, 2004.

Creevey, Thomas. *The Creevey Papers: A Selection from the Correspondence and Diaries of the Late Thomas Creevey.* London: John Murray, 1904.

Cundall, Frank. *The Press and Printers of Jamaica Prior to 1820.* Worcester, MA: American Antiquarian Society, 1916.

Curtain, Philip. *Two Jamaicas: The Role of Ideas in a Tropical Colony.* Cambridge, MA: Harvard University Press, 1955.

Da Costa, Emilia Viotti. *Crowns of Glory, Tears of Blood: The Demerara Slave Rebellion of 1823.* Oxford: Oxford University Press, 1994.

Dallas, Robert Charles. *The History of the Maroons* [. . .]. 2 vols. London: T. N. Longman and O. Rees, 1803.

Davidson, Jonathan. *Downing Street Blues: A History of Depression and Other Mental Afflictions in British Prime Ministers.* London: McFarland, 2010.

Davies, K.G. *The Royal African Company.* London: Longmans, Green, 1957.

Davis, David Brion. *Inhuman Bondage: The Rise and Fall of Slavery in the New World.* Oxford: Oxford University Press, 2006.

Day, Thomas R. "Jamaican Revolts in British Press and Politics, 1760–1865." Master's thesis, Virginia Commonwealth University, May 2016.

Declarations of the Objects of the Liverpool Society for Promoting the Abolition of Slavery, 25th March 1823. Liverpool: James Smith, 1823.

Dick, Devon. *The Cross and the Machete: Native Baptists of Jamaica—Identity, Ministry and Legacy,* Kingston, Jamaica: Ian Randle, 2009.

Diouf, Sylviane A. *Servants of Allah: African Muslims Enslaved in the Americas.* New York: New York University Press, 1998.

Douglas, George H. *The Golden Age of the Newspaper.* Westport, CT: Greenwood, 1999.

Drescher, Seymour. *Capitalism and Antislavery: British Mobilization in Comparative Perspective.* Oxford: Oxford University Press, 1986.

———. *Econocide: British Slavery in the Era of Abolition.* Pittsburgh: University of Pittsburgh Press, 1977.

Dunkley, D. A. *The Life of Rev. George Wilson Bridges.* Lanham, MD: Lexington Books, 2011.

Dunn, Richard S. *Sugar and Slaves: The Rise of the Planter Class in the English West Indies, 1624–1713.* Chapel Hill: University of North Carolina Press, 1972.

Egerton, Douglas R. "A Peculiar Mark of Infamy: Dismemberment, Burial, and Rebelliousness in Slave Societies." In *Mortal Remains: Death in Early America,* edited by Nancy Isenberg and Andrew Burstein. Philadelphia: University of Pennsylvania Press, 2003.

———. "Slaves to the Marketplace: Economic Liberty and Black Rebelliousness in the Atlantic World." *Journal of the Early Republic* 26, no. 4 (2006), pp. 617–638.

Equiano, Olaudah. *The Interesting Narrative and Other Writings.* New York: Penguin, 1995.

Falconbridge, Alexander. *An Account of the Slave Trade on the Coast of Africa.* London: J. Phillips, 1788.

Farrell, Stephen. The Old Palace of Westminster. The History of Parliament, http://www.historyofparliamentonline.org/old-palace-westminster.

Fermor, Patrick Leigh. *The Traveller's Tree: A Journey through the Caribbean Islands.* London: John Murray, 1950.

Ferrer, Ada. *Freedom's Mirror: Cuba and Haiti in the Age of Revolution.* Cambridge: Cambridge University Press, 2014.

Foner, Eric, ed. *Nat Turner.* Englewood Cliffs, NJ: Prentice-Hall, 1971.

Fouchard, Jean. *The Haitian Maroons: Liberty or Death.* New York: Edward W. Bylden, 1981.

Foulks, Theodore. *Eighteen Months in Jamaica with Recollections of the Late Rebellion.* London: Whittaker, Techer and Arnott, 1833.

Fraser, William. *Words on Wellington: The Duke—Waterloo—The Ball.* London: John C. Nimmo, 1889.

Gamble, Samuel. *A Slaving Voyage to Africa and Jamaica: The Log of the Sandown, 1793–1794.* Edited by Bruce L. Mouser. Bloomington: Indiana University Press, 2002.

Gardner, W. J. *A History of Jamaica, from the Time of its Discovery by Christopher Columbus to the Year 1872.* London: T. Fisher Unwin, 1873.

Gaunt, Mary. *Where the Twain Meet.* New York: E. P. Dutton, 1922.

Geggus, David Patrick. *Slavery, War and Revolution: The British Occupation of Saint Domingue, 1793–1798.* Oxford: Clarendon Press, 1982.

———. "Slavery, War and Revolution in the Greater Caribbean, 1789–1815." In *A Turbulent Time: The French Revolution and the Greater Caribbean,* edited by David Barry Gaspar and David Patrick Geggus. Bloomington: Indiana University Press, 1997.

Genovese, Eugene. *Roll, Jordan, Roll: The World the Slaves Made.* New York: Pantheon, 1974.

A Genuine "Dickey Sam." *Liverpool and Slavery: An Historical Account of the Liverpool-African Slave Trade.* Liverpool: A. Bowker and Son, 1884.

Girard, Phillippe. *Toussaint Louverture: A Revolutionary Life.* New York: Basic Books, 2016.

Glasse, Hannah. *The Art of Cooking Made Plain and Easy.* London: T. Longman, 1796.

Godwin, Benjamin. *The Substance of a Course of Lectures on British Colonial Slavery.* London: J. Hatchard and Son, 1830.

Green, William A. *British Slave Emancipation: The Sugar Colonies and the Great Experiment.* Oxford: Oxford University Press, 1976.

Greene, Jack P. *Evaluating Empire and Confronting Colonialism in Eighteenth-Century Britain.* Cambridge: Cambridge University Press, 2013.

Grehan, John. *Voices from the Past: Waterloo 1815.* London: Frontline Books, 2015.

Greville, Charles. *The Diaries of Charles Greville.* Edited by Edward Pearce with Deanna Pearce. London: Pimlico, 2005.

Griffith-Hughes, Elisabeth. "A Mighty Experiment: The Transition from Slavery to Freedom in Jamaica 1834–1838." PhD diss., University of Georgia, 2003.

Grignon, William. *Vindication of the Conduct of Colonel Grignon and of the Western Interior Regiment [. . .].* Spanish Town, Jamaica: St. Jago Gazette, 1833.

Gronow, R. H. *Reminiscences of Captain Gronow.* London: Smith, Elder, 1862.

Gross, Izhak. "The Abolition of Negro Slavery and British Parliamentary Politics, 1832–33." *Historical Journal* 23, no. 1 (1980), pp. 63–85.

Gurney, Joseph John. *Familiar Letters to Henry Clay of Kentucky Describing the West Indies*. New York: Marlon Day, 1840.

Hakluyt, Richard. *The Principal Navigations, Voyages, Traffiques and Discourses of the English Nation*. Reprinted in *Voyages and Travels Mainly during the 16th and 17th Centuries*, reprinted in abridged form and edited by Thomas Seccombe. London: A. Constable. 1903. Originally published 1589–1600 in 16 vols.

Hall, Douglas. *In Miserable Slavery: Thomas Thistlewood in Jamaica, 1750–86*. Kingston, Jamaica: University of the West Indies Press, 1998.

Hargreaves, A. S. "Queen Elizabeth and Her Teeth." *British Dental Journal* 167, no. 333 (1989), pp. 286–288.

Harrison, Mark. *Crowds and History: Mass Phenomena in English Towns, 1790–1835*. Cambridge: Cambridge University Press, 1988.

Hart, Richard. *Slaves Who Abolished Slavery: Blacks in Rebellion*. Kingston, Jamaica: University of West Indies Press, 2002.

Hentzner, Paul. *Travels in England during the Reign of Queen Elizabeth; with Fragmenta Regalia*. London: Cassell, 1892.

"Heroes of the Mission Field: William Knibb," *Primitive Methodist Magazine* 66 (1885), pp. 266–269.

Hewlett, Dorothy. *Elizabeth Barrett Browning*. London: Cassell, 1953.

Heyrick, Elizabeth. *Immediate, Not Gradual, Abolition, or an Inquiry into the Shortest, Safest and Most Effectual Means of Getting Rid of West Indian Slavery*. Boston: Isaac Knapp, 1838.

Higman, B. W. *Plantation Jamaica, 1750–1850: Capital and Control in a Colonial Economy*. Kingston, Jamaica: University of the West Indies Press, 2005.

———. "The West Indian 'Interest' in Parliament, 1807–1833." *Historical Studies* 13, no. 49 (1967), pp. 1–19.

Hilton, Boyd. *A Mad, Bad, and Dangerous People? England 1783–1846*. Oxford: Oxford University Press, 2006.

Hochschild, Adam. *Bury the Chains: Prophets and Rebels in the Fight to Free an Empire's Slaves*. New York: Houghton Mifflin, 2005.

Holt, Thomas, C. *The Problem of Freedom: Race, Labor and Politics in Jamaica and Britain, 1832–1938*. Baltimore: Johns Hopkins University Press, 1992.

Howard, David. *Kingston: A Cultural and Literary History*. Oxford: Signal Books, 2005.

Howman, Brian. "Abolitionism in Liverpool." In *Liverpool and Transatlantic Slavery*, edited by David Richardson, Suzanne Schwarz, and Anthony Tibbles. Liverpool: Liverpool University Press, 2007.

The Humming Bird; or, Morsels of Information, on the Subject of Slavery. London: A. Cockshaw, 1825.

Huntzicker, William E. *The Popular Press, 1833–1865.* Westport, CT: Greenwood, 1999.

Interesting Tracts Relating to the Island of Jamaica [. . .]. St. Jago de la Vega, Jamaica: Lewis, Lunan and Jones, 1800.

Jacobs, H. P. "The Jamaican Press 1789–1865." *Jamaica Journal* 6, no. 3 (1972), pp. 2–6.

Jacoby, Karl. "Slaves by Nature? Domestic Animals and Human Slaves." *Slavery and Abolition* 15, no. 1 (1994), pp. 89–99.

Jamaica Almanack. Kingston, Jamaica: Alexander Aikman Jr., 1828.

James, C. L. R. *The Black Jacobins: Toussaint L'Ouverture and the San Domingo Revolution.* New York: Random House, 1963.

Jefferson, Thomas. *The Papers of Thomas Jefferson.* 44 vols. James P. McClure, gen. ed. Princeton: Princeton University Press, 1950–2019.

Jones, William. *The Diary of the Rev. William Jones, 1777–1821* [. . .]. Edited by O. F. Christie. New York: Brentano, 1929.

Jonson, Ben. *Ben Jonson's Conversations with William Drummond of Hawthornden.* London: Blackie and Son, 1923.

Jordan, Winthrop D. *White over Black: American Attitudes toward the Negro, 1550–1812.* Chapel Hill: University of North Carolina Press, 1968.

Kaplan, Sidney. *The Black Presence in the Era of the American Revolution.* Greenwich, CT: New York Graphic Society, 1973.

Kerr-Ritchie, J. R. *Rites of August First: Emancipation Day in the Black Atlantic World.* Baton Rouge: Louisiana State University Press, 2007.

Kiple, Kenneth F. *The Caribbean Slave: A Biological History.* Cambridge: Cambridge University Press, 2002.

Klein, Herbert S. *The Atlantic Slave Trade.* Cambridge: Cambridge University Press, 2010.

Knibb, William. *Memoir of William Knibb: Missionary in Jamaica.* Edited by John Howard Hinton. London: Houlston and Stoneman, 1847.

Knight, Roger. *William IV: A King at Sea.* London: Allen Lane, 2015.

Kreitzer, Larry J. *"Kissing the Book": The Story of Sam Sharpe as Revealed in the Records of the National Archive at Kew.* Oxford: Centre for Baptist History and Heritage, 2013.

Lawrence, A. W. *Fortified Trade-Posts: The English in West Africa, 1645–1822.* London: Jonathan Cape, 1969.

Leach, J. *Rough Sketches of the Life of an Old Soldier during a Service in the West Indies* [. . .]. London: Longman, Rees, Orme, Brown, and Green, 1831.

Legion. *A Second Letter from Legion His Grace the Duke of Richmond* [. . .]. London: S. Bagster, 1833.

Leslie, Charles. *A New and Exact History of Jamaica* [. . .]. Edinburgh, 1739.

Levy, Mary Catherine. "Through European Eyes: Jamaica 200 Years Ago." *Jamaica Journal* 17, no. 4 (1984–1985), pp. 32–42.

Lewis, Matthew. *Journal of a West Indian Proprietor, Kept during a Residence in the Island of Jamaica.* London: John Murray, 1834.

Linebaugh, Peter, and Marcus Rediker. *The Many-Headed Hydra: Sailors, Slaves, Commoners, and the Hidden History of the Revolutionary Atlantic.* Boston: Beacon Press, 2013.

Lofton, John. *Denmark Vesey's Revolt: The Slave Plot That Lit a Fuse to Fort Sumter.* Kent, OH: Kent State University Press, 1964.

Loker, Zvi. "An Eighteenth-Century Plan to Invade Jamaica; Isaac Yeshurun Sasportas—French Patriot or Jewish Radical Idealist?" *Transactions and Miscellanies* 28 (1981–1982), pp. 132–144.

Long, Edward. *The History of Jamaica: Or, General Survey of the Antient and Modern State,* [. . .]. 3 vols. London: T. Lowndes, 1774.

Long, Gretchen. *Doctoring Freedom: The Politics of African American Medical Care in Slavery and Emancipation.* Chapel Hill: University of North Carolina Press, 2012.

Lord, Russell. "'Faithful Delineations': Rev. George Wilson Bridges and Photography." In *Readings in Caribbean History and Culture: Breaking Ground,* edited by D.A. Dunkley. Lanham, MD: Lexington Books, 2011.

Lustig, Robert. "Fructose: Metabolic, Hedonic, and Societal Parallels with Ethanol." *Journal of the American Dietetic Association* 110, no. 9 (2010), pp. 1307–1321.

Macaulay, Thomas Babington. *The Complete Works of Thomas Babington Macaulay.* 20 vols. New York: G. Putnam and Sons, 1898.

Macaulay, Zachary. *Life and Letters of Zachary Macaulay.* London: Edward Arnold, 1900.

Macaulay, Zachary, editor. *Anti-Slavery Monthly Reporter.* London: London Society for the Abolition of Slavery Throughout the British Dominions, 1831.

Madden, Richard Robert. *A Twelvemonth Residence in the West Indies.* London: James Cochrane, 1835.

Maehl, William H., Jr. "Augustus Hardin Beaumont: Anglo-American Radical (1798–1838)." *International Review of Social History* 14, no. 2 (1969), pp. 237–250.

Mair, Lucille Mathurin. *A Historical Study of Women in Jamaica, 1655–1844.* Kingston, Jamaica: University of the West Indies Press, 2006.

Malhotra, Aseem. "Saturated Fat in Cardiovascular Disease: Friend or Foe." In *Controversies in Obesity,* edited by David W. Haslam, Arya M. Sharma, and Carel W. le Roux. London: Springer, 2014.

Marks, Jeanette. *The Family of the Barrett: A Colonial Romance.* New York: Macmillan, 1938.

Marques, João Pedro. *Who Abolished Slavery? Slave Revolts and Abolitionism, a Debate with João Pedro Marques.* Edited by Seymour Drescher and Pieter C. Emmer. New York: Berghahn Books, 2010.

Marson, Peter. *Belmore: The Lowry Corrys of Castle Coole, 1646–1913.* Belfast: Ulster Historical Foundation, 2007.

Mathieson, William Law. *British Slavery and Its Abolition, 1823–1838.* London: Octagon Books, 1926.

Matthews, Gelien. *Caribbean Slave Revolts and the British Abolitionist Movement.* Baton Rouge: Louisiana State University Press, 2006.

Matthews, John. *A Voyage to the River Sierra-Leone, on the Coast of Africa.* London: B. White and Sons, 1791.

McBurney, Christian. *Abductions in the American Revolution: Attempts to Kidnap George Washington, Benedict Arnold and Other Military and Civilian Leaders.* Jefferson, NC: McFarland, 2016.

McClelland, Keith. "Redefining the West India Interest." In *Legacies of British Slave-Ownership: Colonial Slavery and the Formation of Victorian Britain,* edited by Catherine Hall, Nicholas Draper, and Keith McClelland. Cambridge: Cambridge University Press, 2014.

McDonnell, Philippa. "Why My Great-Great-Great Grandfather Defaced Ancient Egyptian Monuments." *Guardian,* August 2, 2009.

McKee, Helen. "From Violence to Alliance: Maroons and White Settlers in Jamaica, 1739–1795." *Slavery and Abolition* 39, no. 1 (2018), pp. 27–52.

McMahon, Benjamin. *Jamaica Plantership.* London: Effingham Wilson, 1839.

McNeill, J. R. *Mosquito Empires: Ecology and War in the Greater Caribbean, 1620–1914.* Cambridge: Cambridge University Press, 2010.

Mintz, Sidney. *Sweetness and Power: The Place of Sugar in Modern History.* New York: Penguin, 1985.

Mitton, Steven Heath. "The Free World Confronted: The Problem of Slavery and Progress in American Foreign Relations, 1833–1844." PhD diss., Louisiana State University, 2005.

Monrad, H. C. *Two Views from Christiansborg Castle.* Vol. 2, *A Description of the Guinea Coast and Its Inhabitants.* Accra, Ghana: Sub-Saharan, 2009.

Moreton, J. B. *West India Customs and Manners* [. . .]. London: J. Parsons, 1793.

Morgan, Kenneth. "Liverpool's Dominance in the British Slave Trade, 1740–1807." In *Liverpool and Transatlantic Slavery,* edited by David Richardson, Suzanne Schwarz, and Anthony Tibbles. Liverpool: Liverpool University Press, 2007.

Mullin, Michael. *Africa in America: Slave Acculturation and Resistance in the American South and the British Caribbean, 1736–1831.* Urbana: University of Illinois Press, 1992.

Mustakeem, Sowande' M. *Slavery at Sea: Terror, Sex, and Sickness in the Middle Passage.* Champaign: University of Illinois Press, 2016.

Nautical Almanac and Astronomical Emphemeris for the Year 1831. London: T. Hensley, 1829.

Nelson, Louis P. *Architecture and Empire in Jamaica.* New Haven, CT: Yale University Press, 2016.

Newton, John. *Memoirs of the Rev. John Newton* [. . .]. Philadelphia: Presbyterian Board of Publication, 1835.

Nguah, Felix, and Robert Kugbey. *Shackles in Darkness: A Handbook on the Trans-Atlantic Slave Trade.* Cape Coast, Ghana: Nyakod, 2015.

Nugent, Maria. *Lady Nugent's Journal of Her Residence in Jamaica from 1801 to 1805.* Edited by Philip Wright. Kingston: Institute of Jamaica, 1966.

Okagbue, Osita. *African Theatres and Performances.* London: Routledge, 2007.

O'Malley, Gregory E. *Final Passages: The Intercolonial Slave Trade of British America, 1619–1807.* Chapel Hill: University of North Carolina Press, 2014.

"Orthodox History Riddled with Errors—Shalman Scott," *The Gleaner* (Kingston, Jamaica), August 1, 2004.

Ottenburg, Simon. "Humorous Masks and Serious Politics among the Afikpo Igbo." In *Perspectives on Africa: A Reader in Culture, History and*

Representation, edited by Roy Richard Grinker, Stephen C. Lubke-mann, and Christopher B. Steiner. New York: John Wiley and Sons, 2010.

Park, Mungo. *Travels in the Interior Districts of Africa.* London: J. M. Dent, 1954.

Paton, Diana. *No Bond but the Law: Punishment, Race and Gender in Jamaican State Formation, 1780–1870.* Durham, NC: Duke University Press, 2004.

Patterson, Orlando. *The Sociology of Slavery: An Analysis of the Origins, Development, and Structure of the Slave Society in Jamaica.* Cranbury, NJ: Associated University Presses, 1969.

Paugh, Katherine. *The Politics of Reproduction: Race, Medicine and Fertility in the Age of Abolition.* Oxford: Oxford University Press, 2017.

Payne, Earnest A. "Baptist Work in Jamaica before the Arrival of the Missionaries." *Baptist Quarterly* 7, no. 1 (1934), pp. 20–22.

Pearce, Edward. *Reform! The Fight for the 1832 Reform Act.* London: Jonathan Cape, 2003.

Perbi, Akosua Adoma. *A History of Indigenous Slavery in Ghana.* Accra, Ghana: Sub-Saharan, 2007.

Petley, Christer. *White Fury: A Jamaican Slaveholder and the Age of Revolution.* Oxford: Oxford University Press, 2018.

Pettigrew, William A. *Freedom's Debt: The Royal African Company and the Politics of the Atlantic Slave Trade, 1672–1752.* Chapel Hill: University of North Carolina Press, 2013.

Phillippo, James. *Jamaica: Its Past and Present State.* Philadelphia: J. M. Campbell, 1843.

Pinckard, George. *Notes on the West Indies Including Observations Relative to the Creoles and Slaves of the Western Colonies and the Indians of South America.* London: Baldwin, Cradock and Joy, 1816.

Plasa, Carl. *Slaves to Sweetness: British and Caribbean Literatures of Sugar.* Liverpool: Liverpool University Press, 2009.

Porter, McKenzie. *Overture to Victoria.* London: Alvin Redman, 1961.

Ragatz, Lowell Joseph. *The Fall of the Planter Class in the British Caribbean, 1763–1833: A Study in Social and Economic History.* New York: Century, 1928.

Ralph, James. *A Critical Review of the Publick Buildings, Statues and Ornaments in, and about Westminster* [. . .]. London: C. Ackers, 1734.

Ramirez, Israel. "Why Do Sugars Taste Good?" *Neuroscience and Biobehavior Reviews* 14, no. 2 (1990) pp. 125–134.

Reddie, Richard S. *Abolition! The Struggle to Abolish Slavery in the British Colonies.* Oxford: Lion, 2007.

Reid, C. S. *Samuel Sharpe: From Slave to National Hero.* Kingston, Jamaica: Bustamante Institute for Public Affairs, 1988.

Reid-Salmon, Delroy. *Burning for Freedom: A Theology of the Black Atlantic Struggle for Liberation.* Kingston, Jamaica: Ian Randle, 2012.

Richardson, David, Suzanne Schwarz, and Anthony Tibbles, eds. *Liverpool and Transatlantic Slavery.* Liverpool: Liverpool University Press, 2007.

Riland, John. *Memoirs of a West-India Planter.* London: Hamilton, Adams, 1827.

Roberts, Walter Adolphe. "Edward Jordon and Free Colored Jamaica 1800–1865." In *Six Great Jamaicans.* Kingston, Jamaica: Pioneer, 1957.

Robertson, David. *Denmark Vesey.* New York: Alfred A. Knopf, 1999.

Robertson, James. "Eighteenth-Century Jamaica's Ambivalent Cosmopolitanism." *History* 99, no. 337 (2014), pp. 607–631.

———. *Gone Is the Ancient Glory: Spanish Town, Jamaica, 1534–2000.* Kingston, Jamaica: Ian Randle, 2005.

Roughley, Thomas. *Jamaica Planters Guide* [. . .]. London: Longman, Hurst, Rees, Orme, and Brown, 1823.

Rouse, W. H. D. *A History of Rugby School.* New York: Charles Scribner's Sons, 1898.

Royle, Edward. *Revolutionary Britannia? Reflections on the Threat of Revolution in Britain, 1789–1848.* Manchester, UK: Manchester University Press, 2000.

Rugemer, Edward Bartlett. *The Problem of Emancipation: The Caribbean Roots of the American Civil War.* Baton Rouge: Louisiana State University Press, 2008.

———. "Robert Monroe Harrison, British Abolition, Southern Anglophobia and Texas Annexation." *Slavery and Abolition* 28, no. 2 (2007), pp. 169–191.

Rushdy, Ashraf H. A. *Neo-Slave Narratives: Studies in the Social Logic of a Literary Form.* Oxford: Oxford University Press, 1999.

Sanderson, F. E. "The Liverpool Abolitionists." In *Liverpool, the Slave Trade and Abolition,* edited by Roger Anstey and P. E. H. Hair. Chippenham, UK: Antony Rowe, 1976.

Scott, Julius S. *The Common Wind: Afro-American Currents in the Age of the Haitian Revolution.* London: Verso, 2018.

Scott, Shalman. "Sam Sharpe's Journey from Slave Plantation to National Hero." Lecture presented at Calvary Baptist Church, Montego Bay, Jamaica, July 27, 2014.

———. "That Kensington Fire Which Started the Sam Sharpe Rebellion." *Jamaica Observer* (Kingston, Jamaica), January 14, 2018.

Senior, Bernard. *Jamaica as It Was, as It Is, and as It May Be* [. . .]. London: T. Hurst, 1835.

Shenton, Caroline. *The Day Parliament Burned Down.* Oxford: Oxford University Press, 2012.

Shepherd, Verene. *Livestock, Sugar and Slavery: Contested Terrain in Colonial Jamaica.* Kingston, Jamaica: Ian Randle, 2009.

Shepherd, Verene, and Ahmed Reid. "Rebel Voices: Testimonies from the 1831–32 Emancipation War in Jamaica." *Jamaica Journal* 27, no. 2–3 (2004), pp. 59–64.

Sheridan, Richard B. "From Jamaican Slavery to Haitian Freedom: The Case of the Black Crew of the Pilot Boat, Deep Nine." *Journal of Negro History* 67, no. 4 (1982), pp. 328–339.

———. "Sweet Malefactor: The Social Costs of Slavery and Sugar in Jamaica and Cuba, 1807–54." *Economic History Review* 29, no. 2 (1976), pp. 236–257.

Sherlock, Philip, and Hazel Bennett. *The Story of the Jamaican People.* Kingston, Jamaica: Ian Randle, 1998.

Shore, Joseph. *In Old St. James.* Kingston, Jamaica: Aston W. Gardner, 1911.

Smith, Adam. *An Inquiry into the Nature and Causes of the Wealth of Nations.* New York: Modern Library, 1937.

Smith, Andrew F. *Sugar: A Global History.* London: Reaktion Books, 2015.

Southey, Robert. *The Life and Correspondence of the Late Robert Southey: In Six Volumes.* Edited by Charles Cuthbert Southey. London: Longman, Brown, Green, and Longmans, 1850.

Stewart, John. *An Account of Jamaica, and Its Inhabitants* [. . .]. Kingston, Jamaica: Longman, Hurst, Rees, and Orme, 1808.

Taylor, Eric Robert. *If We Must Die: Shipboard Insurrections in the Era of the Atlantic Slave Trade.* Baton Rouge: Louisiana State University Press, 2006.

Taylor, Frank Fonda. *To Hell with Paradise: A History of the Jamaican Tourist Industry.* Pittsburgh: University of Pittsburgh Press, 1993.

Taylor, Henry. *Autobiography of Henry Taylor.* 2 vols. London: Longmans, Green, 1885.

Temperley, Howard. *British Antislavery, 1833–1870.* London: Longman, 1972.

Thome, James A., and J. Horace Kimball. *Emancipation in the West Indies: A Six Month Tour in Antigua, Barbados and Jamaica in the Year 1837.* New York: American Anti-Slavery Society, 1839.

Thompson, Alvin O. *Fight to Freedom: African Runaways and Maroons in the Americas.* Kingston, Jamaica: University of the West Indies Press, 2006.

Thornton, John. *Africa and Africans in the Making of the Atlantic World, 1400–1800.* Cambridge: Cambridge University Press, 1998.

———. *Warfare in Atlantic Africa, 1500–1800.* London: UCL, 1999.

Trelawny, Edward. *An Essay concerning Slavery* [. . .]. London: C. Corbett, 1749.

Trepp, Jean. "The Liverpool Movement for the Abolition of the English Slave Trade." *Journal of Negro History* 13, no. 3 (1928), pp. 265–285.

Turner, Mary. "The Jamaica Slave Rebellion of 1831." *Past and Present* 40 (1968), pp. 108–125.

———. *Slaves and Missionaries: The Disintegration of Jamaican Slave Society, 1787–1834.* Kingston, Jamaica: University of the West Indies Press, 1998.

Turner, Nat. *The Confessions of Nat Turner, the Leader of the Late Insurrection in Southampton, Virginia.* Edited by Thomas R. Gray. Chapel Hill: University of North Carolina Press, 2011.

Turner, Sasha. *Contested Bodies: Pregnancy, Childrearing and Slavery in Jamaica.* Philadelphia: University of Pennsylvania Press, 2017.

Underhill, Edward Bean. *Life of James Mursell Phillippo: Missionary in Jamaica.* London: Yates and Alexander, 1881.

Vasconcellos, Colleen A. *Slavery, Childhood, and Abolition in Jamaica, 1788–1838.* Athens: University of Georgia Press, 2015.

Waddell, Hope Masterton. *Twenty-Nine Years in the West Indies and Central Africa: A Review of Missionary Work and Adventure, 1829–1858.* London: Nelson and Sons, 1863.

Ward, Edward. *A Trip to Jamaica: With a True Character of the People of the Island.* London, 1698.

Ward, J. R. *British West Indian Slavery: The Process of Amelioration.* Oxford: Oxford University Press, 1988.

Warner-Lewis, Maureen. "The Character of African-Jamaican Culture." In *Jamaica in Slavery and Freedom: History, Heritage and Culture,* edited by Kathleen E. A. Monteith and Glen Richards. Kingston, Jamaica: University of West Indies Press, 2002.

Wentworth, Trelawney. *The West India Sketch Book*. London: Whittaker, 1834.

Whitely, Henry. *Three Months in Jamaica, in 1832, Comprising a Residence of Seven Weeks on a Sugar Plantation*. London: J. Hatchard and Son, 1833.

Williams, Eric. *Capitalism and Slavery*. Chapel Hill: University of North Carolina Press, 1944.

Williams, James. *A Narrative of Events since the First of August, 1834*. Edited by Diana Paton. Durham, NC: Duke University Press, 2001.

Williams, Wilma. "Early Kingston." *Jamaica Journal* 5, nos. 2–3 (1971), pp. 3–7.

Willis, Thomas. *The Remaining Medical Works of That Famous and Renowned Physician Dr. Thomas Willis*. London: T. Dring, C. Harper, J. Leigh, and S. Martyn, 1681.

Wilmot, Swithin. "Not 'Full Free': The Ex-Slaves and the Apprenticeship System in Jamaica 1834–1838." *Jamaica Journal* 17, no. 3 (1984), pp. 2–10.

Witherspoon, John. *The Works of John Witherspoon, D.D.* [. . .]. 9 vols. Edinburgh: J. Ogle, 1815.

Wright, Donald R. *African Americans in the Colonial Era: From African Origins through the American Revolution*. Malden, MA: John Wiley and Sons, 1990.

Yudkin, John. *Pure, White and Deadly: How Sugar Is Killing Us and What We Can Do to Stop It*. London: Penguin, 1972.

Ziegler, Philip. *King William IV*. London: Collins, 1971.

ACKNOWLEDGMENTS

In Jamaica, more than a dozen people aided my research and offered insights. I am grateful to Yvonne Fraser-Clarke, Drusilla Grant, Beverley Lashley, and Chantelle Richards at the National Library of Jamaica; Vivian Crawford at the Institute of Jamaica; and Verene Shepherd, Matthew Smith, and Swithin Wilmot at the University of the West Indies. Bob and Ann Betton supplied the image of Richard Barrett and showed me around the estate at Greenwood Great House. For hospitality and conversation, I am grateful to Syd Bartley, Arnold Bertram, Devon Dick, Annie Paul, and Shalman Scott. Special thanks go to Liz, Mariana, and Milton Samuda.

In the United Kingdom, Nick Draper of University College London and Larry Kreitzer of Regent's Park College, University of Oxford, pointed me to specific colonial documents and provided encouragement to keep asking questions.

In Ghana I am thankful to Clifford Ato Eshun and Mark Tetteh at Cape Coast Castle, Rev. Ebenezer Annan at Christ Church Cathedral in Cape Coast, and Emmanuel Ababio Ofosu-Mensah at the University of Ghana in Accra.

Gregory McNamee gave the necessary and final push to write this book during a conversation in his living room in Tucson, Arizona, in December 2016, when he told me that one of the most useful responses to a time of social crisis is to write history.

The manuscript was composed in three locations, and I was fortunate enough to be given a workspace in each one. I owe a major debt to the Lannan Foundation in Marfa, Texas; Dartmouth College in Hanover, New Hampshire; and the Huntington Library in San Marino, California.

Joy de Menil and Thomas LeBien at Harvard University Press provided superb edits, as well as expert shepherding through every stage. I am grateful for detailed critiques made by four anonymous peer reviewers, and especially for the diligent prereading by Enrique Rivera of the University of California–Los Angeles. Karl Jacoby also made invaluable suggestions. Thanks are due as well to Alex Bay, Robert Bonner, Greg Daddis, Joy Deng, Marlon James, Joanna Levin, Nina Nowak, Donald Pease, and Terry Sheehan.

Erin Dunkerly gave loving support to both the book and the author. She made critical suggestions on the manuscript and helped me see things that I did not see. Her imprint is on every page.

INDEX

Italicized page numbers indicate illustrations.

Hanover Parish, 18, 148, 175
Hanover Regiment, 168
Harewood, Earl of, 233–234
Harrison, Robert Monroe, 253–255,
  318n3, 318–319n5
Hart, James, 36
Hart, Richard, 258
Hart, Tony, 321n15
Hawkins, John, 55, 209, 251
Hentzner, Paul, 35
Heyrick, Elizabeth, 30–34, 82, 290n22
Higman, B. W., 226, 258
Hilton, Edward, 186
Hilton, James, 204
Hispaniola, British invasion of (1654), 9
Holmes (militiaman killed in rebel-
  lion), 168, 308n29
House of Commons and House of
  Lords. *See* Parliament
Howick, Lord, 231, 239, 242
Huggup, John, 133
Hunt, Henry, 221, 226
Hurlock (slave), 155–156
Hylton, Edward (slave), 84, 86
Hylton, Kitty (slave), 98

Ibo people, 66, 297n41
Industrial Revolution, 5, 6, 218, 221,
  223–224, 229, 293n4
infanticide, 292–293n1
Inglis, Robert, 237
Irish immigrants, 19

Jackson, Andrew, 6, 253
Jamaica (British colony): description of,
  10–11, 287n21, 287–288n22; earthquake
  (1692), 11; estates in, 14–15, 45–46;
  gradual self-rule, 273–274; labor
  protest and riot (1865), 273; law
  enforcement in, 17; location of, 8;
  missing population of, 267; name of, 9;

parish structure of, 18; as profitable
  British colony, 18, 219; racial
  hierarchy in, 67; scenery of, 60–61;
  seizure from Spanish, 9; settlement
  of, 9–10; slave population outnum-
  bering white population in, 7, 72, 121,
  131, 257. *See also* emancipation;
  Jamaica Assembly; plantation
  system; slave rebellion; slavery in
  Jamaica; sugar industry; whites
Jamaica (Crown colony), 273
Jamaica (independent): descendants of
  slaves as majority of population, 273;
  national anthem of, 274; national flag
  of, 274, 320n2; Parliament, 274;
  sovereignty granted in full
  (1962), 274
Jamaica Almanack (1828), 27
Jamaica Assembly: abolition of slavery
  and, 245–246; apprenticeship of
  former slaves and, 247, 249; Bill of
  Indemnity (1832), 167; composition
  of, 18; members' lack of permanent
  interest in Jamaica, 257; outlawing
  African religious spells, 301–302n8;
  on property damage during
  rebellion, 176; on rebellion conspiracy, 83; sending Barrett and
  Johnson to defend slave system to
  Parliament, 209; Speaker, Richard
  Barrett as, 10, *43*, 44, 196, 265;
  William IV attending, 94
Jamaica Courant: call for killing of
  Baptist and Methodist preachers,
  192, 195; comparing Sharpe with Nat
  Turner, 188; coverage of rebellion,
  308n29; praising militia's dismantling
  of Baptist and Methodist churches,
  193; trading insults with *Watchman*,
  152; warning of slave insurrections,
  97–99

159–160, 278; consciousness among slaves of right to freedom, 79, 81–82, 89, 171, 174, 206, 259; conspiracy formed for, 4–5, 83, 100–103, 107–108; continuing as guerilla conflict, 134; Cotton's proclamation of amnesty, 127, *128*, 129; death toll of blacks in, 176–177; death toll of whites in, 168–170, 308n29, 309n30; disagreements and confusion among rebels, 123–124, 158, 182, 278; economic toll of, 176; executions of captured rebels and other slaves, 125, 139–143, 162–166, 169–170, 173–179, 188–190; final stages, 155–159, 162, 170–173; fires, 111–134; food supplies during, 137–138; impression that whites were abandoning island, 132; king's supposed liberation of slaves and, 85, 89, 92, 109–110, 182, 184, 222; Knibb describing to parliamentary committee, 232–235; Knocklava, battle with rebels at, 133–134; lack of documentation from slaves' viewpoint, 87, 158, 272, 277; leaders in addition to Sharpe, 101, 107, 156–157; loyal slaves protecting master's property, 127–129, 132, 209, 303–304n17; martial law declared, 120, 138–143, 164, 173, 177, 233; militia fighting in, 86, 108, 114–117, 120, 124–125, 129–134, 137, 144–149, 159, 162, 164; motivations behind, 5, 143–144, 157, 161–162, 187; news of, reaching United States and Britain, 205–207; newspaper reporting on, 143–153; nonviolent resistance as part of, 4, 85, 86, 100, 108, 112, 115–116, 125, 157, 168, 183–184, 277, 280; oath swearing by conspirators, 100–101; obstructionist tactics to slow British

forces, 137, 146; property damage incurred during, 318n3; revenge taken on missionaries for supposed role in, 190–198; Rodrigues offering aid to rebels, 153–154; rumors during and after, 85, 89, 92, 109–110, 161, 167–168, 170, 182, 184, 222; saving blacksmiths' shops, 117, 304n18; summary of destruction of estates from, 162, 176; surrender of slaves, 170–173; violence as part of, 85–86, 159–160, 278, 309n30; warnings to white masters, 113–115, 168. *See also* fires; trials after rebellion

slavery: in Akan kingdoms, 55; in British empire, 7; documentation gap from slaves' viewpoint, 87, 158, 272, 277; economic effects in Liverpool from, 212–213; in United States, 246, 253–255. *See also* slavery in Jamaica; slave trade

slavery in Jamaica: abuse charges against slaveholders, 98; Barrett's defense of, 4, 208–212; branding, 64; "buy vs. breed" approach to, 54, 293n1; children of slaves, 54, 292–293n1; communication network among slaves, 83–84; comparison of human slaves to livestock, 51, 62–63, 64, 97, 295–296n21; court testimony by slaves, 167; death rate of slaves, 54, 64–65; English words learned by arriving slaves, 64; floggings, 22–23, 27, 39, 64, 69, 98, 106, 177, 233, 247, 267; growing own food by slaves, 69; hierarchy among slaves, 67–68; infanticide, 292–293n1; king of England held in high regard by slaves, 92; literacy among slaves, 29, 79–81, 145, 156, 253, 290n11; master-slave relationship and "Quashee" personality, 292n31; naming of slaves, 64; number of

Williams, Eric, 56; *Capitalism and Slavery*, 257–258, 293n4
Williams, James, 317n46
Williams, John, 135–136
Williams, Miss (hotel owner), 27, 279
Williamsfield Estate, 166
Williamson, Sophia, 49
Willis, Thomas, 41
Wilmot, Swithin, 317n46
Wiltshire Estate, 116–117
Winn, Isaac Lascelles, 279
women: as abolitionists, 33; British soldiers' treatment of white women, 120; British women's life in Jamaica, 16; execution or punishment of black women after rebellion, 177; flogging of enslaved women, 230, 233, 267; as House of Commons observers, 218; no suffrage, 219; purchase of enslaved women, 62, 296n22; rape of white women, 181, 309n30; white women watching at Sharpe's hanging, 189. *See also* sexual relations with slaves
Woodstock Estate, 157
workhouses, created post-emancipation, 249
Worthy Park (Jamaican plantation), 292n1
Wren, Christopher, 217

yellow fever, 12–13, 119, 261

Zion Hill Estate, 115